PAINTING ZAIDY'S DREAM

with best wishes

Miriam K

PAINTING Zaidy's dream

memoir of a searching soul

Miriam Karp

POPPY SEED PRESS

CINCINNATI, OH

Painting Zaidy's dream
©2013 by Miriam Karp
Poppy Seed Press LLC
7325 Elbrook Avenue
Cincinnati, Ohio 45237
(513) 746-8278
Paintingzaidysdream.com
Poppyseedpress7@gmail.com

Author and cover photo by Roberto Osona
Cover painting by Miriam Karp
Cover design by Yael Resnick
Typesetting by *www.wordzworth.com.*

ISBN: 978-0-9896333-7-6
Library of Congress Control Number: 2013912329
Printed in the United States of America

Credits:
"We Will Remember Her" written by Rabbi Sylvan Kamens and Rabbi Jack Reimer. Reprinted with permission.

"Surprise in Hebron" first published in part on Chabad.org.

"She is Pure" first published in Hadassah Magazine, December 2012–January 2013

"And I Believe" lyrics by Lazer Lloyd. Reprinted with permission.

To Dad, with love,
for showing me what caring and
steadfast endurance mean.

And to shining souls everywhere—
paint your dreams with vibrant colors

CONTENTS

FOREWORD

A memoir must recount the details of a particular life. At
the same time, it must find universal resonance. Without
the details, a memoir would be only vague generalities;
but with only specifics, a memoir would be a collection of dull and
irrelevant facts.

Miriam Karp is aware of the crucial balance. With a sharp sensitivity to the memoirist's task, she tells her own life-story, while
constantly touching the reader with bridging insights. She reflects
on the meaning of what happened to her, and there is a sense that
she is assessing that meaning afresh as she writes. She gives the
sense of a constantly examined life; in her art, she creates familiarity while staying a step ahead of cliché.

Miriam's writing has a disarming feel to it. Her choice of the
colloquial idiom, of common everyday language, is apt and
effective. She avoids its pitfalls with a winning sincerity, so while
at times the reader may fear that the work teeters on the brink of a
winking over-familiarity, one finds in the next paragraph or page
that she is in control, and has used the colloquial style artfully to
vividly establish her mindset.

Crucial to her task is describing her journey into her faith
community. This poses a severe artistic challenge, with
preachiness on the one side and superficiality on the other her
Scylla and Charybdis, her journey between a rock and a hard place.
Her everyday tone allows her safe passage – it makes her revelations seem wondrous in a very accessible way. For she does not
expect us to assume her revelations as our own, but rather to share
the wonder that will accompany our own revelations, as we may be
privileged to have them. In that way, she respects the power of

what she participated in and precisely conveys it to others – there is that sense of authenticity only possible in someone who is not anxiously trying to confirm her own reality by demanding responses from others. It is art, all the more moving for being modest in its tone, in the best sense of that complex word.

This modest tone allows a deep sharing. The story of her finding her husband is illustrative. Readers of modern memoirs are used to writers seeking depth through dark struggles of wrestling the Eros into some kind of coherence. Here instead, her spiritual journey does not involve flirtation with darkness. What she brings instead is an intimacy of another sort, an ease in sharing her journey into marriage and the thoughts and emotions that nurture it.

The read is satisfying, for she is sharing, not manipulating. There is always the freshness, the absence of the preening ego. She shares her life, and though it is unapologetically different from that of most readers, her generosity allows us to feel at home with that difference. In the end, she succeeds: the words tell her story, welcome us to her life, and I as a reader am delighted to be in that inquisitive, whimsical, meditative, honest, reflective, joyous, and loving place.

—RABBI SHMUEL KLATZKIN, PH.D.

Author's Note

This is a work of subjective memory as perceived through the eyes of an impressionable young woman. While the spirit of the story is true, some details have been embellished or reconstructed for artistic if not literal authenticity, and presented through the prism of personal memory and the blurring of time. Some of the characters have been blended, and most names have been changed unless they are public figures or family. No offense to any person is intended. Please treat this book with respect, since it contains God's name.

Searching

"My soul thirsts for You,
my flesh yearns for You,
as a parched arid land without water."

—PSALMS 63:2

PROLOGUE
SPINNING A DREAM

One balmy night, at the ripe old age of twenty-one, I had a startling dream. It was but one brief dream out of the billions hovering over drowsing heads around the globe that April night—some moving and profound, others trivial and nonsensical.

My brief dream was spun in a sparse room on the second floor of a small wooden house shared with three other students, on Broadway Street in Ann Arbor, Michigan.

An ardent New Ager, into psychology and vigorously searching for inner meaning, I was into dreams. We were on friendly terms, me and my subconscious.

I liked swimming under the surface and gliding around those images. I kept a dream journal—a notebook by my bed—and after I woke up, I'd often scribble some images, dialogue or feelings.

The dreams would percolate up during the day. I might be standing in line at the corner store and —flash—green storm clouds floated overhead. Or biking up to the counterculture stores that hung around the edge of the more yuppie campus bars and bookstores, and a hovering figure would appear.

Instead of foaming beer and oversized burgers, I'd drop by Eden's macrobiotic café for some chapati sesame bread, a steaming cup of pungent kukicha tea, and hijiki seaweed served up with steaming veggies and rice. With the twang of a sitar or the rolling

3

rhythm of congo drums setting the introspective mood, I might dive back under and hang out some more with that nocturnal visitor. I couldn't dissect my dreams and tell you exactly what they meant, but they bubbled up in different ways, coloring and shadowing my waking hours.

Earlier that afternoon, I stopped at the food co-op, with barrels of grains and bushels of seeds lined up against the walls, worked a few hours, and took home some quinoa to simmer. I ate it with chopsticks later that night, reading a mystical piece by candlelight, trying once again to quench that ravenous inner hunger. I feel asleep with a prayer for insight and direction on my lips, in my heart. Somewhere before dawn, I had the dream.

It stood out. More vivid and distinct, less mushy and murky than the usual dream. Strangely, it was pretty plain. No storyline or action. Just an image: a still-life tableau, with unusual characters that were totally removed from my preoccupations and waking thoughts. In spite of its simplicity, the scene hit me in the gut and drove me to capture it.

It captured me.

Following the image, following its tantalizing thread as it wound to unusual places, around corners—following, following, to find its spool, its source—led me on a journey of discovery, a journey to destinations that were new and exotic, yet familiar and deeply known.

1

RIPPING SHIRTS AND HEARTS

Thirty years later, on a difficult Friday morning in May, the disparate pieces of my life, the chapters that could be called Before Dream, and After Dream, came together in a funeral hall.

"Do you have a razor or scissors?" I asked Bob, the funeral director. My voice sounded surreally calm on this surreally strange morning.

Several hours earlier I had gotten up, after a night of tossing and turning. In my odd pre-funeral calm I rifled through my suitcase and debated, as if I was dressing for a meeting or other social engagement. What would be the best thing to wear to Mom's funeral? *Mom's funeral?!* I'd have to "tear *kriah*," rip my shirt several inches in the front. An image of Jackie Kennedy, poised in her grief at JFK's funeral, flitted through my mind. I did not own an elegant black suit, pillbox hat, or ladylike veil, however.

"Let's see now," I mused. "Should I wear an old dud that I won't mind kissing goodbye, since it's going to be torn? That would make sense," my practical side urged.

"But I'm going to be speaking and on show," the ego spoke up.

"Remember, you're not even supposed to be focusing on

what you look like, on superficial appearances," my voice of piety gently chided. I imagined a proper mourner, far from such petty concerns, sitting quietly and murmuring psalms.

I finally settled on the black blouse with small sequins down the middle, over a black T-shirt, even though it was a favorite. A reliable goodie—I'd miss it.

"Girl, what's wrong with you? This is your mother's funeral. Are you a robot? Who cares if you're pretty?" a haggard voice cried out from deep within .

Bob came back from his office, and handed me the blade.

Okay, this was it.

No symbolic black ribbon pinned on, as more modern and moderate Jewish mourners do. We Chassidim do the real deal. We take a perfectly good shirt and tear it.

I opened my mouth to say the blessing, but blanked out on the familiar words. I stood there gaping, childlike, helpless. Bob saw my flailing and rescued me, saying them in a quiet monotone. I followed.

"Baruch Ata Hashem Elokainu Melech Haolam, Dayan HaEmes." Blessed are You, God, king of the universe, the true judge.

I started to saw on the stubborn seam for what seemed like forever. It wouldn't give. Finally the razor gripped and sliced through it. Then I took the cut material with my hand and tore it down several inches. The ripping sounded harsh. It was shocking. *Teeaaar.* The destruction was jolting. It seemed the whole room of quietly chatting people was frozen, listening. I had been numb, on automatic pilot, and the violent action startled me, arousing feelings. Feelings, I do have feelings. I am hurting under that blank surface. Feelings of loss, of tearing down in my heart. I do have a heart. Oh yes, it's actually crying under the tired, stoic façade.

But the hanging shreds did not add to my elegance.

When I came out of my world and surfaced back in the old country of my youth, I usually tried to pay a little more attention to my appearance than was my everyday habit. I was not my mother's daughter in that department. Mom always took extra care, her gracious taste apparent in her beautiful attire.

This was never my specialty. T-shirts and jeans, my attire most every day of my teen years, were not just a counterculture statement, they were also comfortable and easy. Now I did it the Orthodox way: jean skirt topped with a long-sleeve, not-too-tight T-shirt or cotton blouse. I could never muster enough sustained interest to accomplish the smooth-and-together look, but I tried to be at least a decent representative of my world—not too frazzled or frumpy, although I usually came precariously close.

Today was different.

I was following the laws of mourning. A mourner can't look in the mirror or adorn herself—which helps her lessen ego concerns, focus on the loss and on the soul in transition, and find the thread of her changed life. It's too easy to gloss over the loss and never really process or experience it.

Those Torah laws help us face mourning head-on, cushioned with caring family and community. Ideally.

But here in West Bloomfield I couldn't completely surrender into that space. I felt I needed to serve as ambassador to the land of the Chassid. Since I would speak at the funeral, I wanted to have something of a smooth, competent appearance. With no makeup or jewelry and three nights of anxious tossing and turning, I was a pitiful sight.

I had asked my daughters to serve as my mirrors as I got dressed and ready in Dad's basement, where we were camped out, and check if I was halfway normal. Compared to me, they were fashionistas. They were used to helping me out, making sure the old girl was in somewhat-acceptable range. Twenty-two-year-old Mushky guided my clothing choices that strange morning.

In my calm and detached, anxious and frenetic mindset, I had thrown myriad possibilities in my bag, before heading up I-75 to Detroit several days earlier. I'd just gotten off the phone with Dad, who called me at work with the doctor's grim timetable. Okay, I'd been thinking, what should I bring to possibly wear to a funeral I don't want to happen, but which probably will?

My fashion barometer was off as usual, not quite calibrated correctly. I first tried a blue peasant skirt.

"Everyone is expecting me to wear black. I'll show them we Chassidim aren't so morose, even now."

My coaches corrected me.

"Everyone else will be probably wearing black; you might look silly if you don't." I dutifully changed.

"There, that's more elegant," Mushky said as she guided me. Esti tugged at my shirt and brushed it a bit.

"You're okay, Mom," the girls reassured me.

We piled into the assorted minivans: Yankel, two sons-in-law, eight children, two grandchildren, and me. We perched coffee in the holders, threw in sweaters, hair brushes, and other possible fix-me-ups, and smoothed down skirts and suit jackets. Our Chassidic caravan drove the ten minutes or so to the funeral home in quiet, subdued camaraderie; our little clan headed out on this surreal morning to see my mom off.

2

———❦———

WE WILL REMEMBER HER

Mom's funeral was an apt snapshot of the jumbled juxtaposition that made up my life. My life that didn't quite fit. Not into the normal borders.

Eight of our ten children, ages ten through twenty-four, had made it, some barely. Only Chaya and Chaim were missing, our oldest two. Chaya had left the day before; she had flown in from Seattle to see her Bubby one last time, and had to get back to her young family. Chaim and his new wife Ayelet were watching via computer monitor from their home in far-off Israel, but we could feel their presence.

No small accomplishment to have the rest of the gang together, pulled out from the daily fabric of school and work, assembled from Cincinnati, Chicago, Baltimore, New Haven, and New York on a moment's notice. Their travel arrangements were a jumbled, last-minute mess of flat tires, bus pick-ups in unfamiliar neighborhoods, and scheduling confusion as I scrambled to coordinate plans through exhaustion and tense worry. I had been alternating frantically between being angry and annoyed that this was dumped on me, and being willing to do anything to have them here. My husband Yankel tried to handle some of it, but he was stuck with a flat tire and three of the kids somewhere on the highway.

What I really wanted was the peace and quiet to sit by Mom's side as she lay dying, under the hospice's ticking clock of prediction.

"She is moving into the next stage. It looks like it will be within about twenty-four hours, though you never know," the hospice doctor said with quiet compassion at the Wednesday morning examination, several light years before Friday morning's service. The social worker nodded her head in assent with a subdued social-worker smile.

But now it was such a comfort to have the kids there. When they filed into the funeral hall, into the front row reserved for family, their black yarmulkes and black hats, modest dresses stood out. (It's the black hatters—the Ultra-Orthodox!) They were unsure and apprehensive. Sad over their Bubby's death, that sweet woman who smiled at their jokes and accomplishments, and taped up their drawings; who especially loved their red hair and freckles.

For the younger ones, this was the first funeral—always a weird thing, even weirder not knowing what to expect at this hybrid Humanist/Chassidic service. The kids hovered around the edges as my parents' close friends milled around, hugging and comforting us in the family room on the side of the chapel.

My aunts and uncle; my sister, brother-in-law, and nephews; my brother, cousins, and the collection of old family friends were more elegantly appointed— women in sleek black sheaths, men in well-cut suits and sport jackets. Maybe a few grabbed a yarmulke as they entered the funeral hall. Some might have thought it an appropriate sign of respect at a funeral. Then again, at a Humanistic one, maybe not.

In spite of the reason we were there, I was glad to see everyone. I had called them the previous morning, some nine or ten hours after Mom died. I feared I cut to the chase too quickly for some of these delicate eighty-something-year-old hearts. Why else would they think I was calling? They'd know as soon as they heard my voice, I had wrongly assumed. I had marched right into my unhappy message, only to hear them gasp.

But once done, it was kind of cathartic for me. Saying it over and over: "Hello, Sharon. It's Miriam Karp, you know, Trudy and Jack's daughter. I'm sorry to tell you but..." With each rhythmic recital, it sank in a bit more.

It started to seem more real, more than those hazy, wee-morning hours in the nursing home, waiting for the police and coroner to make it official, signing papers and emptying out the drawers of her abandoned toothbrush, socks, and nightgowns. Yankel and I sat with sad eyes and quiet with Dad, who seemed dazed and broken, sighing deeply and shaking his head over and over.

When I heard everyone's brief reminiscences and sympathy, it was a needed hug through the telephone line that made my voice break and eyes well up.

The service began. Tamara, the sensitive and articulate Humanistic rabbi, spoke in loving terms about Trudy Driker. It was weird to hear this woman speak about my mom, in the past tense (was this really happening?) and with newfound intimacy. Just the day before, hours after her passing, Tamara met with us to go over the service and learn the details of Mom's life and personality. Mom and Dad's active involvement in the temple had faded by the time Tamara took over the helm, so she didn't know them well.

Like an old friend, a childhood security blanket, Tamara's words, in the familiar style of my childhood temple, were comforting. She spoke with respect and poise, with tenderness too, of Mom's love of the arts, and her style and wit, through poems and reflections. Tamara led us as we remembered her. We pledged to honor her memory by keeping it alive in our hearts. True words, from intelligent, genteel people. Her life is over. We loved her. We'll think of her in the passing of the seasons and the blossoming of the flowers.

Tamara closed with a repetitive reading. At each juncture, the assembled crowd did their part, and affirmed together. "We will remember her."

In the rising of the sun and its going down
We will remember her
In the blowing of the wind and the chill of winter
We will remember her
In the opening of the buds and the warmth of summer
We will remember her
In the rustling of the leaves and the beauty of autumn
We will remember her
And when we are weary and in need of strength
We will remember her
When we are lost and sick at heart
We will remember her
And when we have joy we yearn to share
We will remember her
So long as we live, Gertrude Driker will live, because she is our beloved
And we will remember her.

C'mon. But where did that little lady, those thoughts and words, triumphs and troubles go? Where did eighty years go? Poof— she's gone? All that's left is in that coffin? There's gotta be more.

Such would have been my troubled thoughts, rumbling beneath the smooth and proper surface as the funeral proceeded, under my sad eyes, behind my quiet chuckles as my sister Vivian shared warm memories; such would have been those thoughts that gave me no rest, really, from the time I was a child.

Lying in bed one night, I looked out the window at the starry night. I was about eight. Mom and Dad were out at a party. I loved our Saturday night ritual. I perched on Mom's bed, watching her carefully choose her dress and accessories, matching jewelry, shoes, and purse. A spray of perfume and a blot of her lipstick on a neatly folded tissue. That crimson circle with her lip wrinkles making a pattern. Her black lacquer powder holder had two compartments. The top held the large round puff. The creamy beige powder sat in the bottom bowl waiting for her to put the finishing touch on her made-up face. And sometimes I got to zip up her dress for her, and close that little hook at the top. It felt like an honor to a starry-eyed young girl, like helping the princess get ready for the royal ball.

I wasn't scared. Carolyn, a warm and cozy woman, was babysitting—the one black person we knew well. Carolyn cleaned our three-bedroom home several times a week and stayed over on many Saturday nights. We'd cuddle on the couch while watching TV and eating popcorn. (Well, now it was four bedrooms, because we'd added a bedroom for Vivian, so I had my very own, with gold carpeting and mod pink and orange flowers popping on my bright yellow bedspread.)

It was quiet in my room, a good place to read and think. I lay in bed one hot summer night, looked out the window and thought. I wasn't scared, but Mom and Dad being out late made a slight vacuum, a slight opening in my secure universe.

Like a loose tooth that you just couldn't stop wigging with your tongue, as I looked past the Nichols' roof, past their barking dog, up to the stars sparkling above our suburban oasis of neat streets of modest colonials bordered by pleasant maples and elms, I thought about what happened when you died.

Mom and Dad said, when you die, you're gone. You are a physical body, your brain stops producing thoughts, your heart stops beating, and your body starts decaying. God and an afterlife are old-fashioned silly ideas for people who are too ignorant or too weak to deal with life, so they need a crutch, something they made up to make them feel good. I looked at the unfortunate primitives in National Geographic. Native tribes danced around a fire; uneducated slaves sang hymms because that was the only way to deal with their tzorus (problems). Even today, all those church- and synagogue-going folks needed their myths. But we have science and logic and facts, and we're strong, we can face it: when it's over, it's over.

My tongue kept wiggling that bothersome, compelling tooth. I wasn't satisfied. What's that sense of me, that *I-ness*, that person, Miriam Sarah Driker? What is that? It's not my eye, my hand, my foot—how can it just disappear? Like, gone? Vanished? Where does it go? Is it something or not? Am I something or not? I stashed that gnawing question back, but it hung on the edge of my mind, flaring up from time to time.

As a teen those rumblings gathered strength and drove me to pursue a merry chase—a colorful tour of philosophies, religions, and communes, seeking that something more.

Tamara finished speaking. Yankel, my husband, the sensitive Chassidic rabbi, spoke too. He walked to the podium with his slight figure, his quick, intense walk, and put down his prayer book. He stroked his reddish-brown beard, graying around the edges. He took the mike. He adjusted his yarmulke as he composed himself. He cried a few long moments, and then whispered Mom's Hebrew name into the mike. "Gittel Rivka bas Velvel. Another precious Jewish soul has left this world."

He spoke with earnest sincerity, but he knew this was a foreign language in these parts, in this not too religious, not too anything, suburban funeral home. Yankel was usually disarmingly funny, with legendary puns. Our nightly family dinner included the kids moaning and laughing *"Taaa"* (Dad, stop it!), as he laid another play-on-words groaner on the table.

His first words to me were a joke, over the phone. It was the day before Yom Kippur, a hectic and intense time. Even though we were making arrangements for a first date —mutual friends suggested we meet—and he might be expected to be nervous or hurried, I was struck by his open humor, warmth, and ease.

That Friday, at the funeral, his words were much more subdued and serious. He spoke about God, souls, good deeds, eternity, all that religious jazz. Trying to bring other dimensions to this event; to honor more than Mom's life and the memory of her personality. Trying to honor not only the end of this life, but to help her soul get provisions for its journey, which in our eyes, mine and Yankel's, was only just beginning.

As the mourners, as her kids, there were specific things we had to do and say, and we wanted to include the crowd—at least let them hear the words, even though they were unfamiliar and maybe averse to prescribed rituals and mumbling in Hebrew. So Yankel gave an introductory course in "Death and Souls 101," and said the appropriate psalms and prayers.

I was torn. This Torah stuff was now my home base, the way I really thought about the situation. I wanted it said for Mom's sake, for her *neshama*, her soul—but I was a little worried, too. I knew few of those gathered there shared that perspective, and might think it primitive. I didn't want to alienate them.

Then I spoke. The spacey peace-maker and ruffle-smoother. I danced between Tamara's tribute to the Trudy we all knew, and Yankel's words to help Gittel Rivka on her way in the spiritual realm. My family, especially my Daddy's heart, was raw and dangling like the threads of my ripped shirt. I wanted to do some mending, and sew these seemingly disparate pieces together.

I was a wacky conglomeration of those diametric perspectives. To the born-and-bred Orthodox I was a bit of a free-floating anomaly, not cut of quite the same cloth as them even though we followed the same way of life. In the eyes of the worldly sophisticates, I was a quaint innocent, an idealist trapped in many rules.

I decided to put right up front what was happening, to discuss the very different perspectives coming together on that podium.

Here was the non-deistic Humanist rabbi, followed by the Chassid, who hardly made a move without thanking God and having that move guided by thousands of years of Jewish law and mystical insight.

15

I looked out at the audience and smiled at Tamara, seated on my left. I saw my sister Vivian, my cousin Elissa, and Nacha, my Chassidic buddy, smile at me with reassurance. These were three hip and real women I loved, really so similar, but occupying the two very different worlds I was part of. I wanted to hug them and everyone there in one big squeeze.

"You might think that Tamara and I are on opposite ends of the Jewish spectrum." I think I heard an intake of breath.

"But," I continued, "I don't see it that way at all."

I tried to build a bridge. To show that the things I learned in Mom and Dad's home and at the Birmingham Temple weren't really discarded. I learned to love beauty. To think independently, outside the box; to dare to be different. I had followed those tantalizing gingerbread crumbs, and I wanted more. So I looked. And looked. And here I was.

I wanted these dear ones to understand; to feel connected to my path, not rejected. And maybe see that I wasn't a freaky weirdo, but still part of their planet. And that I didn't speak Swahili, that a step or two into my world might have value to them, too, might have something to warm them on one of those long, lonely nights.

3

———✦———

DRESS BRITISH, THINK YIDDISH

L ooking back, thinking back, I try to trace it.

Why? How?

Which encounters, questions created the brew that percolated to shape this product, this mommy, grandma, teacher, overgrown kid I rub my eyes and see in the mirror each morning?

What little nudging bug got under my skin and drove me to search out this life of faith, ritual, rules aplenty, soaring joys, and loads of work—to land in such a different place than the home that spawned me?

Looking back, thinking back, I sum up a lovely childhood like this:

I was happy, I was normal, I was nurtured—I was starving.

Starving? Didn't my parents feed me? Didn't they know the first and foremost saying of Jewish parents from Time Immemorial: "*Ess, mein kind*—eat, my child?"

Generations. Each has its story, its challenges, its strengths, and its gaps which the next generation is driven to fill, to balance, to correct. The precious children are fed the best diet their parents can scrape together: the finest brew of foods, beliefs, and values the parents can dish up to make them strong and whole.

Mom and Dad and their clan of loyal friends, grew up in the old Jewish neighborhood, near Dexter and Davison Streets, in the heart of Detroit. Children of immigrants, they shared roots well-watered with Yiddish culture.

Dad's 80th birthday, several years before that funeral gathering, was the last time I'd seen most of the *chevra* (gang). Since the party, in a quickly racing blip in my busy life--"Three years? Where did the time go?"--a few more of this precious gang had passed on. A few more had canes, hearing aids, or other signs of the passing years. I was used to them gasping at us kids, at how we were rapidly growing, charging forward with breakneck speed into our identities and lives. During the last decade or so, the tables were turned. Time was unraveling. We kids were at a fairly predictable middle-age plateau, but each encounter with our parents' peers shocked, hurt. I'd do a double take, until I recognized that familiar face beneath the whitening, thinning hair, and slower gait.

"Harold, how are you?" I said as I held open the door.

"Oh, Miriam." He looked up from carefully watching his step. "It's so good to see you, dear. You look wonderful." His weathered face broke into a smile.

Same shining eyes and sweet voice, I thought. *My, he's changing. How could I be towering over these fragile folks, who used to be steady giants?* I helped them ease their way into the hall, gently kissing their elderly, once-firm cheeks.

Viv, David, and I had planned the gathering, reminiscing as we brainstormed to create the party's centerpieces, highlighting the *Yiddishe taam* (Jewish flavor) of this crowd, once over easy, with a light touch.

"Wow, Viv, these pictures are great!" We were busily assembling the centerpieces on the morning of the party, our kids running around helping to set up.

She laughed. "Last time I was in Detroit, I scrounged the photo albums for some good shots. Here are the skewers to mount them on."

"Great. Let's stick them into the challah rolls and salamis."

We started mounting the photos and spearing my contribution: classic Food of the Hood, laid out on old Yiddish newspapers—greasy, reddish-brown salamis, their sausage shape bursting with cholesterol; golden, twisted challah egg breads, shiny surface kissed with sesame seeds; tight, round garlic bulbs with feathery white peels; and pungent dill pickles. Some of Dad's closest cronies sat together round a table on the side of the hall, kibbitzing and singing old Yiddish folk tunes.

The decorative pictures gleaned from Dad's career and yearbook captured the general life trajectory of the clan, though each had its personal variation on the theme. Central High, degrees from Wayne State, military service in the Korean War, wedding picture, newspaper clippings of professional achievements, children, and grandchildren. Dad looked so dashing in his crisp white Navy lieutenant's uniform, with a slight smile just barely breaking.

The gang's lives had followed a similar arc. I loved the integrity of these hardworking, smart, and funny folk. Their parents had fled violent pogroms and grueling poverty in search of a better life. The Eastern European immigrants wound up in Detroit because of HIAS placement, or relatives who'd take them in, an address scribbled down, or rumors of jobs.

They learned enough English, saved pennies with a fierce resourcefulness, and managed to become proprietors of small businesses that ran on sweat and grit. My grandparents put food on the table by selling hubcaps and running hand-laundries and a candy store that my Bubby would say almost did her in. She remembered those days with gentle sarcasm and humor.

"The best part was to make the chocolate syrup," she told me once. "The man that sold us the store showed us how to make it. He had a big black rusty pot. His hands were greasy from fixing his car and he put those hands in the chocolate syrup to mix it up good. The second best thing was to make the banana split. The 'spritzer' never worked good, and the crème used to go all over the counter."

These immigrants were determined that, no matter what it took, their children's lives would be different. No sweatshops for them. The children were the first generation to go to college, Americanize, and become *professionals*. They were bred on an amalgamation of Old Country wisdom, nurturing and suffocating, and amber waves of grain and possibilities, for those who could blend in just enough.

These *Americanisher*—these precious American-born kids—celebrated their ethnicity in small ways. Dad likes to tell how he'd get lots of room on the crowded Dexter bus, by opening up one of Bubby's sandwiches, with aromatic garlic heavily smeared on the rye bread. After graduating Central, the buddies moved en masse to the neighborhood university, Wayne State, on scholarships and nickels saved from odd jobs and factory lines.

An example of their Jewish/American, sometimes precarious, balancing act: Dad and his buddies sold Christmas wreaths each December. Hey, anything for an honest buck. Joe the Greek, a shoemaker, shared a small storefront with Zaidy's hand laundry, and always bought one. He was very friendly, except from Palm Sunday to Easter. Then he wouldn't even look at the boys, since they were "Christ-killers."

Most of the gang went on to graduate degrees. Dad and his crony Jack even went on to Harvard. Not bad for two Jewish boys from Dexter and Davison. Pessie, their Boston landlady, felt sorry for these *boychiks* living on nothing. She kept their stomachs full with baked beans, as their minds were filled with great ideas.

Their parents were so proud.

"Faygel from Toperey," Bubby would say, "you did very well to derive such richness." The American Dream was coming true, right before their eyes.

Traveling the continent was a luxury these worldly kids were able to access.

"During my adolescence, I read many 'coming of age' stories," Mom recalled. "In them, all the debutantes and important people spent at least a summer abroad, learning to live around the world."

When she was twenty-two, her Greek friend Minerva invited her to go along to Europe for the summer. Western Europe, that is. No way they'd want to go to Warsaw or Zhitomir, to their parents' spawning grounds. Eastern Europe was locked behind the Iron Curtain, a massive Jewish graveyard, the ashes still smoldering.

Mom took a ship filled with young contemporaries and Euro-railed around. The world seemed to open up to the protected, skinny only child. The art and history jumped off the pages as she strolled wide-eyed through the Louvre and the Acropolis. Bull-fights in Spain, the Parthenon. As Mom would later say, "The world opened up for the little schoolteacher from Detroit, just like for the 'beautiful people.'"

Dad was a lieutenant in the Navy, stationed in London. As part of his job, he had the opportunity to travel around Europe and experienced that Jewish peoplehood bond—sometimes members of the Tribe smelled each other out where he least expected it.

Dad recalls: "In 1953, I visited the Vatican. As I approached Michelangelo's masterpiece, a man approached me peddling pearl rosaries looped on his arm. I declined interest. He persisted, suggesting he was ready to negotiate. He quoted a very low price. I said I wasn't interested. He asked, 'Are you Catholic?' I answered 'No.' He responded with the classic Jewish greeting, 'Shalom Aleichem (Peace unto you),' to which I replied, 'Aleichem Shalom (To you, peace).' He then cheerfully guided me to the 2,500-year-old Roman Ghetto, within a few yards of the Pope's Palace."

We have a picture of Dad, handsome in a trench coat, feeding the pigeons in Trafalgar Square. Mom and Dad actually roamed the Thames at the same time, seeing Queen Elizabeth's coronation from different vantage points. They figured this out later, when their travel wound down, bringing them back to Detroit and into each other's lives.

No one wanted to test just how far the tolerance of this *goldene medina* (golden land) went. They strove to fit in enough to be able to advance and utilize their talents for more than the small, struggling businesses of their parents; to fulfill the dreams their education and their families, asked, perhaps demanded of them. Be a man in the street and a Jew in the home, went a popular adage. Dress British, think Yiddish.

McCarthyism blazed just as they were starting their careers, in the mid-fifties. It smelled suspiciously like a genteel, white-gloved, suit-and-tie version of the pogroms their parents had fled. McCarthy attacked liberals and Commies—often code words for *Jews*—with a calculated vengeance that seemed not all that different than drunken peasants on a rampage.

At least McCarthy didn't wave a sword or knife—just a black-list. These energetic graduates, ready to make their mark on the big stage, found they had to look over their shoulders and plot their moves carefully. Jew boys weren't always so welcome. Dad wanted to be an architect, but he was advised to look elsewhere. The old-boy WASP network ran most firms, the same people who kept Jews, blacks, and other minorities out of their country clubs and neighborhoods. He switched gears, using his talents in design and sociology in the new field of urban planning.

The product: The gang was mostly liberal, politically active. They knew the value of a free election and a vote, and cared to place theirs carefully, thoughtfully. Their parents grew up under the Czar and taught them to appreciate freedom. Voting was serious business, like a religious obligation in our house. When I stand in line to vote, I remember waiting quietly in the voting booth with Mom, the curtain pulled snugly around us. It was so much fun to ride in the 1965 Fourth of July parade. We were in the League of Women Voters flotilla, in red-white-and -blue Volkswagen Beetles, standing on the seats to lift placards out of the open sunroof declaring, "Your vote makes a difference."

Once the grads got established, their hard work, character, and smarts did them well. They moved to the suburbs and prospered. They collected art, read good books, Sunday'd on the *New York Times*.

Jewishness didn't make too many daily demands in the push to get ahead. I make a special stew for the Sabbath lunch most every week, known as *cholent*. It simmers on low in the crockpot. By Saturday morning when we wake up, the house is redolent of stewed meat, potato, beans, and spices. So, too, this first generation's Yiddish spark. Low key, on the back burner—but it colored and permeated their humor, their attitudes, just who they were: a warm and savory bunch.

Our parents spent a childhood of summer Sundays at Belle Isle, an island park in the Detroit River. They wandered through the picnic tables packed with immigrant Jewish organizations plying their goods, like a deli-style bake sale.

Raising quarters and dollars earned with hard sweat at hand-laundries and small dry goods stores, raising them for mutual aid immigrant clubs, banding together to provide insurance, funeral plots, and schooling. Raising them for hardy pioneers sweating across the ocean, draining swamps and planting oranges in the Promised Land.

"Hot noodle kugel, a nickel," the women from the Sholem Aleichem Institute called. At the next cluster of tables the Pioneer Women were selling knishes. And down by the band shell, the Odessa Progressive Aid Society men were grilling hot dogs.

My Bubby described the scene in the sketches she penned about those days: "Other people that came over to Belle Isle with their children came over to the Odessa picnic. It was *fraylich* (lively). Then it got cloudy and someone suggested selling things cheaper in case of rain. Mr. Bausk stood on a table and called out the bargains. Two hot dogs for five cents, one watermelon fifteen. Everything was on sale now. Pop, bread, cookies, knishes, latkes—everyone used up their checks."

A tight web of communal support, mutual responsibility, and that lilt of Yiddish accents, history, and smells was just there, ingested along with the vitamins, milk, and fresh produce that were carefully spooned into these children of the new land.

But the next generation had a very different point of departure. We second-generation, children of plenty lived in the newer land, north of Eight Mile Road, scattered throughout the whitewashed developments. We spent our weekends wandering around Northland, the first mall in America, where mannequins with perfect faces and empty smiles looked down on us. Cashiers were polite strangers. To the owners of large chain stores, each one almost indistinguishable from the next, we were another anonymous gang of teeny-bopper profit, pockets stuffed with our allowances. "Here's your change, thank you for your business, have a nice day," she says as she smacks her gum and looks at her watch.

I walked into Kresge's, nervous, heart beating wildly. Could I really do it? What if I got caught? Flashes of the Juvenile Court TV show flashed before my eyes. But Bob and Sandy and Frank and Pam and everyone would be waiting. They said it was easy to rip off, to steal something small. Guess if they could, I could too.

I looked up the aisle. Back behind me, super casually. No one seemed to be watching. Fingered several pairs of dangly rhinestone earrings, acting as if I wanted to buy some, and then slowly, so slowly, slipped a pair into my jeans pocket. An excited, tingly, sick feeling in the pit of my stomach. I'm guilty. I'm dirty. I'm cool, I hope, finally. I casually hung the others back on the rack and sauntered out of the dime store, to a back bench in the mall's plaza, behind the fountain, where my comrades were waiting. When the gang of a dozen or so teeny boppers compared their booty, I proudly, anxiously, pulled out those rhinestone creations, proving that I was tough as the best of them.

Next Saturday we were back. I fudged my way out of the ripping off. Once was enough. I wasn't made for that kind of pressure. That week, we headed for the make-up counter and free dos. What about the cool sweaters in Winkleman's?

I didn't get shiny white go-go boots back in fourth grade when *everybody* had them. Our family had to get these practical, ugly shoes with "arch cookies," some dumb thing the doctor said I needed. So embarrassing. I took them off and threw them against the brick walls during recess, then dragged my feet and scuffed my toes on the walk home from school—anything to wear them out. It never helped. Mom would just take us back to that practical, dreary store for more.

Now I was a teen. Time to insist, whine, cry, pout, and sulk, till I finally got platform shoes. I was with it (even if I fell off them half the time). Keeping up with the Joneses, Cohen's, fads, and images blazing across the TV screen and *Seventeen* magazine was hard work. Dress like a model, think like a movie star—that was our mantra.

The Old Country flavor did infiltrate my suburban life. I sat in front of the TV with millions of other good American kids and was promised that if I'd only eat Wonder Bread, it would build Strong Bodies Twelve Ways. But my family ate very different bread, real bread, with flavor and ethnicity: yellow-tinged egg challah, sliced up in the clanging bread machine by the wrinkled Eastern European women that worked at Mertz Kosher Bakery, their hair nets covering their graying curls and flour-smudged aprons tied around their petite, stout bodies.

These women knew the sweet value of a Jewish child, having seen up close what utter destruction means. Many had their families decimated by the vile, ruthless hand of Hitler or Stalin.

"Oy, such sveet *kinderlach*. Vud you like a cookie, *zeiskiets*, you sveet children?"

Goldie or Yenta would smile and wait patiently while we deliberated. Which color sprinkles? Or chocolate chips? Or multi-colored crunchy ball sprinkles? We finally decided, and pointed a mittened hand up at the right one, perched on a doily behind the glass showcase.

"Ahh, the chocolate. Gut von. *Ess gezunterheit*, darlink"—eat and enjoy in good health, she wished us.

Next door was Barton's Kosher Candy, where we got little white bags of mint lentils and coffee- chocolate cocoa beans. Then Spritzer's Judaica, which we occasionally went for dreidels or Rosh Hashanah cards, or multi-colored Chanukah candles.

Dexter Davison grocery store was the anchor of this unique strip mall. The banner sign, turning slowly on its pole, towered benignly above the parking lot welcoming the shoppers. "Where old friends meet to shop and save" was emblazoned above a Jewish star. Truth in advertising prevailed, as this place was a nostalgic step back to Mom and Dad's childhood. They had tagged along with their mommies to the original, on the then-bustling corner of Dexter and Davison Streets, way down in the old neighborhood.

Here in Oak Park we shopped at the upgraded, transplanted sixties version. But the old pickle barrel was still there; you could roll up your sleeve and plunge in gingerly. Schmaltz herring sat waiting at the fish counter, eyes peering at us, and weathered salamis sporting a good measure of grease on their burgundy-colored skin hung from twisted, thick string behind the deli counter.

I loved helping Mom push the shopping cart through the crowded aisles. A warmth, an old-world atmosphere, hung in the air, although Coke and Kellogg's sat on the shelves along with Manischewitz. It was cozier, louder, more alive than A&P, where everyone and everything seemed to politely stay in their sterile box.

Elderly survivors and immigrants staffed Dexter Davison. Mrs. Siegel, Bubby's friend, always greeted us at the butcher counter with a lollipop. And gentlemanly Mr. Cantor expertly helped Mom squeeze the melons; he'd carefully assess the day's shipment and pick out the best produce. If he wasn't too busy he'd fish some pickles out of the brine. The cashier might slip me another candy.

Monday through Saturday was typical—classic 1960s. Burton Elementary School—a large, brick building about a half-mile walk from our house. We came home for lunch every day. Mom waited for us with hot dog, Campbell's soup, grilled cheese sandwiches, Kraft's dinner or Franco-American Spaghetti. Homework, Girl Scouts.

Our end of the block had a hard-playing gang of kids, who were outside whenever there was a chance, running from yard to yard. We made a clubhouse behind the Browns' back hedge, played Kick the Can and army at the Sands'. The Linders had a great playhouse and sandbox. Our smaller playhouse, apple tree with a tree-house platform, and monkey bars were also in high demand.

During the winter months we hit the basements. One year we organized ourselves during winter vacation and made an elaborate production, acting out "Twas the Night before Christmas," complete with scripts, scenery, and parts, which we performed for the parents and elderly neighbors. A few hours of TV. Piano lessons; practicing those scales up and down, over and over. Deep Barbie and Ken dramas at Rachel's house. We laid out all the tiny molded pumps, cars, accessories, gilded party dresses, combs, brushes, mink stoles, and purses. Where was Barbie going today, with her perfect va-voom figure and tiny little waist? Would Ken be there? Big, involved decisions.

But many Sunday afternoons were spent at Bubby and Zaidy's, where we tasted something different. Their Yiddish accents, their old-world ways and lack of modern aesthetic in their dress and decor. Zaidy wore clashing shirts and ties in gaudy colors. Bubby's simple skirts and lacy button-down blouses contained her buxom but compact figure; we second-generation, lanky teens towered over her almost five-foot height.

Some kind of authentic Jewish down-home-ness was as nourishing as the chicken soup and thousands of blintzes, knishes, and poppy-seed cookies Bubby made and we dutifully and happily ingested.

We tussled with our cousins, climbed her cherry tree, roamed through the yellowing memorabilia stashed in old dressers and trunks in her attic and basement. Yiddish classics belted out of the turntable, melodious singing of "Romania, Romania" and "Tum Balalaika." We sat around as the adults debated and laughed.

There were no toys and a few tiny rooms, but we fiddled around, fingering Bubby's crystal candy bowl and little figurines, absorbing that secure, womb-like feeling.

Bubby would babysit when Mom and Dad went away to conventions, and that was the best. We got to bake with her, from scratch, mixing and rolling and cutting cookies with glasses, making a good old-fashioned mess with flour all over the table and a real rolling pin. And the whole house smelled sweet and good as the wax-paper-lined cookie sheets went in and out of the oven.

"Come, *zeiskeit*, sweet one, roll the dough a little thinner, or it won't bake enough. *At azoi!* That's it."

"Like this, Bubby, like this?" David showed her his attempts. The youngest child, he perched up on a high stool to reach. "How's this one, Bubby?" Vivian asked as she carefully shaped her cookies.

Bubby patiently and adroitly added a little dough to our too-thin scraps, and rolled out our giant clumps to make them thinner, while she made us feel we'd done it ourselves.

"Take the *glezzel*, the juice glass, it's just the right size, now cut the circles, twist the glass a little bit. *Gut! Azoi*, just so."

By the time Mom and Dad came home from their week away, we had home-baked cookies and large, scribbled signs to welcome them. We were glad to see them, but sorry to see that *heimishe* (homey) ambiance fade. Our parents enriched our lives with many wonderful things—concerts, parks, sports, museums—doting on us and educating us carefully. But cookie and strudel baking was Bubby's province.

She started to write little stories about her childhood in Toperey, a typical shtetl. We all had photocopies, made that much more vivid with her small, immigrant scrawl and hand-crafted spelling. I was spellbound. Her so-incredibly-different life. After reading the latest installment, I would sit and just stare at her. How could she and I even be sitting in the same room?

My experience of struggle was losing my homework, having mismatched socks, or getting a bad haircut. This patient lady lost both parents at a young age. She watched drunken peasants ravage her town, shouting, "Kill the Jews and save Russia." They burst into her little home and savagely murdered her uncle, stabbing him in the head. He alone was attacked because it was the Sabbath, and he refused to hide with the rest of the family.

She continued the harrowing saga. "From then on it was hell on earth. It was so bad that we had nothing to wear. Aunt Libby went to the sugar factory and got burlap bags, so we made skirts for ourselves. David was drafted into the Bolshevik Army when he was seventeen years old."

And even before that, when life was relatively normal, it looked so different from mine. Bubby ate vegetables and dairy from the garden all week.

"On Shabbos we ate soup with noodles that my aunt made. The chicken or meat was cut up in little pieces on a plate and we each took one or two pieces with challah."

One or two pieces? That little fact blew my mind. I imagined her savoring tiny bites of her small portion. Not us. We ate meat every night, as Mom explained, "In the fifties and sixties, that was considered a proper dinner, what men wanted." Who knew from cholesterol or saturated fat? Lamb chops, roasts, chicken, hamburgers, stews—full portions, no minuscule morsel.

Her hiding, shlepping, running, to make it over the border was traumatic.

"We were on the way to America. We were running and hiding in a barn. It was in the middle of the night. I was coughing and the man wanted to push something in my mouth if I didn't stop. My brother David cried and pleaded with the man not to hurt me."

She finally made it onto a boat and across to Mama Liberty's arms, then bravely persevered to carve out a life in a strange, new world. It was all more than I could grasp.

And the sweet routines she carefully described of her "very religious" aunt and uncle's farm life —breaking the poppy seeds off the flower into her hand, feeding the chickens, waking up early

Friday morning to the aroma of fresh challah and the treat of little *"pletzels"* made from the dough scraps, fresh from the wood-stoked oven.

"Aunt Libby had a few chickens. She would put some eggs in a big basket and let the chickens sit on the eggs for about three weeks. We could actually see the eggs crack and the little chicks come out. It was beautiful to see the mother hen walk and the little chicks follow her.

"When it was time to feed them, my aunt would stand outside and call them. Tzip-tzip-tzip! And they would come running. In the evening they would sleep in the chicken coop. My cousin Eve had to milk the cow and I had to sift about ten pounds of flour. I did not mind so much sifting the flour, but why couldn't I do it some other time? It was nice outside, and children were playing. There was nothing I could do about it but sift the flour,"

I imagined that skinny little girl with big eyes and long, brown braids, banging on the sifter bigger than her.

"The shining samovar was standing on the table and my uncle with his friends were drinking tea, one glass after another, with lumps of sugar—and at the same time reading the Bible and arguing like mad over something."

She painted a picture of the simple pleasures of Friday night and the rhythmic cycle of holidays. Shavuos, marking the giving of the Ten Commandments, sounded especially magical.

"Then came the beautiful holiday Shavuos when the house was cleaned and decorated with green leaves that we brought from the river. Sukkos, that was also a happy time. My uncle had a built- in *sukkah*. All year we had wood there. For Sukkos he opened up the roof and we had to clean up the *sukkah*, carry everything out, paint it, wash the window, and put up clean curtains. Aunt Libby used to light her candles there, and we ate there for a week. After eating, the children used to like to look at the moon and the stars sparkling through the roof."

Bubby's stories evoked a distant melody of a vastly different, yet somehow close-to-me, world.

4

---◆◇◆---

FREED FROM SUPERSTITION

Bubby's house was the site of one aspect of our Jewish education: the sensory, between-the-lines sense of deep heritage and yellowed, vintage, sweet, and melancholy yearning something, pulling something, aching something.

Mom and Dad grew up in a world where *Yiddishkeit* (Jewish culture and values) was an integral part of the background, richly implicit if not completely explicit. Most every shopkeeper swore and dreamed in Yiddish. The very air, the atmosphere, was colored by rich, pungent roots.

But Bubby's house was full of crumbling books, and anyway, Yiddish was dying out. It was for old people, to enrich jokes, and for our parents to speak when they didn't want us to understand—while I was young and heading into the future.

Our formal Jewish education took place at the Birmingham Temple, an iconoclastic, progressive place. Tamara had led our temple for a few years. But we grew up with her predecessor, Rabbi Sherwin Wine, who started the Birmingham Temple and the whole Humanistic Judaism movement.

We called him Sherwin, with casual familiarity. Part of the same Central High gang, Dad and Sherwin were born one day apart; they hung out in neighboring cribs in the same hospital nursery. They smiled from the pages of the Central High yearbook. Sherwin was a leader in theater and oratory, and valedictorian of those accomplished fine minds; while Dad was a debate club member and class president. (His campaign manager, Jack Alspector, who later roomed with Dad at Harvard, blitzed the opponents with his rousing campaign slogan, "Don't be a piker, vote for Driker.")

Mom and Dad joined a big Reform temple a few years after their wedding, but it just didn't speak to them. I was enrolled in the kindergarten Hebrew School, where I cried at dismissal, hovering by the door, afraid that I wouldn't get picked up. The rabbi gave me a Ten Commandments pin during the graduation ceremony. I didn't know what that strange little two humped square with tiny Hebrew letters was. It lay in a little compartment in my pink sequined jewelry box for years, a mystery. We tykes had to walk down a long aisle in a giant sanctuary and climb up on a big stage to get that symbol pinned on us. It was overwhelming and frightening.

The next year they switched to Sherwin's temple, which was still in its infancy, back in the early sixties. They found a community in the handful of radicals who journeyed with Sherwin in his leftward movement from Reform, into a controversial, non-deistic theology.

Humanism shared much of the same impulse as the Yiddish culture school Dad went to as kid. Much of his generation was striving for rational understanding, for coming to terms with the challenges and opportunities of American culture and secular education.

Bubby wrote about the *cheder*, the old world religious school in Toperey, where teachers pulled down the wild kids' pants and *potched* (spanked) or paddled them. Grandma Ida's family was religious, her bearded father in a long black coat, serious little mother in a long black dress. They held on to empty rituals they didn't seem to understand and were always warding off the evil eye.

Could my parents see any reason to embrace or continue that kind of Jewish life? They were attracted to a modern, emancipated Judaism that seemed to step with the direction their world was marching to. Logic uber alles: they were college-educated professionals, and antibiotics, the polio vaccine, and space travel were pushing away dark ignorance and superstition. Humanism seemed like the new Enlightenment, blazing pioneering trails as Reform had become a staid and accepted movement with large, fancy temples.

Rabbi Wine was not alone. Three simple words—"Is God Dead?"—blazed across a controversial 1966 cover of *Time* magazine. The issue quoted philosophers and theologians who were grappling with this red-hot question. I overheard adults scorning and praising the piece. From an eight-year-olds vantage point, I couldn't understand how radical the concept of a deity-free Judaism was. I just took childish pride in being part of something novel and different.

"What temple do you go to? Are you in NIFTY—the Reform Youth Movement?" Suzy's mom asked as we sat at her table, eating Oreos and drinking milk one day after school. Suzy was my new friend. We were in the same reading group in Mrs. White's third grade class.

"Oh, no. We belong to the Birmingham Temple."

"Where's that? Don't you mean Temple Israel or Beth El?" Mrs. Cohen thought for a moment. "Wait. Isn't that Rabbi Wine's place?" Her voice took on an accusing tone.

"Yeah, he's our rabbi," I answered with a hesitant smile, sensing her antipathy.

Mrs. Cohen moved back slightly. "Oh."

Then there came some variation of the shrug, silence, or raising the eyebrows.

I felt a bit uncomfortable, as if I had the cooties, but I developed a defiant kind of pride. I didn't really understand what the issues were and why everyone seemed to think it was weird, bad even, but I grew to like the reaction. I was *cool*, different, not your average, run-of- the-mill person.

I thought of our philosophy as something like this: "We're proud to be Jewish. We like our holidays and foods and songs; they are part of our culture. There's no way we can know if there's a God or not. And it doesn't matter in our day-to-day lives. We make our own decisions and try to be good people. No hidden figure in the sky is gonna save us. We have to take responsibility for ourselves."

(In a way, the observant Jews agree. As one Chassidic rabbi says, "Hey, you know that Stern Judging Father up in the sky, that you don't believe in? Well, guess what? I don't either." It would take some digging to realize that image was indeed simplistic. Only later, after searching assiduously under many stones, I came to realize that the Torah was more subtle, nuanced, and multi-layered than that stodgy religion that Sherwin rejected as irrelevant.)

I went to temples and synagogues now and then for a cousin's or friend's Bar Mitzvah. So big, so sterile. One interchangeable with the next. Some rabbi way up on the podium in a maroon robe, seemed so far away.

"And now let us turn to page 37 and rise."

And people dressed carefully, 'to a T,' with their fashionable holiday finery on parade, perfume wafting and diamonds flashing. They were standing and sitting on cue, on automatic pilot, singing words I assumed they didn't understand, in a strange language. I gleaned that our temple was special, because we had bucked the tide, and we actually thought out for ourselves what we believed. We didn't go along for the ride with tradition just because it was there, just because it was, well, traditional.

Our temple met in rented schools, rather than in fancy, thea-ter-like sanctuaries with plush seats. We did Israeli folk dancing and went on fun winter weekends with some ten to twenty families, sledding down the giant hill at Camp Tamarack. The best year was when Marcia, a professor at the University of Michigan, led the girls in raiding the boys' bunk and victoriously stringing their clothes up the flagpole. Almost a small extended family, with an intimate feel.

Sunday School was pretty blah. There was some quaint little book about morals, along with *The Wise Men of Chelm*—funny stories about a town of *meshugenners* (crazies) somewhere in Poland, whose warped Jewish logic repeatedly got them *oif tzorus* (in hot water). The book seemed to confirm that old-world lore was nostalgic, charming—and basically ridiculous.

In sixth grade I learned how to hide in the bathroom and ditch class, going for walks in the ball field behind the school, something I never would have dared try, but my friend Rebecca guided me. I felt scared, daring, and rebelliously free, actually tiptoeing into my first major venture into trying out being "bad" and breaking out of the normal limits and expectations. No thunder boomed. No lightning crashed on us. We ambled over to the carpool line up at dismissal time, and no one seemed to have noticed or cared. The teacher was probably glad to have two fewer antsy teeny-boppers on her hands.

In tenth grade, my involvement with the temple got a jump-start. Sherwin offered a high school philosophy class that sounded interesting. A deeper look into life's issues and mysteries. Even the very word *philosophy* was impressive. I felt very grown up, sitting around the conference table with a few other students and the rabbi. We read and discussed humanistic philosophers, including Sartre, Camus, Bertrand Russell, and Nietzsche.

Rabbi Wine seemed so self-assured as he strode into the room with his perfect posture and immaculate dress. He sat at the end of the large, oblong table. The half-dozen or so of us students sat around the sides. The atmosphere felt cool and detached, as if we were a privileged elite. Classics and philosophy books neatly lined the library shelves. The Torah scroll had its own shelf.

Other synagogues kept the scroll in an ark in the main sanctuary, in the front of the congregation. It occupied a place of honor, was covered with velvet and brocade covers, its wooden staves topped with a silver crown. Taking the scroll in and out of the ark was marked with much ceremony: special songs, everyone standing. It was carried slowly to the *bimah*, the reading platform, with a protective care, the way grandparents might cuddle and hold a new infant. The congregants would watch it pass by lovingly, reaching out their hands to kiss it.

Our Torah was housed on a shelf in the library, as it was not considered divine, but a significant artifact and shaper of the Jewish historical and cultural experience. The *bimah* in our sanctuary had an artistic rendition in wooden letters of the Hebrew word *Adam*. Man was the shaper of his destiny; he was the being our readings and meditations focused on. I used to gaze at the stylized *Aleph, Daled,* and *Mem* shapes as my mind wandered during services, a short array of readings and discussion of politics or other significant trends.

Each book and item in that library seemed consciously and carefully chosen and granted a space. I have a picture of Mom in a Bible study class with Sherwin. He is far off, at the end of the table, at a right angle to her, and she is taking careful, neat notes. Everyone seems ensconced in their own private space. That's how the temple seemed to a teen: quiet, poised, and cool. I loved being an adult and studying philosophy, but it was presented in neat boxes, organized and defined by Sherwin.

Then it was time for my confirmation, a coming-of-age we celebrated at sixteen. Mom dropped me off for private preparatory sessions. I greeted the secretary, fiddled with a magazine, and was escorted into the rabbi's office. I had some general ideas for my speech, and tried to explain them as Sherwin listened politely. We discussed them. Sherwin outlined bullet points on his yellow legal pad, in angular script, with a long silver ballpoint pen. Then he gave me books to read before our next session. Somehow, during the course of our meetings, my vague ideas were reformulated by Sherwin into a step-by-step proof of the supremacy of

Humanism over backwards and benighted Orthodox, Conservative, and Reform.

I spoke well at the Friday night service. But the run-up to the event was typical sixteen-year-old. I almost didn't make it to the temple, as I was busy having a temper tantrum about my awful hair.

"I'm *not* going," I cried and stamped, about an hour before we were supposed to get to the temple. I stood in front of the mirror, curling iron in hand, scowling at the hideous figure with the yucky hair who mocked me with frantic, bloodshot eyes. But somehow, logic prevailed (Mom's or Dad's, not mine), and we made it to the temple intact. I presented my/Sherwin's talk with poise and dignity, and gained some public speaking confidence. The Kiddush reception was lovely and I had a fun sledding party the next day.

Later, after the gifts were opened and the thank-you cards written, I was left with a squirmy feeling. I didn't necessarily disagree with the rabbi, at least not consciously, but I felt vaguely ripped off—as though I'd been a mouthpiece for his dogma, and had been denied true exploration. (I later realized, fissures and the whispers of mystical ideas were already forming in the back of my mind and heart.)

Camus and Sartre seemed more open-ended and human when we chewed on them in Mrs. David's literature class. The tragedy of Sisyphus, endlessly and futilely struggling to carry rocks up the mountain, only to slide to the bottom and begin again, struck a chord. Work. Marry. Have children, raise them. Get old and infirm. Die. Then they do the same. If it's just about the material gain, what was the point, I wondered. Generation after generation, struggling, saving, pushing, suffering—for what?

Even if they weren't struggling—they were shopping and dining and planning vacations, as we did in our respectable green-lawned and bushes-neatly-trimmed world—what for? The abundance left me starving. *There's gotta be more, there's gotta be more,* that little annoying bedbug voice, kept crawling into my quiet bed, and disturbing my somnolent slumber and making me swat and itch.

But here in the Birmingham Temple I don't remember chewing and exploring the way I did with Mrs. David. It was cool to be reading grown-up material, but we were expected to swallow what Sherwin had chewed for us and dictated in clear, encapsulated outlines, sentence after sentence explaining to us exactly what these thinkers meant.

I did enjoy our study of Mao's *Little Red Book*, more for its cachet and what it symbolized than its content, as I only read a little, and slowly drifted off.

One day I was trapped. Like a proletarian worker, I was exploited by my mom, stuck as a passenger on one of her bourgeoisie-indulgent errands, to an exalted castle of the ruling class, no less. It was too cold to wait in the car, so I sullenly sat by the escalators in Jacobson's, an upscale department store, waiting for Mom to choose which scarf best complemented her new maroon blouse. I felt very self-righteous reading my *Little Red Book* in the middle of all these bustling shoppers. They were buying designer names, as the revolution was fermenting and about to explode!

I held up my little red plastic-covered book as I read, so everyone could see it. They all must have known what critical, subversive-to-their-empty-lives material I was pursuing. It felt hot, like lit dynamite in my hands. They were glancing at my surly, scowling countenance, and seemed to keep a wide berth. They must have been afraid; it's obvious what a comrade reading small red book means; obviously, it was *The* Red Book.

"Where is Mom? Let's get out of here already," I muttered to myself. Finally, after what seemed like forever, I stashed the book in my backpack and sauntered over to the accessory section. Mom held up two scarves. "What do you think? Which color looks better?"

"Oh, Mom," I whined. "Who cares? Let's just go already." Seeing her hurt, I shrugged and reluctantly acquiesced. "Fine.

Show me again. Ummm, I like the gold thread in that one, it gives it more, you know, pizzazz."

"I think so, too," she said, smiling in agreement.

"Can we go now?" You have your silly scarf, lady, I thought, as I obnoxiously continued my refrain. "Give me the keys while you pay. I'll wait in the car. I've gotta get out of here. Hurry!" And I sauntered and slithered out.

The revolution didn't happen. Jacobson's was still standing. But I moved on. By twelfth grade, my interest in the philosophy class faded as I sensed the limitations of rational logic. I was starting to see that logic was a worthwhile tool. It could go good places and do good things. But it couldn't spawn wings, or soar into that dazzling, pulsing world of mysticism and metaphysics. It seemed a veneer, a flat and empty shell. I knew, with growing certainty and excitement, there was another whole realm of existence that Bertrand and Co. just couldn't tap into. And I was gonna learn that language, too.

5

———◦◦◦———

HIGH SCHOOL SEARCHING,
FIRST BELIEVING

I suffered occasional "What is an *I*? Where does that *I* go?"
cracks in the egg my parents lovingly cooked for me, their "be
a good person, be mildly and culturally Jewish, and march
ahead" omelet. That bedbug nuisance burrowed into my skin
from time to time, whispering, "There's gotta be more." But on
the surface, life proceeded with the normal ups and downs of a
child, and then young teen.

My early adolescence was textbook typical: filled with pimply,
self-conscious obsession with peers. I had been working so hard at
perfecting junior-high cool during seventh and eighth grades,
scrunching my being into a meticulously observed and copied
definition of cool, circa 1970.

By the end of elementary school I was getting ready to launch
my career as the new-and- improved, with-it chick. Even though
my parents and teacher thought I had promise, I quit violin before
junior high. There was no way I'd be seen toting that thing
around—everyone knew that violin was an instrument for nerds. I
practiced cartwheels endlessly, and cheered till I was hoarse. All

the aches and pains were worth it; I made the seventh-grade cheerleading team and shook my gold-and-blue pom-poms with gusto.

"A-C-T...I-O-N—Action, speed, yes indeed!"—great stag jump, head tipped sideways with peppy smile.

I strove mightily to hang with the in crowd: thick, black eyeliner and clumpy mascara make-up just so. I dragged Mom to the pre-teen boutique A La Mode, and spent ages trying on each pair of hip-hugging bell- bottom jeans, peering in the mirror for just the right fit, not a hair's-breadth too loose or high or low. I laughed at the right guys' jokes; and choked on a cigarette and sipped on Boone's Farm Wine, down on the corner.

Judaism was all about getting invited to the cool Bar Mitzvahs (I didn't), and knowing all the dances, which the kids learned at Joe Cornell Dance Studio so they could wow the crowds at those lavish-themed parties. (I didn't take the lessons so maybe it's just as well I wasn't invited. What a fool I would have made of myself, not knowing the Twist and whatever other numbers those sweaty kids mastered.)

By the end of junior high, this wearying effort seemed to spin and spin but go nowhere. Never quite with-it enough, I started to get tired of the shallow cliques. *Perhaps* they weren't the be-all and end-all of existence.... I finally started to regain a sense of self and choose friends I (surprise) enjoyed being with. As I entered ninth and tenth grades, the cracks of dissonance with the placid world I knew deepened and spread.

Summer camp was a place I felt more integrated and whole. From the age of about nine, I spent at least a month each summer away from malls, away from square grid-mile roads; on the untarnished hills and beaches of Camp Tamarack that I came to know like the back of my hand.

I can still see the country road curve just so up near Pioneer Village, where the Queen Anne's Lace and Black-Eyed Susans go wild in their August abundance, their last kiss of summer smell punctuating the hot tar of the lonely, one-lane road. The dip of the canoe oar slicing through the blue lake.

I loved the relaxed pace, the natural, simple life, and the communal camaraderie of camp. I didn't just belong to a nuclear family isolated from the neighbors ensconced in their private lives, behind chained doors, two-car garages shut and locked, sitting silently in front of their TVs, the gray light shining through their living rooms and beaming *The Brady Bunch* and *Gilligan's Island* to the mesmerized observers.

I belonged to a bunk, a village, teeming and pulsing. When camp ended, I felt my soul rage like a caged animal, leaving the bus filled with crying and cheering kids to enter a way-too-quiet car: Something deep inside me sighed. I'd take my moldy duffle bag full of wet towels and lovely camp pebbles and filth right into the laundry room, so it wouldn't dirty up the house, and soak sullenly in the bath, viewing all my scabs, bruises, and mosquito bites as badges of honor.

In the lonely silence I heard echoes of cheering village mates. I sat on my neat bed in my solitary room which had been waiting forlornly for my return. I finally wandered down to the kitchen to get something to eat. When I finished my sandwich, I got up from the table, listened for announcements and cheers that never came. I threw away the scraps and started nostalgically singing the after-lunch medley to myself.

A Tamarack goat was feeling fine
Ate three red shirts right off the line!

My lone voice and hand tapping on the clean table were pathetic. Where was the exuberant chorus, the raucous sound of kids banging and screaming to win points for bunk competition?

As I lay in clean, pressed sheets, I felt the splashing water, the baking sun and slimy seaweed between my toes. I heard the roar of shouting kids and lifeguards shrill whistles as they shouted "Buddy call!" during general swim.

But every summer, that spark of my soul would stretch and come to life as I joined the jabbering kids while chatting parents milling around. We shlepped our footlockers to the luggage truck, grabbed our shopping bags overstuffed with nosh, looked for a familiar face, and boarded. The ratty brown school buses pulled out of the JCC parking lot and headed north, up I-75 to the little town of Ortonville, then ambled down the gravel road to our beloved oasis.

At Tamarack, I'd gotten little tastes of a deeper, truer self and a Jewish spirit that reached beyond boring Sunday School and inane Bar Mitzvah celebrations.

At eleven, I was in Sheruth Village. Our bunk was dominated by a few "queens," stereotypical JAPs—Jewish American Princesses. They strutted around with the latest clothes, the biggest boxes of nosh, and Attitude—while we peasants vied to be a lady-in-waiting and gain their approval. They cast their scorn on Bonnie, an unsophisticated, homely girl, and held court while delivering cutting putdowns to her cot, from their perch on the top bunks.

Rest hour was prime time for this activity, when we were all cooped up in the bunkhouse, ostensibly to write letters home. For the first few days, we listened quietly, some of us giggling nervously and offering supporting barbs to the Queens, so that we'd get in their good graces. Bonnie lie on her cot and turned towards the wall, crying quietly.

It was not a pretty scene. One afternoon, my conscience got the upper hand. I decided to take a stand, throwing caution to the wind, knowing I risked becoming prey for their next assault. I took a deep breath, my knees shaking, and went over to vulnerable Bonnie's bed, sat down, and started talking with her, making a point to glare at her attackers. I went out of my way to befriend her for the rest of camp.

I don't know if my intervention made that much of a difference to Bonnie, but it was a defining moment for me. My sense of self seemed to go dormant soon after, as I dove into those glorious pre-teen years of almost total preoccupation with fitting in. But a little glimmer of that moment of truth, shone deep in the pit of my being. It reminded me that I could stand for a principle; it felt like a soul stirring and calling.

A communal sensation was also stirred at camp. Singing, Israeli dancing, celebrating Shabbat with the village—all awakened a vague feeling that being Jewish was some kind of unique belonging, unique peoplehood. Group singing in music class at Burton Elementary or at Girl Scout meetings just wasn't the same.

When I hit sixteen, I innocuously signed up for Camp Tamarack's Western Trip, a month-long touring and camping trip. We twenty kids and three counselors rode a bumpy school bus through the Rockies, Yellowstone, and Tetons and all the way to Banff, circling back across the Badlands. Big time wow. A glorious explosion of snow-capped mountain peaks touching the sky, pristine air, adventure, youthful idealism, and idyllic valleys. We pitched tents, built campfires, hiked breathtaking trails and munched on sticky s'mores.

We swayed and sang "Rocky Mountain High" around the campfire, the sparks reflecting in our dreamy eyes. How did John Denver know exactly what we were feeling and the perfect words to describe the high we were on?

High on nature, that was all we needed. Come to think of it, the counselors let us minors have a sip of beer (Coors, brewed in Colorado, of course) one Friday night. (Shhh, don't tell anyone. Anyway, the statute of limitations must have run out on that one.)

Our bus pulled out of Teton National Park after we broke camp early one morning, and drove under a picture-perfect rainbow stretched across a valley. The majesty and force of nature called and insisted, "There's more, there's more." We put together our Western Trip version of "The Man Who Never Returned," gustily singing during the endless hours on Spurt, our forest green school bus who valiantly chugged up the mountains. Man, this country is *big*, we realized, the distances and spaces amazing.

Oh, they'll never return, yes, they'll never return,
And their fate is still unlearned,
They may stay forever in the Rocky Mountains,
They're the group that never returned.

Now, you citizens of Detroit, don't you think it's crazy,
That your children have chosen to stay,
In the rugged Rocky Mountains
Where there are no TVs, and their stereos they cannot play.

(Well, we sort of forgot those square citizens of Detroit were footing the bill for this glorious expedition.)

At seventeen I returned to my favorite habitat to work as a junior counselor. I finally got one of those way-cool gray Camp Tamarack hooded sweatshirts with STAFF emblazoned on the back. Besides learning to care for kids and plotting color-war schemes and drinking in the warm sun and refreshing lake, I hooked up with Eileen and Doug, two earnest, guitar-strumming seekers.

I already knew a drop about the Eastern outlook from my high-school-dropout buddy Sue. We hadn't *really* dropped out, we trudged through the halls of Berkley High together, but at the same time I was making academic headway in advanced literature, physics, and math, Sue and I had dropped out of the normative social scene. We were elsewhere.

I first saw the purple, magical, inviting, Ram Dass tome *Be Here Now* at Sue's house. Her parents were artists, and her house much more strange and exotic than mine. All kinds of books and sculptures and herbal smells were just around the corner in unexpected rooms and darkened nooks, behind beaded curtains. *Be Here Now* glistened, a little scary, luring. A tickling, entrancing peek into completely different reality. It beckoned, "Come little one, come into—just being, just oneness, a mystical, marvelous space." The simple words teased: step into the silence, the space between the nonstop words, thoughts, chatter of your Western, linear, racing existence. Ram Dass started off from familiar turf, a nice Jewish boy named Richard Alpert who had a Ph.D. from Stanford. He then zoomed off into the stratosphere and opened up the world I was hungry for.

Sue and I hung out in the back when we had to go to the fields for gym and do dumb relays and calisthenics. My starry-eyed pal and I were barely there, just going through the motions. Our fraying, baggy overalls drew disdainful looks from the smartly made-up prom queens and neatly Nike'd jocks. We were hanging in an alternative realm, also dabbling in political action as we picketed stores on behalf of the migrant grape and lettuce pickers. We felt for the underdog, but our efforts didn't seem to add up to much. (I still feel a reflexive pang of guilt when I pick up a head of iceberg lettuce at the store.)

Julie and Sam also hung with us in our zone. We spent long weekend nights driving around and around the 'burbs; up Woodward, stopping in for a coffee or tea. Sometimes we hit our favorite coffee house, where a folk singer strummed, expressing our yearning for something more rosy and whole. We dreamers ambled down one of the mile roads; miles going nowhere, feeling the freedom of wheels as we were talking, wondering, sharing our meandering thoughts and questions.

Every Christmas Eve we found an interesting or different church, and sit way in the back, taking in the music, ritual, pageantry, and sense of awe—so missing from our college-prep lives. We sat under the glistening golden dome of the Greek Orthodox Church one year, the next in the cozy wooden chapel on the grounds of Cranbrook, looking and smelling, seeking and sensing threads of greater mystery and meaning.

But that summer at camp, my searching got a boost, new fuel for the fire. Eileen was a step ahead of us Berkley High kids, as was Doug. Older, wise, more versed in those new views whose door I was scratching at, like a stray kitten out in the cold that senses warmth inside.

They were both studying at the glamorous, mysterious University of Michigan. Eileen was a regular devotee at an ashram, like she worked on that *Be Here Now* stuff on a daily, disciplined basis. She shared little tidbits of exotic Eastern insight, doling them out sparingly, so I was entranced and hungry for more, the way I lure my preschool class to focus with small drops of candy and stickers. I couldn't wait to get to funky Ann Arbor, site of the SDS revolution and hippie happenings, and check it out myself.

As for the gang—the old family friends and relatives—as my revelation revolution gained steam, they watched my progress (downward or upward, depending on your point of view). They saw the sparkly-eyed, straight-A student, the little good girl twirling in her new dress at the family Chanukah parties. Now the sullen, way-cool hippie would occasionally tolerate showing up at a family event in ripped overalls, maybe toting another grungy, long-haired companion so she'd have *someone* to talk to besides these hopelessly narrow-minded squares.

They saw the sweet, typical girl change as the ferment started to brew, as the Miriam Show went through its incarnations and acts.

I brought Brian to Uncle Eugene's Fourth of July barbecue. He was my friend's big brother, and one of the first real counter-culture people I hung out with. In the early seventies, antiwar activism was morphing into mellow-yellow spiritual times. He took me along to some kind of food co-op, where the food was so simple and real: orange lentils, brown rice, seeds and nuts. In glass jars and brown paper bags—no labels, no brand names, no commercialization, no stripping of nutrients or bleaching, colors and textures speaking for themselves.

I was enchanted. He seemed to know so much, talking about friends in India and sitar music and all kinds of exotic things. He indulged the aspiring hippie, the wide-eyed, kid-sister's friend, letting me tag along to a get-together with other Detroit-area free spirits, with yoga, meditation, and Sufi-dancing in the woods of Palmer Park, a lovely urban park. These gentle souls seemed to be popping up all over the place, like elves peeking out of the corners of normative American life. Brian revealed a hidden world I never encountered at the temple or shopping mall.

I'd gone ice skating on Palmer Park's frozen pond, but never imagined that childhood destination of swans and fountains could be the site of such a new and groovy happening.

Afterwards, Brian drove me to the family picnic in his beat up VW van he shared with some friends. Everyone I knew drove shiny new Fords and Chevrolets, purchased from a dealer, with colorful plastic flags waving over the lot and carefully groomed salesmen waiting to help them drive off in the latest model. One just didn't share wheels on their last legs with friends, and patch them together with spit and duct tape. This communal-type reality seemed so dreamy and cooperative. Peace and love, man.

Eugene approached with a friendly, outstretched hand, even if he may have been inwardly rolling his eyes.

"Would you like a hamburger?"

"Oh, no thanks," Brian replied with a condescending smile. "I don't eat meat." I nodded in agreement.

With that disparaging eye cast on their bounty, my carnivorous family anyway tried to engage us moonbeams in conversation. We munched on salad and watermelon, topped off with Bubby's strudel and cookies, before Brian headed off to his next grooving stop, leaving me with the hopelessly earth-bound family and my math homework to finish before my hopelessly boring school week would start once again.

6

—◦≈◦✧◦≈◦—

BEYOND LOGIC

Mom's new scarf had sparkly gold threads. It hung smartly on her shoulder, the colors accenting her dark eyes. Not for me. My threads weren't spun of silk or rayon. They weren't stocked at Jacobson's, Hudson's, or even Saks.

I hungered to find dazzling threads of cosmic light, hints of something big and new. Calculus and physics seemed to be pointing in the direction of shining nuggets of a purer reality. Quantum physics confirmed my sense that this material world wasn't as solid, stolid as it seemed. A dancing field of dynamic energy lay under the roads that were paved across and down the square-mile grid that made getting around the Detroit area so easy. South to north, marking the miles from Downtown, were 11 Mile Road, 12 Mile Road, 13 Mile Road. East to west was also defined by a mile grid—Coolidge, Greenfield, Southfield Roads. All testimony of that human urge to confine and box up an entropic, pulsing universe.

One day I found an entrancing book at Border's. It jumped off the shelf and into my life. *The Tao of Physics*, written by a physicist, explored the parallels between modern physics and mysticism. It verified my intuition about this new stuff, and pushed that dry two- dimensional logic out—too limited by the rational physical senses, languishing in the dust. This book soon became a well-worn favorite; I carried it around and found a way to reference it in most every paper I had to write.

I liked to raid Mom's bookshelves for more fuel. She and her group of well-read friends kept up with the latest. They had monthly Book Group meetings featuring books like *Siddhartha*, *The Electric Kool-Aid Acid Test*, and *Zen and the Art of Motorcycle Maintenance*. Local professors would lecture to the women about these and other cutting-edge works.

Sometimes I tagged along to listen. But I'd squirm in frustration. Didn't these ladies *understand* the words they were reading and analyzing? They'd perch coffee on their knees, enjoy the new art and latest furniture and culinary best of their hostess. She, meanwhile, had been busy, having the carpets cleaned, shopping for just the right dips and pastries; stressing and arranging everything just so for weeks.

Startling revolutionary words were jumping out of those pages! I wanted to jump on the table, throw the quiche on the floor and scream. I was ready to wander the dirt path with Siddhartha, to climb on the bus with Ken Kesey and his gang, in the search for enlightenment and the new, shimmering reality.

Meanwhile, the women just sat there and nodded sagely at the professor's dissecting and oh-so-clever posturing. They seemed to only pay lip service to the ideas; while, in my know-it-all mind, I alone seemed to take them to heart. Some took the analytic approach: "So, Professor, what exactly is Kesey advocating? Is his movement an aberration or are many of today's young people as disaffected? What percentage, would you say?" Claudia crossed her legs, pushed up her glasses, and smiled intelligently, awaiting his insightful answer.

Sylvia, a sensitive woman, seemed to take the words more personally. She quoted meaningful phrases and listened dreamily, writing poetry in her notebook. I was even more perplexed. How could she process these ideas, be affected, and then take her son to his orthodontist appointment? Was Sylvia prudent and mature—or copping out? Maybe, just maybe, she shouldn't throw away her kids, marriage, mortgage, and job to ride that *happening* bus?

It seemed crystal-clear to impatient-for-enlightenment me: how could they read these blazing words and then turn to Lorraine and ask where she'd gotten her hair done? How could the professor pack up his briefcase and go home to grade papers? They put on their fur coats and noted the date of the next month's meeting on their leather-bound, monogrammed pocket calendars. I was left hanging, frustrated.

High school calculus was a respite, a place where something was brewing. We were a small group of more scholarly kids joking, hanging out, and doing formulas that were achingly beautiful in their elegance. Mr. Pearl, our teacher, was a sweet man with an expressive, Woody Allen sort of face, laughing brown eyes, and curly black hair that tended towards the wild and disobedient.

One day he came in late and grabbed a piece of chalk, which broke as he started scribbling formulas on the board. Soon he stopped because of the muffled laughter rippling through the class.

"Alright," he said, grinning, "what is it this time?"

I piped up. "Your belt, Mr. P."

He glanced down, turned red, and burst out laughing. Then he turned his back to us, removed the brown belt that had been buckled on top of the black one, and gave some kind of comeback.

We could just imagine our absent-minded professor thinking over some problem or talking to his kids as he layered on the belts.

Mr. Brown, our pre-calculus teacher, seemed a shy and innocent soul from the realm of pure mathematics. We loved him because he was so egoless, a tall, balding man with quiet, pale eyes hidden behind thick, horn-rimmed glasses. When he lectured, he gazed over our heads at a back corner of the room and explained his formulas in a monotone, not even making eye contact. But from him, the formulas were poetry. His tests were somehow like works of art, so balanced, logical, and precise, while Mr. Pearl's

53

were scrawled in almost illegible hand and a bit loose around the edges, sometimes with little inconsistencies.

Seth, who would go on to study architecture at MIT, came in with a big package one day. During break he opened it, and quickly distributed white T-shirts, with a line drawing of Mr. B. printed on the back.

"Wow, these are amazing!"

"You really got him in those few lines." "I can't wait to see his reaction."

We quickly put them on, and sat quietly in our seats, buzzing with anticipation. Mr. Brown walked in, set down his books neatly, opened to the right page, stood up and began lecturing in his quiet voice.

"We left off on page 178, with the quadratic function."

Seth counted to three. We all turned around, revealing the face of our hero emblazoned on our backs.

It took a minute for Mr. B. to grasp what was going on. We turned back around to see him stare for a few seconds. A blush stole up his cheeks, then he cracked a shy smile.

Score!

A higher world peeked through, down there in room 52. We hung out and did what in Chassidic terminology I now call *"farbrenged"*—sharing humor, irreverence, and wonder, perched up there on the edge.

Then there was physics. Mrs. Plotkin droned on in her flat, thick Polish accent, an older, soft- spoken woman. I got the impression that she may have been a refugee who fled from Hitler some thirty years earlier.

"Clazzzz, pleezzze, today ve are talking about Newton, and how he made ze calculation for gravity."

Spitballs flew and the buzz of whispering grew louder as she went on and on, working her way through page after page.

The Holocaust was hardly ever mentioned back in our carefree American Happy Days. This overwhelming tragedy crept up to the edge of my world just twice.

Tisha B'Av, the quintessential Jewish day of mourning—the day the first and second Temples were destroyed, the Spanish Inquisition started, and other grim historical tragedies occurred—comes in the middle of the summer. The Camp Tamarack staff made an assembly to mark it.

"What's this about?" I asked Lori. "Are they breaking out color war?"

We filed into a stuffy, crowded auditorium. The director, one of the few middle-aged people visible on the camp groups, came out of his office. He seemed so dowdy and out of place among the screaming, bopping, youthful surge of camp energy, the only person in a button-down shirt we'd seen since we left home. He talked about something serious; some kind of modern-day destruction. I couldn't really hear him, and it sounded too much like school anyway.

They darkened the lights and showed us grainy black and white clips of emaciated toothpick survivors hobbling out of concentration camps. But I had no context to stick this in; the footage a random and menacing image. Only years later did I understand what we had seen and what it had to do with us.

My grandparents had one friend, Mr. Schwartz, who was a survivor. He shared Bubby and Zaidy's Yiddish accent and destroyed world. He looked at least as old as them, but more shriveled. He made me nervous; he was too skinny and intense and had some yucky bluish numbers on his arm. He went around trying to find youth groups to listen to his strange and sad experience of some sort. He was scary.

Mrs. Plotkin seemed to know a lot about her subject. But she was born and bred in a different world. Generation gap, cultural differences, thick accent, lackluster materials—added up to a pretty boring class and unengaged students. But somehow, I got some kind of bug for what she was trying to teach us, for the ideas and implications that one could spin off the formulas.

Physics seemed like a path to understanding those tantalizing mysteries; seemed more real than the constructs and the castle-building, postulating world of Sherwin's philosophies.

E=MC2—that means everything really is one! Like all this static separateness really, scientifically, *is* an illusion. Here was solid proof, in scientific language, for the purple, Ram Dass, misty reality. I started thinking about studying physics and advanced mathematics in college, more for the mystical insights that tingled through the formulas than for the practical experiments.

I liked the ideas and theories better than the actual applications. Engines, rockets, mechanics, specifics: just not my thing. Our school had a limited lab program, so I never really got to find out how much I probably *wouldn't* have liked the practical world of a physicist.

But it looked impressive to put physics on college applications. The number of glossy brochures that came in the mail made me feel noticed and courted. Every day I had piles of mail. Eeny, meeny, miney, mo, to which college should I go?

After school, I biked home, grabbed the mail, and scanned the kitchen for some serious food. I'd eaten 280 carefully allotted calories for lunch—a Dannon yogurt, an apple, and a cracker. Gotta fit into those jeans. But by the end of the day, I was ravenous, my stomach growling and the inner void aching.

I wolfed down half a carton of ice cream at our kitchen bar that ran along the window, ripped open the envelopes, and pored over the new pamphlets. As I ate, I sat in solitude, peering down the quiet, empty street. I got a few Ivy League applications, but they seemed intimidating, so preppy and competitive. The urban, intellectual vibe of the University of Chicago was appealing. I was accepted to Chicago as an up-and- coming physics major. Mom and Dad opted for the University of Michigan, since the in-state tuition was a fraction of Chicago's and my plans still vague and dreamy.

I headed to Ann Arbor, almost an hour away from home, with high hopes. Looking forward to life in the "academy," in a higher realm of scholarly pursuit with like-minded seekers and thinkers.

7

GO BLUE!

The searching roamers split up. No more Friday nights in comfortable companionship. Julie and I went to the University of Michigan, and Sam to Michigan State. Sue was off somewhere else altogether, out of touch. I didn't see too much of Julie, since she lived in Alice Lloyd, on the other side of the campus. Julie came from a struggling home, and was mature enough to focus on getting a usable degree and filling science prerequisites. She knew the real-life pressure of worrying about monthly bills and hoped to build a way to get ahead of that wearying cycle.

I was ready to dissect reality with big and earnest bites, while Julie dissected frogs. I came to Freshman Orientation ready to rock and roll. Ready to meet deeper, more evolved people; ivy-covered- type people who flew on the wings of ideas.

I chose a small, experimental program within the big university that had more of an open and explorative bent. The Residential College—and East Quad, where the "RC'ers" lived and took our innovative classes—seemed like it would deliver the goods. The aged brick building had layers of character, a remodeled, intimate auditorium with natural-wood beams over old, exposed brick. It had a richer atmosphere than the newer, sterile dorms of pre-med, pre-making-it yuppies.

East Quad had endless little nooks, rambling hallways, and remote corners filled with intense, intense, intense young people intent on finding the Meaning, man. You could walk into a lounge in the middle of the night, or a hallway, or a weird windowsill up in a corner. Two or three RC'ers might be there, strewn on the floor, or on their backs, feet up on the wall—sipping a beer, or a cup of tea, or strumming a guitar, and talking talking talking.

In early spring, Julie and I decided to travel the hour or so to East Lansing and visit our old crony, who we hadn't seen since the summer after our high-school graduation. Sam was living in a tepee, about ten feet in diameter. He had taken up TM, Transcendental Meditation, and was spending more and more hours meditating.

We took a bus to the town, then walked through the giant, neatly groomed Michigan State campus. Finally, we found our way to the small, overgrown hippie neighborhood, beyond the border of the manicured lawns and rambunctious, tanned frat kids. We followed his directions till we saw it—a large, beige tepee perched in the back of an overgrown yard. Julie and I made our way through the weeds and wildflowers, past the compost pile and little fire pit. What do you do at a tepee doorway? Knock? No real door or doorbell. We poked our heads into the open buckskin flap that served as the entrance.

"Hey, Mir, hey Jules! You guys really came!"

Sam was sitting cross-legged on a faded cotton blanket, looking shiny-eyed, but awfully pale and thin. He waved to us weakly.

"What's goin' on, Sam?" Julie and I gave each other worried looks.

"Great stuff, great stuff. I've been on this juice fast for over a week. Only fresh-pressed juice. I'm cleansing out toxins, feeling really pure and clean, like I'm raisin' my vibrational level."

"Wow." We were both a bit dumbfounded. We were cosmic wanderers and dabblers in comparison. Sam was marching forward with single-minded focus. Clad in a loose Indian cotton shirt and robe-like garment, he sipped water and herbal tea while we talked.

His juicer and several crates of organic fruits and vegetables, along with a few knives and peelers, sat over on the side of his simple abode.

We hung out for a few hours, quietly shmoozing before we had to head back. "Just take care of yourself, guy," Julie urged him.

"Yeah, I will, don't worry, I'm almost done with this fast, dear sisters."

We both concurred: this guy is inspiring; this is a little scary. To see him down about twenty pounds, looking so gaunt. And what happened to our easygoing, laughing buddy? Who's this serene and placid yogi? We wanted to tell him to take it easy, just a bit.

Next we heard from Sam, he had gone off to Israel as part of an international TM gathering, to meditate and bring peace to the war-torn Middle East. Could they really do it, usher in a new reality? I admired the idea, but couldn't help but be a little cynical. Well, good luck. Sadat and Begin, move on over. You got nothin' on these swami guys.

Israel had never really been on my plate as an option. I vaguely knew of its existence, and that it was a Jewish state. And there were some kind of communal farms called *kibbutzim*. And they did some folk dance called the *hora* and wore little cotton sun caps. And rode camels. Something about some old wall and Jewish history? Though I searched for a more natural and community-oriented lifestyle, I never thought of checking out a kibbutz. Julie had been there with her youth group, and continually raved about it, but it just never clicked or connected for me.

Camp Tamarack brought several Israeli counselors over each year, hoping to develop a Zionist bent in us Yankees. But those native-born *Sabras* had a hard edge, spoke and moved too quickly with their staccato accent.

I remembered Zev with trepidation. When I was about twelve, Zev was our tripper, leading our bunk on a three-day wilderness trip. A tall, blond, Israeli army veteran, Zev had a cruel streak and seemed to enjoy making us spoiled softies squirm.

We sat around the campfire after a long day canoeing in the hot sun, pitching tents, collecting firewood, cooking. As we relaxed over s'mores, Zev sat up, a glint in his steely blue eyes.

"Listen, I want to teach you a real army song. Sing after me."

Wow, a real Israeli army song? We listened attentively. Zev proceeded to teach us a grotesque, violent pub ditty that made women into degraded sex objects. Line by line, he sang, and had us repeat it back. He smirked like a cat with a mouse in its claw, watching us struggle uneasily. But we dutifully followed our leader and sang along.

Who knows what he'd experienced? Was it his natural disposition? Trauma on the battlefield, too much war and fear? Maybe I shouldn't have written off a whole country because of one surly person, but when I thought of Israel, I imagined a country of Zevs. Not too appealing.

So, Ann Arbor, particularly East Quad, was my Jerusalem, the focus of my hopes for inspiration. I found a new traveling companion early on. I first eyeballed Maureen during Freshman Orientation for the Residential College, and our group was on a walking tour of the campus. At the foot of a pedestrian bridge, I saw this little thing hovering in the back, with wavy blond hair, faded overalls, and an intense-yet-dreamy expression. We gravitated to each other. A fellow seeker, fun, and different, Maureen and I started hanging out. We shared a natural, mystical, cosmic perspective—candles, herbal oils and remedies; a deep, deep, deeper, probe deeper, kind of path.

We dove into our search for the bolts, the warp and weft of being, starting off the year with Freedom and Structure as Psychological Reality, taught by a handsome, guitar-playing, gaunt young scholar. We RC'ers read, pondered, and pontificated during 2:00 A.M.

impromptu hallway soirees, and at dinners with teachers, whom we called by first name, at their pads. Intoxicating, the ferment.

Maureen was from a small-town, conservative church background, but she stretched her hand and mind way beyond that. From time to time we'd leave Ann Arbor for the weekend and catch a bus to her small, working-class home.

Her friendly parents didn't know quite what to make of us.

"Hi, Mom. Hi, Dad. What's new?" she called out, breezing in the door and dropping her backpack on the neatly waxed linoleum tiles.

"Hi, honey. Who's your friend?"

"This is Miriam. She's from Detroit. Hope you don't mind that she came along."

"Of course not. Welcome." Her mom peered quizzically at me. "What church does your family go to?"

"Oh, c'mon, Mom, she's Jewish."

"Ahh... how nice."

I scratched my head defensively, nervously feeling the top. I wondered if they'd ask to see my horns. Once, I went with my friend Kathy to her church youth group, in a blue-collar neighborhood only a few miles from ours. Her friends cornered her in the bathroom. "Did you see them? Did you touch her horns?" they demanded. Was I the first Jew to cross Maureen's threshold? I didn't ask.

But the family was just about as mystified by Maureen and her highfalutin ideas and grungy get-up as they were by the Jewess. Her younger sisters peered at us from under their carefully blow-dried blond hair and heavily eyeliner.

"Are you coming home for the town festival?" they asked. "Maureen, how could you miss it?" Pictures of young Maureen and her sisters dancing in the festivities graced the walls.

Maureen laughed and brushed them off with a non-committal shrug.

"Maybe, I'm not sure. It's during finals so I might not be able to."

Maureen's sisters saw her roll her eyes. They grumbled and gave her a blistering look. Her mom looked hurt that her daughter had flown so far out of the coop.

Her handsome, ex-football-star dad took us out in Lake Michigan in his speedboat, and we laughed and sang as we soared across the waters, mist spraying in our faces. He glanced back from the helm and smiled, happy to see us lightening up and having a bit of normal fun—taking a break from philosophizing, meditating, and crunching sprouts instead of his fresh- grilled burgers. Sweet people, her parents tried to understand these strange creatures and politely accommodated us.

As the year rolled on, Maureen started getting into Anthroposophy—a Gnostic, Christian, nature- oriented, mystical brew, developed by a late-nineteenth-century Austrian esoteric/social philosopher named Rudolf Steiner. I tagged along to bits and pieces of lectures, painting classes, and celebrations. It seemed a bit dark and mysterious. I liked that it was intellectual, not just about transcending the mind.

Steiner's schema diagrammed the spiritual worlds and was populated by angels, soul levels, reincarnation, and destiny. There were practical applications in medicine, farming, education, and the arts. But something didn't quite jibe with me. Steiner looked foreboding, dark eyes peering out from under shaggy eyebrows in his portrait. Something seemed askew; some kind of emotional, essential element was missing. But maybe the lack was with me.

Back at the U, the larger university mostly disappointed and left me feeling raw and very small, almost invisible. I started out with good intentions, but quickly lost my way. As a dewy-eyed freshman, I was excited to join a community of scholars pursuing "Knowledge for knowledge's sake, pure pursuit of wisdom." The RC classes were more open and inquiry-oriented, but we had to supplement with classes out there on the big main campus. The mega–state university seemed like an assembly line producing trained technocrats.

The 'academy'? What kind of dream world was I dreaming? Keggers, frats, razing, massive *Go Blue* football games with thousands of frenzied fans. A busy campus with swarms of productive, driven people rushing rushing rushing on their way to their degrees, careers, and busy, purposeful lives.

Walking across the crowded Diag, the main pedestrian thoroughfare was intimidating, yet exciting. Thousands upon thousands of students going in every which way.

I felt like an anonymous ant scrambling through the ant farm of schooling and preparing for the ant farm of society. I couldn't quite latch onto the right crumb for me to carry, to claim as my little piece of the complex task of moving the world forward.

I loved honors math in high school, a small group of students wrestling with calculus. Felt like we were cracking nuts of the secrets of the universe. I looked forward to more of the same at the big university, and signed up for Calculus 2.

It took place in a giant lecture hall filled with hundreds of pre-med and engineering students racing through the material to get on to their next prerequisite. The instructor was a teaching fellow from India, barely understandable as he rattled through the formulas. After a while I stopped asking questions because his stilted, thickly accented language was too hard to decipher. The joy of learning and discovery became a vague memory in this mechanistic world.

Lori was a high school buddy. We embarked on Calculus 2 together. I was hoping she could give me the support that I couldn't get from the teacher.

"Lori, did you get those formulas? Can we go over them together and try to figure out what he's really saying?"

"I have a big biology exam next week, I don't have time. Just go to a study carrel, get a big coffee, and keep going over and over them till you memorize the formulas and can buzz on through the problems. Don't worry about whether you really get it," my savvy friend advised.

"Okay." I shrugged forlornly, grabbed my books, and headed down for the suggested caffeine and carrel key.

I'd hole up in my dorm room with the giant book of course offerings as a new semester loomed, marking, folding down corners, flipping back and forth, changing my mind once again Being interested in too many things made simple course selection overwhelming, especially since the question "What do I want to be when I grow up?" lingered in the background.

It seemed like everyone had been asking me that loaded question since I was old enough to talk. It loomed as the quintessential way I would prove my worth, and be interesting and important enough. I wasn't methodically filling prerequisites, the logical thing to do. I couldn't, since I didn't know which direction I was marching in. Building a pragmatic way of earning an income? How pedestrian. I wanted to discover who and what the universe, souls, and consciousness were. Which class would do that? Not too tall of an order!

Other students seemed to find their niche with ease, and could accept that these were, after all, just college courses—not the pot at the end of the rainbow, the secret to cosmic wisdom that I was more and more preoccupied with finding.

"Okay, psychology is the place to find more about what makes people tick, what goes on beyond the conscious, logical mind."

I flipped the course catalog to P.

"Psychology 101. Boring. I know that from my own reading. I can't sit through that, spelled out so step-by-step. But everything else needs that as a prerequisite... Oh, here's the only one you can go right into. Child Development. And I already took it. And it was stupid. All those draggy articles that took gads of pages of wading through research to say what seems obvious. I want to jump right into something meaty." I took a few upper-level and graduate courses that didn't need the stream of dreary prereqs, but just couldn't settle down.

I loved kids, but I didn't have the patience to sit through tedious education courses and methodologies; they seemed like common sense with a lot of paper shuffling. I didn't bother to see if my stereotyped image of education students was valid: neatly coifed teachers-in-training who would greet their young charges with a chirpy, "Good morning children. Let's mark your names in the attendance book with a red check."

As the year wound to a close, I was excited for summer, to get away from the city and books and get back to camp, dirt, and canoes. I'd try something new, working as a tripper. We handful of hardy trippers lived at a small base camp in northern Michigan, consisting of a few platform tents, small storage buildings, and outhouses.

Busloads of kids from the main camp came up to us for a several-day immersion in wilderness living. We gave them a crash course in camp crafting basics and took them on hiking and canoe trips in the neighboring Manistee River area woods and fields.

Those summer months were the longest stretch I'd spent out in the woods. The sustained time away from the twentieth-century, concrete maze of hustle and bustle was magical. I heard the birds call, became sensitized to nuances of sun, moon, stars, wind, foliage color and variety. Living in peaceful harmony with slow days and hands-on, simple tasks, opened a window.

One day, mid-summer, it happened.

All of a sudden, all my earlier dabblings and mystical ventures imploded, exploded, and exponentially intensified.

I was ambling slowly through the woods, on the hushed pine needles that cushion the delicious northern Michigan forest floor. Moss-covered logs and soft green ferns abounded, making a magical place, where elves and fairies might reside. A few determined rays of sunshine made their way through the canopy of pine branches that arched overhead, reaching infinitely high. The stillness was interrupted by a squirrel scurrying, a breeze rustling. A lone bird flitted from branch to branch. I came into a small clearing.

All at once, unexpected, unsolicited: I experienced a quiet, roaring flash.
Sparkling.
Revelation.
Heightened awareness: zinging.

I could feel, taste, *know*— the flowing energy that united all the trees.
I saw, *got*—as obviously and completely as I knew my name—
knew, as a concrete fact—
these trees, leaves, stones—
didn't just randomly evolve, by blind forces of nature.

I could practically see and touch the intelligent, purposeful,
vibrant energy that made/makes/ is—pulsing, shimmering—
"Hi! I'm here!" the energy seemed to smile, to whisper and sing.
There is a harmonious, dynamic unity pervading all this.

I'd met up with this revolutionary, turn your world upside down
impish insight,
It had taken tentative root—

But this was different. Stepped up, a powerful surge: golden,
suspended, connected, flowing—
a blast of sure knowing
I knew it wanted something from me, that I had to strengthen,
and be part of it.
I knew that unequivocally.
And I needed to find the bestest-rightest-truest way to live in
harmony with it,
as much as I needed to take another breath.

I was amazed, but not overwhelmed; calm, yet energized; in
harmony with creation and the creative force surging through me.
Excited, open, and connected.
Radiating, tingling.
Alive.

This blazing moment catalyzed my search. It ramped up the
absolute intensity and burning need to find a way—the true
way—of serving and furthering that divine energy. "Kind of,"
"more or less," wasn't gonna be good enough. I was ready to go
for the gold, do whatever I could to find the real goods, the
truest truth I could uncover—whatever or wherever it would be.

This vision/experience took my breath away. It was both gentle and obvious and not a big deal— and a totally electric, enormous big deal. Spirituality could no longer be a side interest or nice pursuit. It was life and breath. All that mattered. Front and center stage.

The rest of the summer was cast in the afterglow of that moment, like the luminous golden intensity right before twilight. I was warmed by those rays. The crashing waves and vast blue expanse of Lake Michigan, gulls crooning and dipping, all seemed to echo and confirm that glorious oneness, the beautiful energy I could flow with too.

When that summer ended, both pastoral and intense, I ventured back to Ann Arbor and my sophomore year. I was still trying to pursue these tangents within the university, but wearying. I wandered through courses that might offer glimmers. Mythology, Psychology of Thinking, Phenomenology of Childhood, Theories in Religion; what *was* that "I," that sense of consciousness, where did it come from?

But my fellow tripper Karen said something that lodged in my mind, echoing over and over, the more reading I did, the more courses I took: "In college everyone just talks too much." I was getting tired of over-analysis and objective dissection that somehow never hit onto where I was trying to aim.

At least I had a partner in crime to scrounge the university with, trying to squeeze out the scattered drops of light and energy. Maureen and I took many courses together, but it was hard to find professors with time and patience for our quest.

One day at the end of a mythology lecture, we hurried down the aisle of the lecture hall to ask the professor some questions. He glanced at his watch looking weary, as though he wanted to get to lunch and not be derailed by these earnest boppers. "What do you think about Jung's theory of collective unconscious?" Maureen asked. "Is that where these myths emerge from, with heroes, villains, and other similar archetypes in every culture?" He paused briefly, pushed up his glasses and sighed, then gave us the name of something to read as he gathered his books and scurried off.

Others also seemed to wish we'd stay in our box, not ask too many questions, and go study for our tests.

As my frustration with the university increased, I focused more outside those ivy walls: the Holistic Health Council, food co-op, Jung study groups, Anthroposophy, and periodic dabbling and venturing into a hodge-podge of ashrams and New Age gatherings. I also frequented Arbor Alliance meetings, where we planned our actions to protest nuclear power. Sufi dancing and chanting in the tree-filled arboretum and learning the basics of reflexology with other serene star-gazers seemed more relevant than wandering the stacks to find dissertations and research about this or that hypothesis. The university seemed frozen in the old model, where harried professors saw the brain as a singular organ cranking out ivory-tower theories—isolated from the heart, body, and soul, remote and removed from real life.

Towards the end of my sophomore year I felt overloaded, stuck. That back-to-nature clarion call sang louder. "Sun, water, wind, moon. Forget this academic jazz!" Whatever the true path was, it seemed obvious that living in tune with natural rhythms and cycles was an important element. Some kind of farming, camping, simpler life of harmony beckoned.

The bit I read and heard about biodynamic farming sounded intriguing. A form of organic farming developed by Steiner, it was more than avoiding chemicals; it was a whole stew of complex practices that claimed to be in harmony with the seasons, the moon, the cosmic calendar.

Did I really understand it? Not at all.

But it seemed to have a whole theory and methodology; it was more than simple grooving.

8

―――∽≈✦≈∾―――

DOWN ON THE FARM

ollowing intuition more than anything, following the vibe,
I asked Maureen for some contacts in the Steiner world
and got in touch with the Hazelwood Farm in upstate New
York and asked about apprenticing as a farmhand. Took an
Amtrak east to see it and fell in love with the calm, rural beauty of
the rolling foothills of the Berkshires.

Splashes of rust, magenta, and oranges, splayed patches of
early fall were spreading through the hills and forests. A winding
road led to the farm and small village of Steiner-oriented families,
school, farm, and small craft industries nestled in a valley. The
green fields were slowly browning as the trees turned and gently
shed.

Karl, the middle-aged farmer, made hand-crafted, raw-milk
cheese the authentic way he'd learned in his native Switzerland.
He had brought his copper-lined cheese vat with him to America.
It was about the size of a small Jacuzzi, the warm copper metal
kept shining and clean.

The people were an interesting, family-oriented group, dedicated to implementing a holistic lifestyle. Their kids were more
spontaneous; healthy, spirited, country-raised children, their

laughter and simple antics a spark of life in this sedate community of European reserve. Katy, a carefree five-year old tree-climber with sparling brown eyes, was captivating. "I want my kids to be like her," I thought. I was excited but hesitant. These folks seemed more grounded and directed than super-mellow New Agers. But there was a dynamic energy or spiritual buzz that was either missing or curiously subtle and muted.

I loved waking in the still dark, as the first call of the rooster rang through the hushed valley, pulling on my flannel shirt, army pants, and knee-high black rubber boots, then walking to the barn. We pitched hay down in the barely stirring barn. The cows and horses would moo and bray gently, with the innocence of babies coming to after a peaceful night. They were fed and milked in just-breaking light.

Nan, a senior farmhand, and I filled the vat with the fresh, warm milk, heated it to just the right temperature, stirred in rennet, and let it sit and coagulate. We went back to our trailers for a farmer's breakfast of hearty whole-grain bread, spread with our creamy, fresh butter. We sliced pungent hard cheese, with its thick edge, and scrambled up some of our free-range chickens' brown eggs. By then daylight had broken and the rest of the village was stirring. The dawn found us with a few hours of work already under our belt.

Quiet times. Farm life was simple. It was hard physical work, with sore muscles by the end of the day. Leisure was spent in study groups, reading Steiner's dense texts that were a bit obtuse, and gloomily mysterious. I played in a recorder ensemble in the evening, our simple Baroque melodies echoing through the valley. Read. Sketched. Walked. Thought.

Sometimes I was happy in this peaceful, simple, task-centered world; sometimes a thread of melancholy wove through. I sat in my little home, a small trailer with rusty exterior but clean and simple interior, and looked in the cracked mirror to sketch a self-portrait; wondering, sad eyes staring back.

Every Saturday, Karl and one or two of us farmhands loaded up the pickup truck. His wife and children gathered to give us a large lunch and wave goodbye as we headed off before dawn. We drove down the quiet parkway into another world—the smoky, congested, boisterous Big Apple—to sell our wares at a farmer's market in downtown Brooklyn, off of Atlantic Avenue. The energy and static increased as we headed down the parkway and approached the city.

I relished the contrast, bringing a touch of genuine country food to the city folk that flocked to taste our cheese and read our farm's write-up in the *New York Times*. The buzz of the city gave me a needed charge and lift.

"Would you like a taste of our organic cheese?" I asked a woman with dangly earrings, frizzy, wind-blown hair, and a paint-spattered shirt. She was on a lunch break from Pratt, where she taught painting and graphic design.

"Oh yes, thank you," she responded. "Hmmm, such a rich flavor."

The next Saturday she was back, artist friends in tow. I'd explain a bit about our authentic, nutritious product. Gourmands loved its unique flavor. Earthies loved its handcrafted quality and that we treated our small herd of cattle well.

At the end of an exhausting day, we'd pack up and head north. I loved escaping to the rural stillness, the colors on the hills deepening in rich outpourings of crimson and chestnut hues as the autumn progressed.

I tried to be a good farmhand. I tried to understand and relate to the Anthroposophy. But the Christian overtones and undertones rankled somewhere in my being. No overt word was ever said, but I felt very Jewish, and somehow an outsider.

And I was a little too spaced-out, messy, all-over-the-place for the stoic, organized farmer. One day I left the spigot to the whey tank open during morning tasks. Whey, the liquid part of the milk left after the curds were separated to form the cheese, was vital nutritious food for the animals. Each drop was valuable. Whoops! We returned from breakfast to find a watery puddle running all over the barn floor, the tank almost empty by the time we got to the barn. Embarrassed and humiliated, I apologized profusely for my major screw-up.

Youch. Sorry, boss.

After several such faux-pas, Karl called me over, one chilly January afternoon. I was finishing my afternoon task, carefully turning the cheese wheels in the small, climate-controlled cellar where they aged.

"Miriam, please come here. We have to talk," he said quietly.

"Oh, yes, Karl, one minute, I have to finish this shelf."

I felt I was starting to get the hang of the cheese process, carefully marking the dates as we turned the aging wheels, and noting any that didn't seem to be progressing quite right. I expected some small praise, or maybe to be given some new responsibility.

But Karl seemed serious. He gently but sternly let me know I wasn't quite right for the job, and perhaps I wanted to go back to helping with the community's environmental education program, where I'd worked when I'd first arrived in September and been much more successful.

"There have been too many things that have gone wrong. I don't think this is the right job for you," he said, not unkindly, but with a firmness that booked no arguments.

"But, but... I am really trying... and being much more careful... and I thought I was getting better..." I mumbled, my words falling away in the afternoon silence.

My tears welled up and caught him by surprise. We both were embarrassed by my leaking emotion. I felt the sting of failure. I quickly finished my jobs and shuffled out of there, hurrying back to my trailer, my little den, to nurse my wounds and hurt.

I knew right away. I wanted out.

The work with kids had gone well, guiding city kids and turning them on to nature and farm life. It was more up my alley. I really was a better teacher and inspirer than a methodical detail person; Karl was quite right. But I didn't want second best. The real deal, hands-on farming, had been my objective, a coveted goal I wanted to achieve, and I hadn't made the grade.

A few days later I slung on my trusty backpack and waved goodbye. Karl and his wife came to the gate to see me off. Nan drove me to the Amtrak station, where I caught a train for Philly. I visited another Anthroposophic farming community in the area, which focused on working with developmentally delayed kids. Neat. But I realized, I was done, at least for now. Sort of looked around the community, but couldn't even muster the energy to try to connect.

I headed home, to nurse my back. It was severely strained from a recent afternoon's folly, when I had tried to prove my mettle by emptying the silo and lifting too much grain. And to just be home, just on my own turf. Just that.

9

══════◦❦◦══════

THE JEWISH AMISH

ll this time I had wondered, what happened to my meditating buddy? As far as I knew, peace had not yet dawned
in the Middle East. Was he still there? I heard a vague
rumor, something about studying Torah in a *yeshiva* (rabbinical
school) and becoming *Orthodox*?

One afternoon, a small white envelope arrived at my parents'
house. (I'd spent a few months there nursing my back, with copious
amounts of Tiger Balm Chinese ointment that stunk up the whole
house and other various and sundry natural remedies.) The stamp
had Hebrew writing and was postmarked *Israel*. Mom sent the
letter on to my new pad in Ann Arbor, where I'd recently returned
to study art. I ripped it open to find a short letter and a picture.

Dear Miriam,

*Shalom from Jerusalem. I'm having an amazing time. I'm studying
Torah in a yeshiva, a school for guys like me who are just getting
introduced to it. It is really really deep and interesting. How you do like
my new looks, ha ha. Seriously, there's some very great stuff here and you
might want to check it out sometime.*

All the best, Sam

Who is that guy? I peered at the picture. Same big smile, but what happened to his curly long hair? And where is the Indian robe or at least loose cotton shirt? His hair is cut short; he's wearing a dark suit and white button-down shirt. Huh?

Finding out that he had gone to Mars would have been less of a shock.

Orthodox. The word evoked old-fashioned, puritanical, naive, unworldly. Quaint, completely time-warped—Jewish Amish or something like that.

I had gone into an Orthodox synagogue once, as part of a Sunday School trip to visit the various backwards denominations, like a visit to our ancestral roots. Maybe it was the fall holiday called *Simchas Torah*; I sort of remembered some dancing with the Torah, clapping and singing, and flags with apples on the top. The Orthodox neighborhood was only a few miles from my home, but I never interacted with them. One Orthodox kid came to my high school, but he stuck to himself. Like, he didn't even eat food from the cafeteria. What was his problem, why was he so aloof and weird? He seemed to be from a separate universe, behind glass, untouchable and irrelevant.

Had they kidnapped my buddy? I couldn't quite grasp the whole thing. But Sam wrote again.

He was happy, it was great and meaningful, and I should check it out.

Very, very warily, but to honor my friend, I scrounged up a Jewish calendar and noted which day was Yom Kippur. Maybe I'd dabble with fasting, and even peek into the Hillel Student Center's Orthodox service. Sam did make me curious. Maybe, just maybe, there was something to all this, improbable as it seemed.

The Yom Kippur I knew from the Birmingham Temple was short and sweet. Some choral singing. Joyce sang in a dramatic, minor-keyed soprano, to the plaintive, haunting, traditional melody of *Aveinu Malkeinu* (Our Father Our King):

We look for the right thing to do.
We look for the right thing to do.
The right thing to do is, to love one another, that is the right thing to do.

We read, some responsive and others silent—short, meditative pieces about being sorry and starting anew. I liked the pensive mood. It made me think and reflect. But in moderation. I'd heard about those fanatics who stood through services lasting hours and fasted all day. Mom's grandparents and mother used to, and she groused about how dangerous and extreme it was.

Day of Repentance sounded morose, as did fasting for your sins. What's a sin? Pretty medieval thinking.

Should I check out that archaic Orthodox version? It sounded intimidating. But Sam was so enthusiastic. I wavered. Alright, I'd be bold, stick my toe in the water and take a quick, cross-cultural anthropologist's look. By mid-afternoon, when I hesitantly walked in, only a few sturdy souls were still praying at the Hillel. The service was held in a small side room, which was divided down the middle to make a men's and a women's side. Why they are segregating us, I wondered.

The women sat on folding chairs, reading a set liturgy from a prayer book, standing and sitting, standing and sitting. They didn't seem to be praying all together, like they did at temples, with an organ and choral singing. Everyone hummed along at their own pace, and was looking into the books with intensity, some quietly swaying as they read. A cantor droned on in unintelligible Hebrew as he led the prayers.

I felt sorry for these rigid, narrow-minded people. How could they read someone else's words? Wasn't Yom Kippur supposed to be about looking into your own soul? A personal, spontaneous expression would be better, I thought.

I sat in one of the back rows, took off my shoes, folded my legs lotus-style, and perched across several of the gray metal chairs.

I closed my eyes and tried to focus on the rhythm of their

chanting, the droning sound, and meditate, sending light to these poor, ritually bound souls.

"Hmmm, hmmm, hmmm," I hummed, filling the air around me with peace.

Several women looked at me across the aisle a bit askance—bad vibes. I continued to send them harmonious energy.

"Would you like me to show you the page?" one offered, smiling slightly.

"Oh, thank you, it's fine. I'm not really reading, just being here, you know, just taking it all in," I responded serenely.

They all stood at the same time, for something that seemed important. I stood for a minute or so, then resumed my meditative pose, closed my eyes, and hummed quietly. One of the women looked over with a mixture of pity and scorn, but hey, it was Ann Arbor, where much weirder creatures and ways of being were floating all over the place. Even these Orthodox women, praying on Yom Kippur—I didn't think they saw me as more than mildly wacked-out; maybe a three (alright, fine, maybe a four) on a scale of one to ten.

I smiled benevolently at them and left after an hour or so, feeling mostly bored. Maybe, somewhere, way under the surface, I felt a little connected to Sam. Maybe even some kind of "Hey, I'm Jewish, it's Yom Kippur and I took a little time out to acknowledge it," sort of connection. I went back home, but continued fasting for another hour or two; occasional fasting is healthy, after all.

But for the most part, whatever Sam saw in all this escaped me.

Tasting

"Taste and see that God is good."

—Psalms 34:9

10

━━◦❦◦━━

THE DREAM

I never heard about the Jewish people wandering in the desert; yet I felt like I was wandering in the desert.

Searching for that wellspring of living waters, that oasis that wouldn't dry up. Searching for a rock to stand on, somewhere to put down solid roots that could hold fast and endure in the arid soil.

Somehow, I stubbornly grabbed onto the idea there *was* going to be a place and a way that would ring true.

Where was it?

Though my heart sought The Place, my mind had pretty much resigned itself to accepting that there wasn't going to be a singular path; there was going to be an eclectic piecing together of shards of light.

I had ventured to the ashrams, to the Anthroposophic farm, and checked out UC Santa Cruz—only to end up disappointed.

I assumed the fault was with me. I couldn't divorce myself from the ego and mind chatter enough for the ashram; and that framed portrait of the guru with flowers placed before it just annoyed me.

I was too spaced out, too neurotic, had too much feeling for the dry and calm, yet strange and detached, study of Steiner.

Santa Cruz was a gorgeous paradise, but somehow too perfect, ecological, and hip; all laid out, no struggle.

Wherever I went, there were fellow hippies living an organic life. Some might eat sprouts while others ate raw-milk cheese, some focused on meditating and others on compost; but nothing dramatically stood out, or grabbed more than a fleeting hold of me. I figured it was my cowardice or lack, and I felt condemned to wander.

But I was tired. Weary. And still so hungry for some kind of unique connection my heart sought, that I was driven to continue seeking.

That night, I lit a candle. I sat in my darkened room— my simply appointed, mattress on the floor, crumpled jeans and sandals thrown in the corner, sketches on the wall and dried flowers scattered, scruffy little chamber of solace. I cried and prayed.

The silence was interrupted by shrieks of laughter from down on the first floor, as my housemate levitated several inches up, coming down with a bang that shook the floorboards—her nightly practice. The smell of fermenting tempeh wafted up the stairs.

I closed my eyes and moved beyond the distractions. It wasn't a calculated effort to surrender or focus; it was desperation.

I cried, simply, from the heart, from exhaustion.

God, I know You are there.
I want to know You. I want to get close to You, and serve You.
I can't find the right way. I can't find it.
Show me.
Guide me.

And I watched the candle burn and cried myself to sleep.

Hours later, I woke up, startled, after a vivid dream.

It was...

(dum da dum)

...a MESSAGE.

THE DREAM

The dream:

My *Zaidy*, my grandfather, was in the forefront. With his thinning white hair, stout, clean-shaven face, and thick glasses, Zaidy was the most modern figure. A long chain of elderly sages with white beards and wise eyes was coming down from the misty past, from the top right and left corners, getting larger and more defined as they came forward. Zaidy was in the middle, the most prominent, as if he were the charm in the center of a necklace, going back in time and in size.

A three-dimensional image.

I don't remember any talking or storyline, just this vivid image—this tableau.

I woke up knowing.

Not guessing, not associating...

Knowing.

This was the chain of Jewish history and continuity, coming out from the ancient past, through the generations to the late twentieth century, and Zaidy was the most current link.

Now, I had hardly ever seen pictures of old bearded Jews. Maybe Bubby had a little painting of a gnarled rabbi tucked in a corner of her overstuffed living room.

Monks, gurus, Zen masters: those were the images that peopled my world. But I just knew this was a Jewish message and those men were Jewish sages—whatever the heck they were.

I never heard the analogy, which in my current zeitgeist comes up all the time, of the golden chain of Jewish connection and continuity—the links sometimes rusty, sometimes stretched thin, but never snapped—as our people wandered through thousands of years, persecutions, continents, and cultures.

And even if I had, I couldn't have cared less. Why differentiate yourself, anyway?

Universal oneness was my credo.

I was obsessed with living spiritually, and the only "Jewish question" on my plate was why on earth did my parents harp on the backward and provincial, perhaps even racist, notion that I marry a Jew.

(And I didn't think about their request much, as marriage was an obsolete, bourgeois institution that ensnared women into domestic slavery.)

Even though I was sure no rabbis had anything to offer me, especially the ancient, bearded, black yarmulke'd ones that appeared that night, still, somehow, I was swept up and compelled.

This dream grabbed onto me with surprising force.

I wanted to capture this image, not let it fade away. I wanted to express it and bring it out into the world.

The soft images in muted colors, the three-dimensional quality of coming forward in space and time seemed like a sculpture, a paper sculpture, with soft, fraying edges that could blend into the past, coming forward with stronger definition. I had made paper once, mixing the pulp with natural dyes and pressing in wildflowers, and I loved the soft, pliable medium. That was at a studio in northern California.

But I wasn't a sculptor, and didn't have access to the materials or know-how to go about creating such a thing. I was in the midst of several drawing and painting classes, so I decided to paint it.

I jumped on the bus to go to a good source for Jewish material— back home to Mom and Dad's—to do some research, something I'd never done for a painting before. This was the first time I moved beyond explorations of brush strokes, energy, and shapes based on still-lifes or landscapes right in front of me. I wasn't sure exactly what I was looking for, but figured I'd find some family and Jewish images to help me convey something of the dream.

Mom and Dad were glad but surprised to have me show up on such short notice. Since I'd returned from California, I holed myself up in Ann Arbor, crossing the Twilight-Zone, Iron-Curtain barrier to the suburbs infrequently.

"Where are the photo albums? And do you have any books with Jewish texts?" I asked with urgency.

"What are you up to? Some kind of research project?" Mom

asked. Glad to be needed, she helped me find the right shelves.

I scrounged through photo albums, till I found one from a family Chanukah party, with Zaidy lighting the menorah. I pulled back the plastic protective page, lifted off the yellowed picture and put it in my stash to bring back to Ann Arbor.

I started looking through my parents' Jewish books. Most of the items in their fairly scant Judaic library were the Judaism I felt I had left behind. Yiddish jokes, boring history, Philip Roth-style neurosis. Other contemporary novelists using their Jewish background as grist for the mill. My birthright. The secular, intellectual Judaism that was a familiar culture zone but nowhere I would remotely think of looking to quench the compelling thirst that left me parched and desperately searching. I don't think I ever heard the word *spiritual* (except for black church music) till I met up with the hippies.

I leafed through a large, coffee-table-size *Hagaddah for Passover*, illustrated by Ben Shahn. There was a spark of life in the dancing Hebrew letters. All of a sudden, in the middle of the page, a verse caught my eye, and captured my heart.

"Those who sow in tears will reap in joy."
I read it again.
Yes.
I read it again, with growing excitement. Something so true was being laid out there.

Whatever this Jewish thing was—this bothersome, burdensome, somehow always there, nagging-at-the-edge-of-one's-consciousness thing—this verse spoke to it. Sowing in tears; that was it. Perfect description. Being Jewish was sowing in tears—more worried, more neurotic.

Never quite smooth, easy, cheerleader-blond or cool; not seamlessly gliding in. There was a mournful dirge to it, like that squeal of the klezmer violin. But there was a hidden beauty to it too. Some kind of depth and joy hidden under that cloak of heaviness. Some unique light that was yet to unfold. They *will* reap in joy. Not quite yet. But it was a hint, a promise. Something wonderful is in there, the words whispered.

I thought of Bubby and Zaidy. Their little G.I. house, near Eight Mile Road, overflowing with books, papers, and *tzotchkes*— little statuettes and decorative knickknacks. We spent many hours there. Eating, singing, arguing; absorbing something deep.

Everything was a little too intense for the condensed space— and the reams of Jewish food that almost obsessively poured out of that tiny kitchen. The onion, garlic, and sugary cottage-cheese-blintz-filling smells you could peel off the walls. Under their worrying, their debating, the yellowing Yiddish classics, there was a hidden gate to a realm of delight; more than looking back to a lost world, more than nostalgia and grieving.

Bubby would often stroke our cheeks with her velvety soft, yet weathered hands. Those hands had poured her love into thousands upon thousands of carefully rolled and cut poppy-seed cookies, had formed so many blintzes and strudels to fill us with warmth, tradition and some subtle ingredient of Jewish consciousness that got mixed into the dough.

"*Guta yingele. Tiere maidele,*" she'd murmur. She'd peer at us with her worried, proud eyes. It was a description, a challenge, a promise. We would of course do anything to be those "good boys" and "sweet girls" and give her the *nachas* she'd crossed the ocean and endured hardship to receive; *nachas* and pleasure from grandchildren who would flourish and do the right thing.

This verse put words to it. Even more, it opened my eyes to the possibility that there was something essential, beautiful, even positive to that Jewish pull; that *nudnik*, nudging inner voice. It wasn't just a tug back to a lost world and down with weighty guilt. There *would* be a reaping in joy. All they stood for would grow and flourish and culminate— somewhere, somehow—in a fruitful harvest.

I copied the verse, trying to write the Hebrew letters, though I didn't know their names or formations, which way the wiggles were really supposed to go. But these words were what I had come home to find.

11

———◦⊰✦⊱◦———

THE PAINTING

Back at school, in the second-floor, glass-walled, warehouse-styled painting studios of the University of Michigan School of Art and Architecture, I tacked the photo of Zaidy's menorah lighting and my scrawled version of that evocative verse next to my blank canvas and got to work.

I stood in the vast studio on poured-concrete floors, and imagined myself back in their crowded living room, with, matted, dusty carpeting. As I squeezed blue and purple paint onto my palette and got my turpentine and brushes ready, I looked around to see what others were doing.

Jane, a willowy grad student, stood squinting at her work, a large, abstract montage with angular, cool colors. She exuded Bohemian confidence with her cowboy boots and streaked blond hair pulled back with a bandana. She consulted with Rick, a bald and bony professor, who coolly dissected her idea and shared her passion for the stark and extreme.

I tried to visualize and capture something of tiny Bubby's flour-smudged apron, Zaidy's garlicky breath and grunts as he'd rise to make a *l'chaim*, a toast, amidst belly laughter and dissention.

I didn't try to paint the sages. Instead, I used the Hebrew verse to represent the past wisdom and tradition that Zaidy was linked to and nurtured from, that he was bringing forward in time to the next generation.

The image of the chain, with solid links from the past was fitting. Zaidy was the Jewish patriarch in our family, the keeper of the flame, trying to bequeath his sense of Jewish destiny to us kids. No family gathering was complete without him making a brief speech and leading a formal singing of Yiddish favorites. He'd clear his voice to signal the ceremony, with an "Ahem!" We giggled, but knew to sit at attention and sing along. He wanted us to grab the chain and make our own new links, not leave it lying broken or abandoned.

A blue purple flow developed in the back of the picture, with the Hebrew letters peering in and out of the past, out of the dream. Those letters were barely recognizable, blending in and out of the background with irregular formation. I copied the lyrical shapes without knowing their proper form, as I might innocently try to copy a Chinese character: "To the right, three strokes, down a bit on an angle."

Zaidy came out of the mist, a flame in his hand, ready to light the menorah with his candle, ready to light the next generation with his precious heritage.

My professor strolled over to see what I was doing. He saw the photo clamped on my easel, the beginning sketch of Zaidy emerging. His reaction was benignly paternalistic.

"Oh, a nostalgic family picture. How nice." How cute and dumb, was what he implied. I felt like an awkward wannabe, patted on the head and given a cookie. He tried to give me critical direction, to make the work more painterly and less canned. "If you focus less on the image, more on the underlying structure and the picture plane, you will be able to come back in a few years and do a painting of grandpa that works."

I'd entered art school as a refuge from all the words and theories, hoping it would be a place where I could stay in the university without so much academic floundering. I loved to draw. And paint. But I had never focused on it as a primary activity. As a teen, I spent many hours roaming the Detroit Institute of Arts, sitting in the large courtyard and gazing at Diego Rivera's giant murals of the assembly line. I often leafed through my very own pocket-sized booklets of artists from Impressionism on. But I had bought the starving-artist notion that "real" people were professionals who supported and collected art, but were never those crazy artists, who struggled and were often outside normal limits. Van Gogh's ear, Gauguin's escape to Tahiti. Not what nice girls did.

Once I stepped inside the studio, however, things started fermenting. The magic of creativity was enchanting. Working on a music composition during my sophomore year was an amazing, freeing experience, allowing me to enter a suspended state of flow, intuition, and expression— something deep and personal, transcendent and real. I hungered for more.

But painting was more my native turf. Dad was an accomplished amateur painter, so shmearing colors came naturally. I spent many happy hours painting and coloring. On family vacations, I watched Dad. He'd sit on the beach, with a white watercolor pad on his lap, squeeze those little tubes of colors on a palette and dive in. With a brave brushstroke he'd start to create a horizon and work in the lake, the waves, and presto; there it was. I even won a blue ribbon for a clown I colored with Crayola crayons back in kindergarten, as a decoration for the Big Tent Circus. Every time I passed that framed picture with the proud ribbon, hanging in our house, it shouted out to me, "Hey, you are an artist!"

During high school I started reading the theories of modern masters such as Mondrian and Kandinsky and was fascinated by their attempts to symbolize meaning beyond the superficial and physical. Maybe art would be a way to tap into that deeper place I sought. And maybe other artists were uncovering the keys.

The art school had a well-stocked library, where I poured over biographies and insights penned by great artists. Some did seem to tiptoe into a province of the divine. Rothko's majestic mood-murals struck a deep place, as did his thoughts and feelings.

Color healing also beckoned. It seemed fascinating, a holistic field where color was utilized for more than its aesthetic appeal, for its healing qualities and vibrations.

Being in art school allowed me to set aside prime time to paint. Working into the wee hours of the night exploring—following intuition, texture, trying to express and gently guide but not crush the delicately evolving something—was exhilarating. My finished products were pretty raw, though, looking more like dreamy blobs of color than anything. Art mimics life: the paintings were full of color and movement but lacking structure and definition.

Several professors who seemed to get and appreciate where I was coming from, that my work was as much or more an inner process than a visual accomplishment. I wasn't quite there yet, getting my hand and eye to fully express what was brewing inside. But they liked that something *was* brewing inside. Dan, a friendly teacher, helped nurture a transition that just happened in the middle of a painting of dancers. Somehow the piece started working more within the tension of the picture plane, not just floating on top of it.

I often felt cut down by many of the other instructors, who focused on visual adroitness (or, in my case, lack thereof). Rick's kind but patronizing suggestions to help jumpstart the fledgling beginnings of the dream painting started to elicit my usual reaction— defensiveness and a feeling of queasy inferiority.

This time I paused and realized: I just didn't care. The strength of the dream outweighed my teacher's slight. Yeah, it would be nice to paint it with more mastery. But too bad. This was important to me.

The dream piece might not make it into the Museum of Modern Art, or make an important artistic statement. But it made a soul statement I needed to formulate, and led to a soul place I needed to go.

This Zaidy creation ended up changing my life. Drastically.

A painting?

Working on it brought the Jewish thing out of the dusty corner of unfinished, nostalgic, and largely irrelevant business I had relegated it to. In my mind, being Jewish was kind of like your high school yearbook or kindergarten picture. Good memories you wouldn't want to throw out. Keep it in the attic or a back closet in a stash of memorabilia. I gained a lot of social consciousness from it; I gained a certain inquisitive intellectual drive and courage. It gave me valuable perspectives and tools for dealing with the grounded real world.

It had always been there, this question of Jewish identity and what on earth it all meant. Why did Mom and Dad always harp on which entertainers, politicians, and casual acquaintances were Jewish? This annoyed me to no end. What's the difference? Don't you judge each individual on their own merits? This is America, land of equal opportunity and rugged individualism. What's with the tribalism?

But on the other hand, how come, in truth, most of my close friends were Jewish? What was that elusive quality that drew us together? I had largely ignored that unresolved issue, that nagging question, but it simmered under the surface and never completely went away.

There was one thing I knew for sure. Jews had nothing to say about the hidden realm, the mystical, the spiritual. The Judaism I knew left me empty-handed in that province.

Whatever spiritual force the Jews might have once had, it was now passé. After all, I had learned with the Anthroposophists that the Jews' purpose was to be the vehicle for bringing the "Christ consciousness" to the world. That done, they taught, the Jews are extraneous, outdated baggage —which I now can't believe I blithely swallowed with hardly a burp. (Actually, the idea did give me a bit of indigestion, but I figured that was my lack of true understanding.)

One of Maureen's friends, some funky combination of Anthroposophist and Punk Rocker, used to push my Jewish button. "You'd be soap or a lampshade," he'd mutter as he slithered past.

I was so minimally aware of the full scope of the Nazis' demonic deeds, and so willing to try to ditch any Jewish differentness, that I just giggled uneasily and shrugged. I thought maybe he was trying to shock me into a nascent Jewish pride. More likely, he was saying, in more visceral, nasty words than the Anthroposophists used: "Steiner was right, the Jews are a done-for deal." Looking back, I'm horrified, pretty sure he was giving me a vitriolic verbal kick in the teeth.

I still bought into Steiner's proposition--the Jews were an outmoded relic of history. I could see it. The Jewish world I knew of was rational, completely non-spiritual. It seemed like everyone else was zooming beyond an abstract God and dry ethics. Instead they were grooving on cosmic beings and worlds, souls, quests, reincarnation, and all kinds of juicy stuff.

It was blossoming April, a year before, when I visited Donna and checked out UC Santa Cruz. My back had healed from the farm injury, and I was off in search of the next step on my soul development curriculum, the next place to find that elusive something.

"Hey, Miriam, you gonna be around next week?" she asked, as we sat sunning and drinking in the glorious spring sun out on the deck.

"I'm not sure. Why?" I lifted my head from the hammock.

"It's almost Passover. We're gonna put together a progressive *seder*. Got any ideas you want to share?"

"A seder?" I sat up in disbelief. "Why? This is California. I thought you left all that in Detroit."

She was surprised at my hostility. "Hey, it's not grandma's. We're gonna mix in our own readings and have a good time," she said defensively.

But fresh from my jaunt with the Anthroposophists, I was sure the seder was nothing more than outmoded nostalgia. Not worth the time of a serious spiritual seeker. I grew up with enough Jewish memorabilia, filling time and going nowhere. I wanted Truth. I checked the calendar and found that Easter and Passover coincided that year.

I packed up my backpack and vaguely, self-righteously, told Donna, "I might be back in a few days. Enjoy your seder. I'm going down to the Big Sur to meditate on the Christ consciousness."

And I hitchhiked down, hung out on that magnificent shore, thinking my deep and confused thoughts. Out in the raw elements, I was happy, inspired, and maybe, just maybe, a little bit nervous being out there all by my lonesome.

The waves crashed, their passion never abating. The powerful rocks and cliffs piled high. The sea lions were sunning and chirping with their unique call. Everything was in rhythmic, dynamic harmony. What was my place in it all?

I hiked and sunned, daydreamed and pondered, breathing in the briny, invigorating fragrance of the sea, gazing at that blue, blue, endless skyline. Gulls swooping and soaring. I huddled in my sleeping bag on a patch of grass behind rocks and ate granola bars, praying for guidance.

Crazy? I now tremble at what could have happened to a spaced-out young woman hitching into a largely unpopulated expanse. But I was naively oblivious to mundane concerns like safety and precaution.

On the way back to town, I stood on Highway One—another West Coast bold and beautiful day, backpack on, thumb positioned. The road was quiet. An older woman drove past. I saw her do a double-take. She stared, pulled over, and motioned for me to come into her compact wagon. Sue was pleasant, intelligent, and mildly artsy-looking, with graying curly hair. "I don't usually stop for hitchhikers," she explained after I piled in, threw my pack in the hatchback, and got comfortable. "But something in your face was different." As we talked, we found lots of common interests, including art and color healing.

"You just look so familiar," Sue kept repeating. "Have we met before?" But it didn't seem likely.

After a while Sue said, "Hey, I'm actually headed up to a Steiner center in a few days. It has a color-healing school. Maybe you'd like to come along?"

"What?" I answered, startled. "I wanted to visit that very center on this trip. And you know about Steiner? I was working at a Waldorf community in the East a few months ago."

She turned with a jolt.

"Now I know where I've seen you! Were you at the Hazel-wood Farm this fall? In New York?"

"Yeah! Wow—I remember you, too. You visited, right?"

We sat back in smiling silence. What were the odds of us crossing paths on a lone highway, clear across the country?

Thank you, Cosmic Force, for guiding me, I sang silently with joy.

(And as I later came to realize, with deepest gratitude, thank you, God, for throwing me a lifeline of safety and protecting a young and foolish hitchhiker from who-knows-what).

The Passover/Easter season ended. So did that trip. I decided to return to Ann Arbor and entered the art school, instead of transferring to Santa Cruz or the Steiner color healing program. It was on a starry night soon after my return that I had that vivid dream. Why did it move me so?

I never seriously thought about checking in with a rabbi or adding a Jewish book to my collection from the metaphysical bookstores, which I visited often, scanning the shelves to find/feel/sense my connection. I'd once grabbed a book of Chassidic folk tales, but that was from Borders, not my source for serious searching material, and it evoked nostalgia more than anything else.

Jews don't believe in God, I thought. I guess I knew some Jews did; that *Baruch Ata* business we sang at camp and that Aunt Elaine sang when she lit candles had something to do with God. But it seemed an empty formula that you rattled off to show you knew how to say Jewish stuff.

In English it was a turn-off. The blessings all started with these same unappetizing words: "Blessed are You, O L-rd our God, King of the Universe, who sanctifies us with Your commandments, and commands us to..."

Yuck. What is sanctifying? Sounds like sterilizing. Commandments? Ain't no one gonna command me to do nothin'.

What is God, some kind of dictator? This is no path for me. And no Jews I knew actually would admit caring about faith or what God might want from them on a daily personal basis, beyond maybe a general, global sense.

But that evocative verse I had stumbled upon, the one about sowing and reaping, tickled, opening the musty attic door just a crack, to this unresolved Jewish-identity thing.

We usually worked alone, each student at their own pace, as the professor circled around. Every week or two, there was a group critique. We'd all go from easel to easel, and each student would explain what they were doing—their progress, their problems— so others could offer suggestions and comments.

During the next group critique, I noticed a quiet, sort of boring-looking girl who must have been in the class all along. Her neatly pressed skirt, her small paintings, her unobtrusive comings and goings had been under my radar. She was not expressively throwing paint on a large canvas, standing out in her intensity or cutting-edge work like the others.

When her turn came she explained her nice and pretty piece to the group. "I have friends who had a Chassidic wedding this summer, and I made painting of it as a gift for them."

Oh, Chassidic, I thought, *that's nice. I have a book of Chassidic tales.* So I ambled over to her and started shmoozing. "I'm working on a Jewish-themed painting, too," I mentioned casually.

"Jewish? You?"

Her Jewish outreach radar went up. She looked me over, seemingly surprised. With my wild long hair and paint-stained overalls, she probably had assumed I was another artsy Zen, Hindu, whatever. Maybe she'd overheard my impassioned debates with Jenna, the custodian, who kept plying me with Jehovah's Witness pamphlets.

"Did you say your name is Miriam?"

Brocha looked shy, but determined. She dutifully latched onto me and started inviting me. Come, come to a class. Come learn. Come meet my rabbi.

Now, I was aware of the Chabad House near my dorm. Not cool. Not my speed.

I had noticed the rabbis sitting with their table on the Diag, giving out brochures and trying to get students to go into their cute little sukkah and eat a piece of honey cake. Like seeing the Amish: a curiosity, another world that had no connection to mine.

And Sherwin had taught us that all movements of Judaism were outdated and irrelevant, most especially and absolutely the Orthodox. I mean the term *Orthodox* said it all. Dogmatic. Primitive. Xenophobic. Not on the radar of remote possibilities. And Chassidim were ultra-stone-age Orthodox. Did they even know how to read, I wondered?

They had tried to connect with me. Maybe they'd gotten my name from some list. I'd sometimes come home from Holistic Health Council happenings to find their flyers pushed under my dorm door, weird squiggly Hebrew letters and all.

With their black yarmulkes, white button-down shirts tucked neatly into dark suit-pants, pale complexion, totally uncool look and vibes, there was absolutely no way I was ever going to go to any of their programs, talk to them, or go into their building.

But Brocha wanted me to come—like really, really wanted me to come. Come to a party. Come to a video. Come learn. It seemed I had to field some kind of invitation most every time I was in class.

Okay, okay, I finally relented. I'm supposed to be open-minded and tolerant. One time can't be that bad. I'll chalk it up to an interesting experience and try to guard myself from catching their cooties.

So I went with sweet Brocha—with her carefully groomed hair, intense eyes under plastic glasses, and neat skirts, stockings, and sandals—to a class discussing *Pirkei Avos*, the Ethics of the Fathers. The three students, the rabbi, and I sat with a text: black Hebrew block letters on the right side of the page, English translation on the left.

The synagogue had too many books jamming the book-shelves. The fluorescent light droned and glared and the beige carpet was cliché suburban sixties.

No candles, incense, wood, or soft lighting. There was no chanting, meditating, dervish dancing, ooohmmming, or groov-ing, like the Holistic Health Council picnics in the Arb.

It was intellectual, using the mind to discuss a text. But it wasn't a university class, where objective analysis ruled. The text was discussing some kind of spiritual perspective. The ideas were interesting but out of context to anything in my life.

Weird.

One doesn't discuss God; one melts into the godhead in an ecstatic merging with the oneness. Did not resonate.

Learning— as these Jews called this activity, as an active, pre-sent-tense verb—did not connect, certainly not as a way to reach my burning goal, to come close to the cosmic energy.

Okay, at least now Brocha will leave me alone, I figured. I learned with her and the rabbi.

Done.

12

—❧—

MEETING UP WITH THE SHABBOS QUEEN

I tried to minimize our contact, but Brocha wouldn't bug off. *Come for a Sabbath meal. Have you ever celebrated Shabbos? It's very special. Come. When are you coming?* She kept at it with single-minded determination. I didn't want to go. But since I was floaty miss universal, no boundaries, all oneness and goodness, I could hardly keep saying no.

And the word Shabbos did evoke a warm tingle. On Friday nights at Camp Tamarack, we were supposed to wear something a little nicer. We entered a different, hushed dining room, utilitarian tables covered with white paper tablecloths, lit candles, twisted challah loaves, and bottles of grape juice. We ate raisin-studded noodle kugel and roasted chicken, mouthed some Hebrew songs. Something subtle but special hung in the air.

Saturday morning had been one of my favorite times of camp. No running off to crafts or camping skills. We often just slept in, but from time to time the staff led discussion groups with ethical themes in honor of the Sabbath. Once I was with a group sitting on the beach. The leader taught us a Joan Baez, consciousness building song about humankind's interdependence, based on John Donne's "No Man is an Island."

After we sang the slow, serious song a few times, so different than the usual rowdy, rafter- raising camp cheers, the leader tried to launch us into a discussion. What is our connection and obligation to others? Her lead-ins were met with mostly blank stares. Some kids looked bored, and were busily scratching mosquito bites, pulling on grass, and deciding what nosh to eat from their goodie box that day. A few of us were mesmerized. I loved thinking such big and meaty questions. I wanted to belong, beyond my stubby, chunky pre-adolescent body—I wanted to belong and give and care.

But then "Shabbos" was over. Time to re-enter regular camp zone. We ran to lunch and grabbed our bathing suits for general swim.

And more.

The Friday-night scene in *Fiddler on the Roof* had seeped into my bones. My family was fairly obsessed with this nostalgia-evoking show. We saw Zero Mostel, Topol, the Broadway production, the movie, tons of amateur ensembles; and knew the lyrics, even the places where there were skips in our phonograph, by heart. The Sabbath scene, mothers praying over their candles, shining on the darkened stage, never failed to evoke sentimental tears and some kind of intense longing in me.

The haunting melody, sung over the candles, hung in the air, asking God to "hear our Sabbath prayer. Amen."

Even though we didn't believe in prayer, and only Christians said Amen, as far as I knew... still...

Something was there.

And the "Welcome to America, greenhorn" classic, *All of a Kind Family*. As a kid, I was intrigued with the description of the *havdala* ceremony, where the family gathered to end the Sabbath and usher in the new week. Something about the braided candle and the pungent spices stood out, lodging in a corner of my memory.

Growing up, Mom and Dad did mark Friday night fairly often. We lit candles, drank a sip of syrupy-sweet Manischewitz wine and ate a slice of challah before running off to Friday night's

100

menu of basketball games, movies, or parties. We uttered the Humanist version of the blessings:

We bless the light in all the world / We bless the light in every man / We bless the light of Sabbath peace.

None of that *Baruch Ata* mumbo-jumbo. But a drop of that evocative, elusive something hovered there too.

Sabbath peace. Hmmm...

So, I finally agreed. "Fine, I'll come," I told Brocha, and she happily told me where and when to appear.

I somewhat apprehensively knocked on Brocha's door at the appointed time, before sunset one Friday night. She ushered me into her nondescript student apartment. I gave her a bag of organic trail mix I had picked up at the food co-op. She scanned it carefully. "Thanks, I don't know. It doesn't have a kosher certification. I'll have to ask if I can eat it."

Whaddya mean—it's vegetarian, organic, healthy. Why do you have to ask some rabbi? You can't even think for yourself? Another sure sign this whole whatever-it-was had nothing to do with me, that was for sure.

In Brocha's enthusiasm, she had invited me not only for the evening meal, but for the full twenty-five-hour experience, a lot for a first time. She seemed glad that I had come. She was intelligent and sincere, but I couldn't understand why she took all these nit-picking details so very seriously. "Chill, honey," I wanted to say. She showed me the bathroom and said something about brushing my teeth before sundown and leaving the lights on for the whole Shabbos. A small piece of masking tape secured the switch in the on position as a reminder.

Okay. This is getting weirder by the minute. All these rules. I just want to melt into the oneness. What does the bathroom light have to do with anything? I was annoyed at myself for letting myself get talked into this bizarre experience.

We went to the rabbi's house for the Shabbos meal. It was pleasant but kind of boring, served up with way too much food.

Rabbi Goldstein and his wife, Esther, seemed nice enough.

There were twenty or so students gathered around their dining room table, which was bedecked with a crisp, white tablecloth, the house permeated with good smells. They sang, joked, and seemed to be enjoying themselves, but they didn't fit into my definition of spiritual. They were too neatly dressed and groomed. The guys had crocheted yarmulkes clipped on. Some girls wore skirts. Polyester might even have been seen, perish the thought! And a clear plastic cover over the tablecloth? I mean, c'mon. That's not for mystically-minded people, that's what middle-aged Jewish women have covering their couches in their living rooms that no one's allowed to go into.

I was a universal child of the universe and lover of humanity; however I couldn't help but rank the chatting people gathered round the laden table. Way below me on the hip-and-cool barometer. In fact, they were scraping the bottom, I assessed unjudgmentally with non-judgmental compassion.

I made it through the night, bathroom light still on, and got ready to face the Sabbath day.

After morning services we walked to Rabbi Goldstein's brother's house. Levi had come to Ann Arbor several months earlier to help his brother develop the community and to teach his children. We shared desultory conversation as we strolled in the direction of North Campus, a good mile or so away. I lived in my organic hangout just past North Campus, so I figured I'd make a polite escape if things got too draggy.

We opened the door to Levi's dimly lit basement apartment. A young, simply dressed woman looked up with a warm and inviting smile. "Good Shabbos! Welcome!" she sang as much as spoke, with a lilting French accent. Her greeting felt like a blast of golden, radiant sunshine.

There was something magnetic about Levi's wife, Bella. A radiating, compelling energy of depth, sincerity and most of all, *simcha* (joy). Maybe because I tend to be a melancholic sort, my negative pole was instantly attracted to her positive spark.

It sounds silly. It sounds canned.

I walked into that flat with no expectations, or negative ones, ready to endure and get out. Suddenly, I could feel, almost taste the Shabbos Queen. Could feel the *Shechina* (divine presence) though I knew not of the concept. Bella kissed the *mezuzah* scroll on the doorpost. That slight movement caught my attention. What was she doing? I could sense something profound and real. She said a blessing with focus and joy, the words almost flying up to the God she was passionately thanking.

I got it. I felt, I intuited what I later learned words to describe. Godliness was there, all around her, and these actions and words celebrated or enhanced or revealed that energy, somehow grounded it and made it more tangible.

I had gone along with Brocha and Levi to that luncheon date, figuring I'd sit through some schmaltzy conversation and yet-schmaltzier food. I sat there in that little, drab, sparsely furnished apartment in shock.

There were only the four of us, Brocha, Bella, Levi, and I. They were far enough from campus that people didn't just drop by, like they did at Aharon's larger and more centrally located home.

So they concentrated on me. Asked about my studies, my interests, my background, and tried to explain the basics of what they were doing, as it was all Greek to me. Making *Kiddush* on the wine, washing hands, was unusual and awkward; only the blessing *Hamotzi* thanking God for the bread was familiar. I don't remember any particularly fascinating explanation or insight. I just remember basking in the intense feeling of light—well, *Shechina*—that glimmered and shone.

After shlepping for so many years to *so many* centers, lectures, ashrams, and happenings, finding a drop here and another morsel there, piecing together a collage of bits of spirituality that rang true, it seemed that was as much of a "path" as there was going to be: an individualized, ever-changing, eclectic mix. I was wary of a too-easy or complete answer.

As I sat on the gray folding chair, at the small folding table covered with a white tablecloth, picking at my plate of gefilte fish and potato salad, something was different.

Somewhere deep inside me, my soul stretched and smiled. "Surprise! I know you're probably cynical, but honey, guess what? Girl, consider well, this *could* be it: an integrated path, your long-lost and ferociously sought-after path. Dorothy was right. Yes, Toto, there is no place like home, and, hey, you just might be in Kansas!"

There was a *ruach*, a spirit, and one of those Hebrew words that doesn't translate well, with too many negative connotations in English: *kedusha*, holiness.

Bella had a purity and sweetness about her. No worldly sophistication—not in her simple dress, the apartment decor, her mannerisms. At first glance it seemed like naiveté, but she was highly intelligent, full of deep insight.

There was something unadorned and honest. Straight from the source.

I started, on that Shabbos afternoon, to get an inkling of something authentic and ancient; something I was connected to.

Our family once attempted a camping trip, to Tahquamenon Falls, in Michigan's Upper Peninsula. (The cozy family wilderness adventure didn't unfold as planned. Poor Mom and Dad slept on air mattresses in the tent, while we kids refused to budge out of the back of the station wagon, where we had a restless and rowdy night.) The beautiful waterfalls sparkled and rushed, but few tourists flocked around, as the falls were tucked in a backwoods location.

Another year we went to Niagara Falls, which showed off her bountiful might and splendor to the multitudes, razzling and dazzling with Maid-of-the-Mist boat rides and souvenir hawkers. The delicious and pure spring water of Tahquamenon Falls couldn't match up in glitz, and remained obscure, unknown to most travelers.

So, too, with these Chassidim. Relatively few students made their way to their open Shabbos meals. To access the delicious, pure spring, you had to travel the less-known path, dig, and get past the rocks—the cultural differences and peculiarities, the insularity. But a roaring wellspring of the freshest water gushed forth. I didn't realize all that in one afternoon, not consciously at least; but something stirred in a crevice of my soul.

It seemed the heavens had conspired to get me to come back again. Bella and Levi lived in a fairly large apartment complex, with two-story buildings spread around the valley below University Hospital. It was far from the dorms and main student population, far from their brother and his Chabad House. They lived on the ground floor, half a flight down. Maybe they were there because the basement apartment and the far-off locale were cheaper, I guessed.

Maybe, but I can't help but see their address as a bit of cosmic engineering. I had outgrown beer parties, frats, too-crowded and teeny-bopperish campus life, and lived in a "townie" non- student neighborhood on the fringe of remote North Campus. In the back of our teeming organic garden, behind the compost pile, was a trail going down the overgrown hill, our shortcut to the main campus. At the bottom of that hill, an apartment complex was nestled. Out of the whole complex, which wound around a few acres, the very building and window closest to our trail, that I passed right by each time I hurried up to class, was Bella and Levi's.

At the end of Shabbos lunch, Bella enthusiastically invited me back again. She flashed her megawatt smile. "Miriam, it has been such a pleasure to meet you and talk with you." She slightly bowed her head with European graciousness. "When will we see you again? Please come soon. Maybe next Friday night?"

I retreated a bit from our connection, and was vague. "Thanks, maybe, we'll see..."

Hey, don't corner me or pin me down. Let's see which way the wind's blowing.

I might have let the experience drift off as a blip, an interesting detour, because it was just so far out of my context. I mean, she served potato salad with mayonnaise, her challah was baked with 100% bleached white flour, and she had tacky pictures of old rabbis hanging with little handwritten explanations tucked into the corners of the plastic frames. How un-organic, how unsophisticated, how gauche. And the Jewish Jewish Jewish thing—they kept talking about Jews this, and being Jewish that. Why so exclusionary?

I walked past Bella's kitchen window often, so I didn't forget about her. As I hurried up to campus, I glimpsed her, clad in colorful babushka headscarves, washing her dishes. Her image evoked nostalgia for Bubby and her Ukrainian past, beckoning me to stop, which I did from time to time.

Those that sow in tears will reap in joy.

A seed had been planted. I was hardly aware of it; it lay dormant. It would have to fight many weeds and rocks. But the tiny speck of a seed had been sown.

13

❦

THE CRYSTAL GPS

On the surface, the search continued. A few weeks after that Shabbos encounter, I went to a lecture at the Zen Center for the first time, hoping to find some enlightenment. The lecturer and quiet, reserved audience seemed dry and detached. But one bopper in the audience caught my eye. She was smiling and laughing. We drifted to each other and started to talk. If you're living in the light, you should be openly joyful, I figured. But that radiance was hard to find. So few seemed to have it. Lori did.

Lori and I skipped out of there, two soul sisters wanting to live in the light, buds leaning hungrily towards the sun. We headed up State Street, giggling and laughing, sharing a bubbling mirth, going beyond the mind to a place of delight.

One Friday evening, we ended up in some little room, meeting with a pony-tailed guy with intense eyes that Lori considered almost a guru, her mentor. She was excited, as he was going to take us to the next level, to taste some kind of nirvana. I was full of anticipation. Fasten your seat belts, get ready for takeoff!

The lights were dimmed, a few throw pillows on the floor. A candle was lit. Indian atonal music droned in the background, a cloud of incense hovering in the air. I centered myself with mostly calm, touched with a drop of excitement and a smidgen of apprehension. The guru guy led us through a series of meditating, chanting, deep breathing, and hyperventilating till we blacked out and went into a heightened state. I felt a quicker pulse, a kind of lightness, slowed thinking, intensified colors, and almost an aura around my visual field.

Enlightenment!

(Well, probably from lack of oxygen, I now wryly realize.)

We went through many hours of this. Over and over. Exhausting, monotonous, and exciting. What level would we zoom to next?

Chant, breathe, bend over, kneel, stretch, black out, breathe.

Chant, breathe, bend over, kneel, stretch, black out, breathe.

Chant, breathe, bend over, kneel, stretch, black out, breathe.

Chant, breathe, bend over, kneel, stretch, black out, breathe.

The night slowly gave way to first glimmerings of dawn. We persisted, in a hazy, rhythmic routine.

Chant, breathe, bend over, kneel, stretch, black out, breathe.

In the middle of a chant, pretty lost in the zone, a detached perspective suddenly settled in my brain (or what was left of it), coming in unexpectedly for a landing.

All of a sudden I pulled back emotionally from the incense haze, and had a clear, time-related thought. "It's Saturday morning. This isn't where I should be. I'm gonna go to the Chabad House, that Chassidic center, and join in the Shabbos."

I had been dropping in now and then, on quiet weekends when no more-exciting happenings were unfolding, and it was slowly becoming a real go-to for me.

The melodies and images of the services had been slowly seeping into my bones. The surprisingly deep insights of Bella and her sister-in-law Esther were real food for thought: nutritious, solid food. Even the nerdy students who frequented the Chabad House weren't so bad once you started to get to know them. But I still thought of that whole deal as background music for the real search. After my night on Mars, however, I wanted comfort food, something grounded and straightforward.

"I'm done here," I realized with surprising clarity.

I got up, stretched, and started to pull out. I walked toward the door, to the protests of my intergalactic traveling companions.

"Miriam," Guru Guy said, his resonant, deep voice serious and compelling. "I'm sorry to see you leave. We've come so far tonight and are laying the groundwork for deeper and deeper awareness."

Lori looked a bit crestfallen and hurt. "Are you sure? Don't leave now..." she implored, putting her hand on my shoulder, and then giving me a hug. I stood there mutely.

I didn't want to try to explain. I didn't understand it myself. Wasn't this what I wanted? Focused, personal guidance—with promised fruits of bliss dangling almost within my reach? No. I just knew it was time to go. I nodded, pushed back the Indian tapestry hanging in the entrance, and pulled open the door. I waved, murmured thanks, and turned to go. "See ya around," I offered, and left.

With mixed feelings, I wearily closed the door and walked to the street. Am I just chickening out? Am I really missing the big breakthrough that's just about to unfold, I wondered? Questions nagged, but I kept walking. It was a bit of downer to come back to the everyday world, but mostly a calming relief to smell fresh air and see daylight and normal pedestrians going about their business on planet Earth. I trudged up the hill to listen to the Torah reading, had a bit of lunch at Bella's, and then went home and collapsed into a deep sleep.

A few weeks later I got a call from Starburst. A senior, advanced free spirit—like a Ph.D. in Free Spiritology—she was probably in her late twenties, sun-aged skin and crow's feet crinkling when she smiled. In my eyes, a sage mentor.

We had met a few months earlier at a New Age gathering in northern Michigan. Adorned in sparkly, Indian-cotton, flowing skirts, barefoot to feel the good Earth, sun-kissed streaked hair blowing freely in the breeze, Starburst was confident and fun. She lived with zest, trying to tune her being into the vibes of Mother Earth and Spirit, like a resonating tuning fork. Running Deer, her little blond love-child, was an easygoing toddler who traveled along with his mom in her sling or backpack.

"Hey, Miriam," Starburst greeted me and let me in on her latest. She was passing through Ann Arbor on a burst of wind, on her way out west to travel with the Spirit, and did I want to come along?

No carefully laid plans, no travel agent or itinerary. We would meet at a healing center in Arizona and follow the "GPS" of the divine intent, traveling by pendulum. (I'm now thinking we really did have a GPS—Godly Protective Spirit—since we say God protects fools and innocents; a protection I have drawn on way too heavily.)

Free-spirit faker that I was, I cheated and reluctantly enriched the corporate machine. I bought a plane ticket and flew out to Phoenix with money saved up from camp counseling, lifeguarding, selling bagels, and other odd jobs. Since I lived simply, I was able to finance my quest adventures without asking Mom and Dad for money (or approval!). Their knowledge of these jaunts was minimal, and the pre–cell phone era made dropping out of contact easier. While waiting at the airport, I stayed true to my principles as best I could. I sprawled on the floor in the terminal waiting area, not in one of those molded plastic chairs. I munched my granola, instead of buying a Styrofoam-encased Mac Meal.

In Arizona, I took a bus and bummed rides, and finally got to the healing center, set back from an isolated dirt road in arid desert-and-cactus country—vast, open skies and pink-orange-golden ribbons of color. It was built around hot springs, whose healing waters had been enjoyed by Native Americans.

Found Starburst in the healing center's main building, a pleasant adobe structure.

"Hey," I scurried over to give her a hug, happy and relieved (okay, I was a bit chicken to be wandering alone; don't tell anyone) to be in the right place and see her familiar face, and excited to begin our adventure.

Starburst hugged me back, gave me a big grin, then grunted and gestured.

Huh? Does she have laryngitis, I wondered? She held her finger to her lips making a *shhhh* motion.

A bubbly woman came over, introduced herself as Suzanne, and clued me in.

"Is Starburst sick?" I asked.

"Oh, no, love. She's just fine. How was your trip? Did you find the center easily?"

Starburst motioned to her mouth and shook her head, then pointed to Suzanne. I looked on quizzically.

"She's doing a fast of silence," Suzanne explained. "Are you familiar with that?"

I'd heard of this meditative technique. As Suzanne chattered on and on, Starburst's silence seemed dramatic, elegant—so quiet and still.

"Once she's quieted and emptied her mind for a few days, she'll rejoin you. Do you want to try our yoga class, use our pottery wheel, try some other classes or healing mandala collaborations while you wait?" Suzanne said, showing me the bulletin boards—a smorgasbord of New Age delight.

Starburst smiled, blew me a kiss, swept up Running Deer, and headed to the deerskin tepee, set back on the less-developed part of the land. I watched her skirts fluttering behind her, kicking up the red desert dust.

Hey, man, I'm cool, I thought. I hung out, hiked around the center's striking land, and soaked in the hot springs while she did her thing.

A few days later we set off on our journey. Starburst had a small crystal, the size of a cherry, suspended from a purple string. When we wanted to know which way Spirit was directing us to go next, we hung the pendulum from one hand above the cupped palm of the other hand.

It hung in still suspense, as the pent up energy waited to reveal our destiny, the many smooth facets reflected the bright southwestern sunlight like a prism, for a restful moment. We stood waiting in quiet, meditative suspense, like birds before they soar, waiting to receive our instructions, waiting to receive the intention of the cosmos for us. The pendulum then picked up some kind of energy and started going either clockwise or counterclockwise, first with the very slightest movement in tiny, barely visible circles, and then picking up momentum. The almost imperceptible circles would get faster, bigger and stronger till the pendulum was almost swinging.

Did the movement come from magnetic force, from subtle, subconscious movements the holder was making, or from the Universal Spirit Force—as we were sure?

(I've seen women use the pendulum to determine if a pregnant woman is carrying a boy or girl. There seems to be some kind of enduring folk wisdom or folklore here.)

We asked the pendulum questions or directions.

"Should we rest today? Move on? Should we head left or right? Should we stop now? Is this a safe place to sleep?"

Clockwise meant *Left!*

Counterclockwise—*Venture right!*

Clockwise—*Yes!*

Counterclockwise—*No!*

"Thank you, Spirit!" we chimed together, once our swinging crystal divined the answer. I hoisted my orange Camp Trails backpack onto my shoulders and tightened the waist belt, jostled the weight to balance it. Starburst tucked Running Deer into her sling and slid on her backpack.

Off we went, till the next question or choice arose.

And so we traveled. On and off buses, hitching, walking. With a joyful abandonment and trust, our "GPS" was never unhappy with our moves and could handle spontaneity.

The GPS in my minivan doesn't like an unexpected turn, and lets us know in its annoying drone that we fickle dummies upset it and it is "recalculating, recalculating." But there were no errors on that trip with Starburst; each step was karma unfolding. That pendulum turned one way or the other, and off we blithely went. Starburst, Running Deer, and I: the three musketeers dancing on the cosmic breeze.

One night, around dinner time, the crystal guided us to 372 Clark Street, on the corner of Main, in a small working class town. Our predestined destination was a small, nondescript house, with a noble attempt at making a lawn grow under the relentless Arizona sun. Two lawn chairs perched on the concrete slab of a porch, and a twelve-pack of Budweiser waited under the small awning that shielded the welcome mat. The name on the aluminum screen door said Jones. We knocked. The stocky Mizzus came to the door, wiping her hands on her apron, pulling her gauzy scarf down over her pink curlers. She peered at us quizzically, then summoned her husband.

"Fred, there's some strange girls here, come see what they want." Fred grumbled as he was pulled away from the ball game. We could hear the announcer solemnly declare, "Two balls and a strike." Fred's raspy voice sounded annoyed as he started to yell, "Why ya need me? Can't you jest tell 'em we're not interested?" But he heard the urgency in his wife's voice and rambled over. He joined her in silently gaping at the apparitions that had shown up uninvited on his doorstep. The couple peered through their screen door as Starburst explained that we'd been directed to just this very house, and we were humbly asking if we could share a meal with them. Her confidence, charm, and our strange sincerity seemed to evoke trust enough—maybe.

They closed their door and conferred a few minutes.

We stood quietly and waited. I shifted the weight of my backpack onto my other hip and ran my hand through my waist-length hair, absent-mindedly smoothing the waves.

"I don't know, Starburst, I'm not so sure they, um, feel comfortable with us," I said as I fidgeted.

"Don't worry," she said, tickling Running Deer and serenely assuring me. "It's all meant to be. We'll just take it as it unfolds."

After a few long minutes the Joneses opened the door and, with guarded smiles, let us come in, wash up, and have a cool drink. After that, they pulled up two more lawn chairs to their card table and served us a hospitable dinner. The small-town, rifle-totin' Arizona folk seemed a bit in awe of our freewheeling focus on Spirit.

We sat at their humble table, in their modest stucco home perched in their stubby little yard. They even shut off the droning TV for us.

"Where you girls from again?" the man asked as he nursed a beer.

"Oh, from back east, from Michigan. Sure is beautiful out here," I shyly offered, trying to make connection.

"And how'd you say you decidin' where to go?" the wife asked as she dished out macaroni and cheese. She eyeballed Starburst's calloused brown feet, and Running Deer happily nursing, with a mixture of scorn, disbelief, and perhaps a tad of admiration for our gutsy faith.

Starburst didn't hesitate. "We just call on Spirit to guide us. Our pendulum swings left or right, and that's where we go. We are roaming in the light of the One Great Force. Look, it brought us here," she smiled sweetly, "to such a welcoming family."

They smiled back, hesitantly, and then with genuine warmth, making their sun-worn faces crinkle. They seemed honored to have such prophetesses in their midst.

That's all I can glean out of the murky mist of memory. How long did we cavort? A few days? A week? Roaming, sleeping in fields, community centers, homes, parks. Eating this and that in coffee shops, restocking in small groceries, enjoying unexpected invites here and there. We literally took one day, one move, at a time.

Eventually this fine journey wound to an end. Starburst went off to the Bay Area to hook up with a friend who only walked and biked throughout the area, refusing to enter a carbon emitting vehicle as he floated through the urban sprawl, up and down those steep hills. He was the real deal in her eyes, a true purist.

Free-spirit-in-training that I was, after we wished each other peace and parted, I headed up to a center in Idaho, circled and starred in my well-worn, dog-eared *Communities* magazine. This periodical had replaced the U of M course catalog as the document I frequently scanned in search of the next move on my quest.

I'd leaf through it, reading descriptions of different spiritual, intentional communities. I carefully pored over their mission statements, narrowing it down to ones that sounded about right, like promising candidates for my next watering hole, a place to put down some roots for a while.

I managed to get out there, to a remote community of forty or so hardworking folks in a rugged, mountainous area. They had a communal eating place, where a woman was busy chopping and cooking up udon noodles and colorful veggie delights. I was directed to sleep in a loft in a beautiful meditative structure they'd built, a geodesic dome crafted with simple, natural woods. I had quiet and privacy and rummaged through a wide variety of interesting mystical books, from Thomas Merton to Gurdjieff to Eastern tomes.

The Idaho folks farmed, gardened, and had some small businesses going with their crops and crafts. Some were involved with environmental political action. People were friendly, but not pushy. They shared the land and community resources, but had their own families and private residences. There didn't seem to be an overriding dogma or doctrine, rather a general ecological, spiritual, political mix, with each member finding his or her own place in the brew. A mature and realistic air. A feeling of depth and quality. A real possibility.

After a few days visiting, walking the land, helping out with various tasks, I roamed away from the cluster of buildings, a mile or so out in the woods, to think. I tried to garner the courage to face the big question.

As they say in the seatbelt campaign, "What's holding you back?"

Could I see myself here? Did I feel I could connect and grow? I liked everything I saw, but an inner pull was missing.

I sat on a mossy log. As I reflected, an image formed in my mind's eye.

It wasn't Buddha. It wasn't a new state of revelation or tranquility.

Oh my gosh, what are *they* doing here? Can't I get away from them? My guilty Jewish conscience is haunting me, pursuing me!

I saw them both.

My father. My Bubby Fayga.

Bubby's sad eyes just don't understand. "Miriam, *maidele*, dear girl," she implores. "She wants to find herself," she murmurs. "But really, *zeiskiet*, my sweet one. Don't you think your parents will be worried?"

I was transported back to Detroit, sitting on the couch in her studio apartment. Whenever I visited Bubby she patiently listened to my newest adventures, stroked my hand, and absently murmured, "She wants to find herself, she wants to find herself," with some sympathetic understanding and an implied prayer for my safety. I felt comforted by her efforts at acceptance.

But I internalized a bit of her deep sadness that my life was not unfurling smoothly and according to plan, and her concern for my parents, her dear children, who were surely pulling their hair out over my antics.

Oh, man, I yelled at myself. I am *such* a baby and *so* chicken. Enough with the Jewish guilt already. Now is a defining moment on my quest path. Can't I cut the cord and step out of my good-little-girl, Midwestern past? Here in the rugged Northwest, it's time to step forward bravely to create the new me. Time to fly the nest, and burn those bridges of middle-class mediocrity and compromise.

I wouldn't learn about Abraham, the first Jew, for another year or so. But I intuited the challenge that he was given, back in the land of Haran, in the early chapters of the Torah. *"Lech Lecha,"* God instructed him. "Leave your birthplace, your father's home, and go to the land that I will show you." I, too, felt I must step forward, trust, go—no looking back. Step boldly, it's time to grow. Bubby and Dad represented all the past chains and conformity, all the Jewish, nice, mediocre, same-old same-old that I needed to spread my wings and fly away from.

But I just couldn't. I begged them to leave me alone, and I walked a little farther into the pine forest, paced back and forth and sat on a rock.

Focusing inward again, I saw an image of Bella. That cute lady in her babushka. With that gleam and light I couldn't quite disregard.

As I looked at her smiling face, I remembered the intensely tranquil feeling of that first Shabbos afternoon in her apartment. I still tended to dismiss it, never owning how special it was. That unique radiance washed over me.

Okay, Miriam, weird as it may seem, there's something there. Really. Something you need to face head-on.

As I sat pondering, I started to realize that I genuinely liked being with those Chassidim, incongruous as it seemed to my hippie mind. *Hey, I do want to find out more about what that's about. It's worth approaching with the same open-minded effort I'm putting into all this other stuff. There might be something of substance, and the only way to find out is to give it an honest chance.*

With a mixture of relief and shame at being such a wuss, I thought, *You are one chicken, one cowardly Jewish kid. Alright, guess I'm not ready for the Big Time yet.*

I sat there for a while longer, absorbing all this, turning it over, letting my change of direction settle in. Slowly, I accepted and digested it. My mind couldn't quite see going back to Ann Arbor as progress. I was mentally programmed to see my return as a cop-out, a failure. But even so, deep down I was a little—maybe even more than a little—excited.

It was good to have some resolution, a clear direction, even if it was very different than the new, brave, western chapter I had been almost sure I was heading to.

I slowly rambled back to the scattered cabins and buildings at the edge of the forest. I ran into Toni, who'd been showing me around. She was pushing a wheelbarrow of newly split firewood. "Well, whaddaya think?" she asked.

Embarrassed to be retreating back to safe and known borders, I mumbled something about thinking about it and tying up loose ends back east, back in the Old Country.

I slid outta there, stuffed up my backpack, got back to Boise, and grabbed a plane back to good ol' Detroit Metro Airport, back to Ann Arbor. Was ready to hang around Bella and the Chassidic Jewish thing, tune into it, and see where it would go.

14

—⁕—

BUBBY'S MELODY

Back from Idaho, I started coming around more. I figured if Bella's image followed me all the way out to the Northwest, I'd follow through on my resolution to check these folks out. Occasional Friday-night meals with the Goldsteins became more regular during the lazy summer months. I got used to the copious amounts of food, and would settle in, pull up to the table, and bombard them all— mostly Bella —with questions, arguments, and challenges.

"Why don't women hold the Torah and lead the services?"

"Why do we sit separately?"

"Isn't serving God all about the heart, the intention? What difference does it make what you eat?"

"What's with the dresses? Aren't they more attractive/sexual/provocative, if the intention is to be modest? I feel more on display when I wear a dress than I do with baggy pants."

And I asked the questions most everyone asks about free choice, evil, and especially the Holocaust.

I was cynical, enchanted, turned off, and impressed—all mishmashed together. Even though my barrage of questions, they were hard to ruffle. Sometimes I cornered Aharon and Levi, but I generally felt a more comfortable kinship with Bella and Esther. During occasional weekday visits I sat around their kitchen table, drinking tea or coffee, watching them deal with their kids and settle the little arguments. We chatted while I helped with the dishes, the laundry, or other daily routines.

I had Shabbos lunch with Bella often enough to have a set job. I helped prepare her trademark vinaigrette salad while we spoke, peeling and slicing the cooked beets, potatoes, and carrots. I enjoyed the rhythm of chopping a fresh onion and dill pickle and mixing in mayonnaise, a little vinegar, salt and pepper. My purple-stained hands branded me a regular.

Whatever angle I came from, they had something interesting to say. The whole thing had a coherent logic and rhythmic harmony; mystical yet systematic, intense yet orderly. I didn't always agree or understand, but I had to admit that the ideas and explanations were thoughtful and substantive. Their faith and enthusiasm were palpable, contagious even. I could feel them rub off, tickle my soul. I slowly became less of a detached observer and more of a somewhat-engaged participant.

These people had some special keys that could open the lock to a different way of looking at life. Different—yet somehow familiar. I felt I'd heard this soothing melody before. A bubby had been singing this to my soul for generations. The many hours listening to nostalgic records at Bubby's used to leave me touched but sad; annoyed, too, thinking, *That was lovely. But so what? Now what?* This new Chassidic melody didn't just look back in longing, like that music from a lost world; it looked to the future with a compelling map for our aching and magnificent globe.

Sometimes it seemed like too much of a closed system. The logic, the way of thinking, worked as long as you were willing to stay within that system, with its own reasoning that justified itself. I knew they probably hadn't been exposed to many of the things I'd read and studied. Sometimes it bothered me. Are they just thinking this and doing this because it's all they know? It's beautiful, but would I ever be comfortable staying completely in that magic circle? Would I start to feel claustrophobic or suffocating, or too cut off from everything else out there?

I'd occasionally come home from a study session on edge. Things just seemed too sweet and balanced. All the lovely answers, Bella's perpetual patience and smile, her glowing eyes, got on my nerves, eliciting mistrust. Don't be so angelic. A little more existential angst, please. Lay on the bass and the minor twang, I wanna hear some blues, I railed.

But that very wholeness, that sense of an ancient authenticity, continued percolating into my bones and thirsty soul, drop by drop, week by week. I was starting to feel satiation after years of wandering in a veritable desert. I tentatively tried out various *mitzvos* (commandments). The way they were explained, enriched and turbo-charged with insights of *Chassidus* (Kabbalah-based mystical philosophy), made them resonate. I felt I had stumbled upon a luxurious banquet of resplendent colors, tastes, sensations of the soul. My previous gleanings seemed like scrounging in the clearance vegetable section for a few scraps and morsels in comparison to this succulent abundance.

One Saturday morning, I was in my usual place in the Chabad House, reading along in my blue bilingual *siddur* (prayer book). The synagogue was cozy. I sat in the middle, with the few other now-familiar women who were there. I was attired in a long, turquoise housedress with dark blue flowers from the Salvation Army—funky and fairly modest—with my waist-long, thick, wavy hair freely flowing and my Birkenstock sandals buckled over my wool hiking socks.

As I skimmed through the prayer service, I enjoyed the imagery the psalms of praise evoked. "Praise Him with the call of the shofar; praise Him with the harp and lyre. Praise Him with timbrel and dance; praise Him with stringed instruments and flute." It was, well, Biblical, lyrical; a dancing, singing kind of poetry, different than e.e. Cummings.

I was in the middle of the Song of Miriam, sang after the crossing of the Red Sea, as the midmorning sun streamed in the window. Suddenly, I was transported; I was there—almost physically—walking in the barren Judean desert, mountains of sand and desolation, the hot sun baking down. There, with my tribe, my people, in that primordial time in the middle of nowhere.

A few seconds, minutes, some unknown measure of time passed as I was suspended; the vision faded and I came to, and settled back into my chair in the large former frat house, the Chabad House, perched up on a large lawn on Hill Street, 1980.

As the service wound to a close I started preparing myself for another argumentative discussion with the Chabad House cook, an insular young man steeped in Brooklyn-style Torah Judaism. This seemed to be his first exposure to other types of folk. During most every Shabbos lunch, he'd peer at my getup and try to get me to eat some animal flesh. (A Jew that doesn't eat chicken? How could it be?)

"According to *kabbalah,* we are supposed to elevate the animals, by eating them on Shabbos and using the energy for *mitzvos,*" he'd implore. "You are actually helping the chicken fulfill its purpose when you eat it this way. That's what it's here for."

He glared at my plate piled with salad, eggplant, and hummus.

I tried to protect my colorful veggies from his withering glance. "I don't know, I just don't like the feeling of heavy animal products, the grease and fat weighing me down and making me feel so much more sluggish. I think vegetable foods have a higher vibration and are healthier." I explained, smiling diplomatically. He grumbled and backed off.

But the next week he'd be back at his campaign to turn the freak into a carnivore. He just couldn't let it go and tried some version of his animal-flesh pitch most every Shabbos. To no avail.

Leave me alone, buddy, I thought after a few rounds of this. It was increasingly annoying. *You so do not get where I am coming from, and I don't think you either want to or are able to.* I held strong to my seven years of vegetarianism. All part of that funky Shabbos mix: Brooklyn meets Ann Arbor meets California dreamin'.

(Years later, I continued the tradition, teasing one of my daughters who got nauseous from partaking of our fine feathered friends: "Are you sure you're really Jewish? You don't like chicken? But chicken soup is Jewish penicillin!")

As one of the few kosher havens in a prominent university town, the Goldsteins often hosted visiting professors, lecturers, and researchers who needed a kosher place to eat. We often got to meet these figures casually around the table, and sometimes more formally when they were featured as guest speakers. I remember an urban planner, a mathematician, a biologist, and a musician.

I hardly listened as the urban planner spoke. His beard, yarmulke, and *tzitzis* (ritual fringes) were from one world, while his tweed jacket and khakis were from another. I kept thinking, in surprise, *urban planner—like Dad. So normal, college-educated professionals do this Torah thing, too. Not just flower children and removed-from-the-world yeshiva students and rabbis.*

I still wondered if this intense involvement with the Torah was born of a naiveté and other- worldliness that I kind of liked, but was also afraid of. Maybe they hang onto this because they've never been exposed to anything else, I figured.

But this guy was a nice professional, the kind I and every Jewish kid was groomed to become from earliest infancy. Guess he knew the score out there, and still was doing this bit; he was earnestly excited about the insights on the Torah portion he shared with us.

He didn't have the bored or cynical attitude toward religious duties that I associated with being a degree-toting professional. I had assumed that the amount of cynicism toward faith one had was directly proportional to the number of letters and fancy degrees after his name. Another stereotype was abruptly crumbled.

As I hung around this land I met many different personalities and dispositions, from the passionate to the quiet, dreamers to the analytic. Scientists, business mavens, fashion plates, homey mommies with broad, soft laps, simple townsfolk types who back in the *shtetl* (old-country village) *might* have been the wood choppers and water carriers.

I would have dismissed the Torah as a highly intelligent product of its times, incredibly progressive for way back then in those ancient days of yore: the first culture and literature to advocate for universal education and literacy, women's financial and sexual rights, just courts of law, and other radical concepts.

Perhaps, I might have figured, it was written or at least codified by rabbis who held and wanted to keep the power. But this *Chassidus,* this Jewish mysticism was something else altogether. It went way beyond dicing apart and reducing to some postmodern analysis. It delivered, big-time, the goods I'd been so arduously seeking.

It was Mystical and Spiritual, in capital, bold, and underlined letters. All the juicy good stuff— way more of it than I ever imagined existed. Exponentially more.

Who knew?

What a shocking surprise to start to find out what delicious treasures these black-coated Jews were hiding in those dark books with gilded Hebrew letters on the cover, myriad volumes packing their overflowing bookshelves. I had to laugh—I'd thought that Jews didn't believe in God and were devoid of spirituality. The stuff in these books took the scattered glimmers and threads of New Age lore and wove a luxurious tapestry. More than how to go out towards the light, it showed how to bring that light way down here, into everyday humdrum pockets of gray. There were discourses exploring aspects of Godliness I never would have even dreamed existed, beyond anything my little brain could ever have formulated.

One night Esther gave me a thick book with a dark blue cover. "Here," she said. "I think you'll really get a lot out of this, though its hard to understand on your own. It's the foundation book of Chabad philosophy, called *Tanya.*"

I leafed through the pages, left side with English translation in small, neat font, and right in Hebrew block letters, with no punctuation or vowels. I turned the pages and held it. Took it in. Felt the vibes. Don't ask me how, but I just knew. This was a treasure, a fundamental one.

This book has the answers, to those biggest and innermost questions, this book is a true guide, I said to myself. *Hold onto it.*

Back in my room, sprawled on my mattress, I opened the *Tanya* and read, but it stubbornly refused to be skimmed or read lightly. What's going on here, I wondered? This nut wasn't easy to crack; pretty undecipherable at a casual glance. Just having it felt good. But that wasn't enough.

I went back to Esther, asking, "Umm, what am I supposed to do with this book? I don't really get it, but it seems very profound."

She nodded. "You're right. Tanya really needs to be learned with a teacher. It's extremely dense and needs lots of explanation. Let's make a time to learn some together."

We spent several sessions reading and discussing. Esther held my hand in the early beginnings; she and many other teachers were the tour guides that helped bring me into the language and Kabbalistic, mystical approach. I slowly got familiar with the unique lingo and imagery.

This work shed a beam of light on dealing with our dual nature—an animalistic drive that wants pleasure, power, ease, and comfort *now* joined in an uneasy marriage with our divine essence, which is naturally altruistic, humble, connected. This struggle made the partisan divide between Democrats and Republicans, or Labor and Likud look like kid stuff. How could these two seemingly diametrical forces coexist, and hopefully thrive?

Rabbi Shneur Zalman wrote the *Tanya* to provide answers to the multitudes seeking his sage advice. He packed it in: struggles, depression, joy, faith, how to steer through life and come closer to God. This was heavy dude material: deep, psychological insights, glimpses into God's essence and purpose in creating this paradoxical world. How the infinite comes into the finite. Why and how God can seem so hidden. Why and how we people have egos and free will and can do terribly awful, screwy things.

Like a slow and sonorous cello sonata, the ideas were elegant and resonant. They didn't promise cosmic bliss. Darn. No shortcuts here. Life was still going to be hard—very hard. But I could start to glean that the Creator did throw us a clear map and direction, not just for my little life, but for humanity and the cosmos. It was subtle, deep, and broad.

This was different than the simplistic and dogmatic, "opiate of the masses" kind of religion I had been raised to be so wary of. It *was* a paved way, not bushwhacking through the wilderness with only my own raw ingenuity, *Communities* magazine and granola stuffed in my backpack; intuition on high alert for hidden light. Yet, I started to think that perhaps I *could* walk it. I could imagine following these road signs with a sense of integrity, without feeling I had sold out to an easy, pat answer.

I almost felt like a little child, when they first pull themselves up and begin to walk on wobbly, drunken sailor legs with exuberant, innocent joy. I could even run and manage being a big person in this here world with this kind of information.

Finally. I reveled in these insights. "My soul thirsts for You like a traveler in a parched desert," the Psalmist declares. I felt like I'd wandered into a verdant oasis that quenched my thirsty soul, like I was served spoonfuls of the finest chocolate, invigorating nectar; satiating the questions, aches, and intuitions I'd strung together all these years.

15

—⸙—

AT YOUR COMMAND!

Cosmic philosophizing wasn't enough. One of the main premises of this Torah jazz was the unique importance of *mitzvos*, the 613 commandments, most involving physical actions.

First, we had to clear up my allergy to the word *command-ment*. Bella assured me I wasn't becoming a mindless robot, or a West Point cadet. "Aye, aye, sir, at your command," the cadet says, as she salutes smartly and waits for orders, face blank, uniform immaculate.

Hmmm, not me. *If* I would wear a uniform, it would surely have a button missing, be held together with safety pins, sport a crinkle or wrinkle, and mismatching socks or funky individualiza-tion. And I'd probably be a little out of the line, leaning too much to the right or lagging behind on the left. Sigh. West Point flunky would be more like it.

Fortunately, that wasn't what was wanted here. They ex-plained that *mitzvah* came from the root of the word that meant "connect." These "commandments" were special vehicles for connecting with God in a unique and charged intimacy. Okay, that sounded lot more appealing and digestible.

Esther gave me a small aluminum box. It had a slot in the top, and a key hole to open and empty it on the bottom, kind of like a plain, square piggybank. But this was not for saving; it was for giving. She started telling me how important it was to give charity regularly, trusting that God will give us what we need, and actively connecting with the collective and the needs of others.

"Great," I said, and pulled a twenty out of my pocket. "No, slow down," she said. "It's not just how much you give; it's about the daily routine. Better to give a penny or a dime daily than a lump sum once a week or month.. The act of giving, loosening your grip on your own possessions, every single day, is a big part of this *mitzvah*."

"Hey, I'm a charitable person, this should be no big deal," I said and smiled. But charity wasn't exactly the same thing as *tzedaka*, Esther went on to explain. *Tzedaka* meant "justice"— what was fair and right—not about how nice and benevolent I was. God expected it from us.

So I took the metal box home and set it on my shelf with my fledgling Judaica collection —prayer book, *Tanya*, candlesticks with the white candles—next to the patchouli incense sticks, paintings, pastels, charcoal, old careworn *Communities* magazines (hadn't bought a new one since I got back from Idaho), and various and sundry esoteric and New Age books. Got in the habit of emptying my pocket change, some right into the *tzedaka* box, and some into a blue, hand-built ceramic bowl so there'd be a few coins ready to get deposited in the morning.

It felt good. Clink, clink, the pennies rattled as they hit the bottom of the can.

As of this writing, I teach preschool. In some ways I feel so similar to my little charges. I remember what it was like to get introduced to these prayers and deeds. I try to share the inspiration I felt when I was in my early twenties chronologically, but a small child in Jewish life.

I guess I was more mature than my current students, at least when it came to giving *tzedaka*, coloring inside the lines, and sharing. In my three-year-old class, the daily giving of pennies is a challenging and fun training in giving, a whole routine which many of the dear children individualize with their shtick. Little Avi waits till he thinks you're not looking, and furtively tucks the penny in his pocket. Sara might be cute with those golden curls, but she's no pushover; she clutches the copper coin tightly in her fist and doesn't want to give it up. Leah scours the penny basket to be sure to give the shiniest one.

But day in and day out, they are slowly trained to think about others. To uncurl that tightly clenched palm, let go of what seems like it's *mine*, and painstakingly... give... it... up. "Yay, Sara!" We encourage her shyly smiling, altruistic soul and try to give it strength for its next round against the ever-present voice of *Me, Mine, I Want*. We complete the cheerleading with song, enthusiastically singing new words to the tune of "For He's a Jolly Good Fellow:" "The very best place for a penny, the very best place for a penny, the very best place for a penny, is in the *pushka* (charity box)!" Another rousing number goes: "*Tzedaka, tzedaka, tzedaka,* that is what we give, to poor people to help them live, so they'll have food and clothes, so they'll have food and clothe. Even a penny a day before we start to play."

Does all this automatically make them kinder or more generous? Well... it's not so easy to change inborn character tendencies. But the training, the regularity of daily giving, and at least once in a while thinking about it, can only help. My own kids know that's just how it is, *tzedaka* before cereal is the morning routine. Yankel, the earliest riser, sets pennies out on the table, along with the bowls and spoons.

It soon got to the point where my morning didn't feel right without depositing a few coins before I headed out the door. And it's funny: something about the *tzedek* (justice) idea—that I'm not such a nice, pat-me-on-the-head person; I'm just doing my normal obligation as a hopefully humane Jew—deflated the ego a bit. I couldn't feel that pride in being so saintly and noble.

Another mitzvah that was easy to incorporate because of its beauty, and excruciatingly difficult because of its strict structure and time limitations, was lighting Shabbos candles. I'd seen the classic Sabbath painting of the kerchief-clad mother waving her hands over the silver candlesticks. Esther told me that this *mitzvah* was entrusted to women; not just lighting the candles but ushering in the transition from weekday, humdrum space and time to lyrical, sprinkled-with-gold-pixie-dust Shabbos.

Okay, I agreed, I'd give it a try. First few times, I showed up at her house early enough to do it with her. The ideal time was eighteen minutes before sundown. If I was running late I could do it sometime during the next eighteen minutes, she assured me, but once sundown passed, it was too late. Sundown was the official beginning of Shabbos; after that no fires could be lit.

She showed me what to do. I followed like a little girl follows her big wise teacher. She guided me to strike the match, and light the wick on the white taper. I copied her and waved my hands three times over the candle. She told me to imagine I was bringing the light into my heart and home, a lovely vision. Then she said I should cover my eyes with my hands. Word by word, I followed her example and said the blessing. She told me that the moment after the blessing was a special, private time to pray and commune with the Almighty.

I did my best for a few minutes. I let my hands fall down by my side and just watched. A softer light seemed to fill the space. Not just the shining candles, but as I turned away from them and walked to the couch, everything seemed suffused in a subtle glow. Esther stood there longer, swaying as she prayed. I could imagine that a mother had more on her mind and heart, so much to wish and ask for, so much to thank for.

We all stood around in suspended waiting while she finished. Then that long, lingering moment in front of the candles ended. You could almost sense Esther letting go of the exertions of the week—the rushing, organizing, doing—sense her muscles relax as the pulse of the world seemed to slow. She seemed to drink up fortitude and replenish —then she took her hands slowly down, turned to us, and slowly mouthed the words, savoring them like candies: "Good Shabbos."

Sometimes I wasn't at her house at that late-Friday-afternoon time. So I decided to give it a try on my own. It wasn't a strange or uncomfortable act; as a good hippie I did my thing by luminous candlelight quite often. But this had a formal structure. A set time, procedure, and blessing. Ouch. That's scary. Set, defined times are not the specialty of flower-child cloud- jumpers.

Even today, the stress of getting to an important appointment on time—not kind of, not rolling in ten minutes after the hour with a "sorry I'm late" as I breeze in the door with a smile and excuse — is hard. And meeting that deadline for starting Shabbos poses a never- ending challenge.

"Three minutes past candle lighting!" Fayga yells through the bathroom door. "Okay, thanks!" I yell back.

I jump in the shower as the clock furiously ticks. I luxuriate for thirty seconds. One minute to dry off, two minutes to throw on clothes and quick makeup, run down, and check the lights and all the settings in the kitchen. I start lighting my candles a good eight minutes before sundown. Again. Darn. I was really trying to be on time this week. What happened? The Friday afternoon weasel sneaks into the house and runs away with those extra minutes, most every week. We always make it, but it's usually an anxious race against that continuously ticking clock before we can relax into that peaceful lull after the candles are lit.

One balmy Friday evening, during that first summer of diving into observance, I was walking up State Street I had started to leave my wallet and backpack at home, letting go of sneaking in a few quick errands, even though I walked right past the store where I needed just one or two things. It would have been so convenient to quickly stop in... it wouldn't really break the Shabbos spirit, would it? Just that one box of tea and that new notebook, so I wouldn't have to go out again next week.

No. I was going to try weaning myself from weekday life cold turkey. No monetary transactions. I strolled through the Friday-night throngs of buzzing kids gathering in front of the theater, going in and out of bars and cafes, hurrying and hustling. They laughed and jostled. I could relate. It would have been so natural to join them. Hey, I'd been waiting to see that movie. It finally came to town. Not tonight. I was in a different space. I might have looked like any other Ann Arbor kid, but I was in a different zone. I had the distinct feeling I was there, and not there: floating through the crowd in a soft golden bubble, a bubble of Shabbos.

And that was before cell phones and internet and round-the-clock connectivity, rings, beeps, and demands on our inner space. Way back in the unimaginable dark ages of pay phones and snail mail. Last Friday afternoon I stood impatiently at the copy machine and saw my exhausted-looking principal rub his eyes and answer yet another demanding text.

"TGI-*shin*! Thank God it's (almost) Shabbos," I encouraged him.

He smiled wearily. "What do people do without a day where they have to turn all this off?" he asked.

I told him something I'd heard in an interview on NPR recently. I'd been in the car, racing to pick up some denim skirts on sale, but I had to be back for 4:00 carpool. I hit a snag in traffic on 71. "Darn, I knew I should have left earlier. I'm gonna be late now."

I impatiently fiddled with the radio dial as I waited for my lane to open up. Some singer was being interviewed. The usual yakety-yak; another guy struggling to make it, grabbing his chance to tell the world why he's so great. I listened distractedly as I scanned the rear mirror to try and switch lanes. Fresh Air does sometimes find interesting artists, and listening to them gets me motivated to get my creative act into higher gear.

"So I relish the Sabbath where I can shut it all off," he said.

What? I reached over and turned up the volume.

"You don't perform on Friday nights or Saturdays?" the

interviewer asked incredulously.

"You know," he replied, "my career is very intense. My agent, my producer, my band—someone's always texting or calling or needing a response. I crave, I need, a day to center, to restore myself, and get off the grid." *You got it, dude,* I thought and took a deep breath as the traffic finally unsnarled.

Standing at the copy machine, I excitedly shared that phrase with the principal: "That singer said he needed a day to just get *off the grid.*"

My principal smiled, sighed, and glanced at the clock. One hour more till the school day and week could close, three more hours till he could turn off the phone completely and step onto Shabbos Island. He nodded in agreement. "Absolutely. Well said."

Shabbos, the seventh day, had been my first taste of the sweet nectar of this hidden universe, and it remained the anchor. *"He garbed the day of rest in beauty; He called the Shabbat day a delight."*

I first tasted this sweetness in Bella's dingy flat. I sometimes wavered, wondering, was this *mitzvah* stuff really the ultimate in connecting with the Creator, or someone's complex, put-together invention? I'd remember that blast of light that hit me in the kishkas when I first stepped into her home. And I held it up as my litmus test.

Strange as it seemed, I was beginning to see how all those weird minutiae were an integral part of creating this golden space—all the details that sound so bizarre, like leaving the bathroom light taped on, not turning up the stove, only using cold water, and breaking bread on two (not one or three) challahs.

Once an old friend confronted me: "What's this craziness about? I hear you can't use scissors on Shabbos, and you can't even carry a tissue outside." He laughed cynically. What kind of bizarre and arbitrary ritual is that, he scornfully implied. I just made some kind of shrugging-it-off remark. It's hard to explain "on one foot," in a sound bite, how these seemingly nitpicking rules come together, how they really did open up a weekly paradise of luxurious holiness.

Shabbos was really true; I knew it in my bones. It couldn't have been invented by some ancient dude who figured out a plan. "People will work more efficiently if they rest periodically. Hmm, every seven days sounds about right." And over time the Jews became habituated to doing it on Saturday. Lovely, sensible practice.

Nice try, rational religious reductionists, but there was something more here—something tangible and from another dimension altogether. That *Shechina*, the divine presence—no one could make up that heavenly sweetness. And if this Shabbos holiness was so real, this kiss from above, maybe the other stuff in those Five Books of Moses and those five million books of debate, commentary, mysticism were real too. Maybe even the parts I didn't quite understand or connect to yet.

Around the same time I started coming around the Goldsteins', two other comrades showed up. Avraham and Nacha were coming from a similar place. We sized each other up–our clothes, stance, gestalt—and thought, yeah, I can relate to you.

One day Avraham told me his last name. It rang a bell. Man, I ruminated, that sounds familiar. Leaf. Leaf... Leaf! One of Zaidy's later business ventures was a small real-estate business with a guy bearing that unusual name. I could hear Zaidy exclaiming in his gruff voice, "Leaf did this. Leaf said that." I asked Avraham if he might be related. He was stunned. "Charlie Driker is your Zaidy? Of course I know him. Leaf is my dad." It turned out that Nacha and I also had intertwined roots: her grandparents were from a *shtetl* close to Bubby and Zaidy. They came to Detroit around the same time and were involved in the same communal Yiddish organizations.

Our common perspective and our shared background felt good, and made this whole thing seem less foreign. Two other kids from my neck of the woods; nice, suburban Detroit hippie-dippie kids were also sticking their toes into this brew and were strangely, magically drawn to these Chassidim. And there was an irony to the Driker's and Leaf's offspring trying to re-graft themselves onto their roots, the roots that had been largely left to wither in the arid sun, in the thrust forward into America. We three musketeers hung out together, and tried to help each other understand, and translate into our terminology, the amazing essence under the weird food, clothes, and other distractions that didn't fit into our cultural milieu.

We often spent many Shabbos afternoon with a macrobiotic and groovy observant couple, David and Rachel. Sprawled on pillows and futons around the shaggy rug, sipping peppermint tea, we earnestly planned how to fix the Chabad House.

"Those plastic plants have got to go. Live ones would freshen up the atmosphere and cleanse the air," Rachel insisted.

"And do you think we could get Aharon to get rid of the fluorescent lighting? Incandescent ones are softer and healthier," I added, stirring organic honey into my tea.

"Maybe we could help them pull up the carpets and put in hardwood floors," David suggested. "The Chabad House energy would be so much better."

I don't remember if the *ad hoc*, uninvited, Interior Improvement committee got up the chutzpah to present our proposals to our patient hosts, who opened their homes, taught and fed us for nary a penny. Maybe the Goldsteins politely said they'd consider it. It's possible they had bigger concerns than the crucial importance of these aesthetic and earth-friendly improvements. Little things like paying the mortgage and keeping the place running might have come before hardwood floors and organic kosher free-range chickens. But we stayed on anyway, even though we had to put up with so much synthetic material.

Hanging out with these two buddies helped bridge my transition to a world of a different focus. We gradually came to realize our burning issues were largely stylistic preferences and relatively transient cultural morays. An eco-friendly environment is important, and healthy eating is part of the *mitzvah* of guarding one's health. But a little white flour or sugar wasn't reason to jump ship. Our barometers were changing.

I still tend to be naturally attracted to "flower children." My eyes light up when I spot one in a crowd. *Hey, a soul mate is here!* There's often a meeting of the eyes, a moment of mutual recognition. Is she wearing the uniform—-maybe a Kabbalistic *chamsa* hand-shaped necklace, earthy shoes, a gauzy cotton skirt, and a frizzy hairdo? There's a certain perspective we tend to share that's visible in the way we dress and carry ourselves. Yet I've come to know so many unique souls don't fit into that mold.

With time, and as the integrity of this new/old land revealed itself, I was able to see beyond my very limited parameters, and appreciate that *even* clean-cut people in suits and white shirts, polyester and nylon, even polished, pointy shoes that clickety-clack with confidence could have deep faith and dynamic relationships with God. Spirituality meant a whole lot more than what percentage of cotton your clothes were and how much tofu you ate, how long you sat in stillness and emptied yourself, or whether you could pretzel yourself into a lotus position.

One Saturday morning I left the Chabad House with Levi and a few other students, to start the jaunt to his and Bella's house. We walked up Hill Street, past an outdoor café. Levi was garbed in his *kapote*, his traditional black, knee-length Shabbos coat, with his *tallis* (prayer shawl) draped over his shoulders. With his black fedora, he made quite the different sight, along with the rest of us in our Shabbos attire. By then my Shabbos getup was some kind of Indian cotton dress thing —my army pants and hiking boots relegated to weekdays.

I glanced at the café and saw my old Tamarack friend Eileen nursing a cup of tea. We'd lost touch for many months. She'd been off on a sojourn in India, at the main ashram of her group. *Guess she's back,* I realized. We were a bit far, but I called out, "Hey, Eileen!" to try to catch her attention. Eileen looked up from her book. I waved. She started to smile. Then her eyes widened in shock as she saw the old-world rabbi. She pushed back her chair and jumped up.

"No, no, no!" She mouthed the words and shook her head emphatically. She pointed to the rabbi and mouthed it again. "No, no, no!"

I froze.

Looked at Eileen. Looked at Levi, Brocha, and the others. Reassured myself: I know they're okay. She doesn't.

"It's okay," I mouthed back, with a big smile that looked surer than I felt.

I waved and kept going, to the North Campus valley and the Goldsteins' apartment.

She shook me up. I mulled it over as I walked. Did Eileen know something I was trying not to see? Maybe I was walking down the hill to a place leading nowhere, getting pulled into a myopic and chauvinistic world. Was I fooling myself? Was there real spirituality here—one with grit, one you could lean on in hard times? Or was I lulled by sweet sound bites that these smiling, maybe too-content and heavenly people sprinkled with sugar?

I used to see Levi and Aharon the same way Eileen seemed to. Old- world, naive, rigid, backwards. And I had valued her opinion and guidance. She helped jump- start my spiritual search; back at camp, as we talked and dreamed, perched up on the top bunk of my cabin, and in my first year in Ann Arbor when she introduced me to many soulful searchers.

I had popped into her ashram now and then for evening meditation. I walked in tentatively; see a picture of the guru on a table in the front of the meditation room. There were flowers on a little altar table, and incense gently burning. I went back and got comfortable on a large mat on the floor, closed my eyes, and joined in. I heard quiet sighs as people settled into their practice. It was peaceful, slowing my breathing, slowing my mind. But somewhere deep inside, I was on edge.

Detachment into an empty space, even emptying the ego into

a deep down connected space of oneness, didn't seem like enough, didn't satisfy—though I figured I was lacking and must be a failure. I knew in the back recesses of my mind that the same India with the gurus with sparkling, serene eyes had millions of starving people and a caste system.

It bugged me. I cared. I wanted to roll up my sleeves and do. I couldn't sit impassively back and watch the wheel of karma turn. What I used to think of as my weakness, I was starting to see might be a healthy Jewish perspective. I loved the phrase *Tikkun Olam*—we were all needed to repair and shine up our little ol' world.

Bob the Builder, yes we can! Maybe my worn army pants with all the pockets and places to hang tools were a precursor of who I was really supposed to be: a fixin' lady, extracting and lifting up those sparks of holiness. "Hmm, this one's wedged a bit tightly, bring over the thinner drill bit."

These Jews seemed to have a different goal than peaceful serenity, a novel slant on spirituality. They didn't teach detachment. They tried to use food, intimacy, the whole freakin' material word in a carefully guided way that they claimed would raise it up, and bring the heavens down to shine into it more.

Maybe it was easy for a suburban girl to say. I'd had a pretty gilded life; I loved this world and never wanted to see it as an illusion or distraction. If I'd grown up in a starving slum in Calcutta, or in violent anarchy in Sudan, I might think differently. But engaging, sifting, and working the world just spoke to me. And here was a tempered way, which seemed to guide one through the maze and multiplicity: being physical without getting lost or buried in material pleasures, in desires, in the very denseness of Stuff.

16

≈≈≈≈

THE HOME BASE: 770

Mid-summer, the Goldsteins started talking up a trip to their home base: Crown Heights, Brooklyn. They wanted us to experience their spawning ground, commonly known as "seven-seventy," because of its address, 770 Eastern Parkway. This sprawling group of Tudor buildings was the headquarters of their Chabad Chassidic group. They must have spoken about seeing their *Rebbe,* their leader, but it washed over my head. I basically trusted them enough to go along on a long weekend trip that they were excited about. Why not?

We got the travel details together and headed off, a small group of us students, squashed into the older sedan together with our tour guide, Levi. Cruising down the Pennsylvania Turnpike, we read, dozed, and passed the time. A few grumbled since stopping for Big Macs wasn't on the itinerary. I was used to bringing food on travels, since organic vegetarians didn't frequent Burger King. Esther and Bella's thorough, motherly planning assuaged the grumbling, and our hunger pains. They made sure we were well-stocked with kosher delicacies to nosh on.

All of a sudden, trouble struck. The red engine light went on. *Oy vey.* We pulled over and started freaking out.

"Oh, man, what are we going to do?"

"I knew we should have rented a newer car instead of taking this clunker."

"Levi, do you have road service?"

"Yeah, we'd better call them. How are we gonna find a phone out here?"

We freaked out, but Levi seemed only a little ruffled. "It's okay. We're all safe, and it's all meant to be."

"Meant to be—yeah, right! This is a royal pain in the rear," someone *kvetched.*

We sat on the hill by the shoulder of the road, while Levi and Sam trekked over to the nearest home, a farmhouse perched up on a far-off ridge. They called a road service, and came back to wait with us.

Once the logistic details were dealt with, Levi realized he had a golden opportunity to teach some practical Jewish philosophy. He tried to use this teaching moment to talk about divine providence, as we sat on the roadside, absently plucking wild daisies and clover.

"You know, guys, there are no accidents. It was meant for us to be at this very place," he declared. "There are sparks of holiness buried here, hidden, waiting for us to elevate them."

"Whaddya mean, Levi? Sparks? Like sparks from the engine?" Josh asked.

"Well, if we learn Torah here, or give *tzedaka*—if we do a *mitzvah* here—we're actually purifying and elevating the potential, the holiness in this place. This exact spot must need it, or the car wouldn't have broken down here. This little patch of highway might have been waiting, all the way since the beginning of creation, for someone to come here. We can't let this opportunity go by," Levi insisted, smiling, hoping we'd catch a bit of his inspiration.

We sat there mutely, on that grassy bank, looking at him, not quite sure what to think. It was just a broken down car... didn't seem to be any great cosmic happening. Was this really part of some grand divine orchestration? I looked up and down the road, and, honestly, didn't see any sparks implanted in that patch of highway— somewhere in the middle of Pennsylvania, as we sat there waiting for the tow truck—not even a flash or glimmer. Except for sunlight reflecting off shards of broken beer bottles.

Levi's earnest conviction was charming. We chuckled, a bit indulgingly, thinking, "Isn't he sweet?" Maybe a bit nervously, wondering, "Is every little thing that happens really such big stuff?" Um, yeah... maybe. These sparks have been waiting for us all the way since the six days of creation? My, my... *maybe* a bit presumptuous?

But echoes of my travels with Starburst were resonating. Traveling in harmony with the One. Wasn't that what our pendulum-inspired rights and lefts were all about? Listen, rabbi, you don't have a monopoly on seeing your travels as divine guidance unfolding. Yeah, we *are* guided by the great force. Of course, we are exactly where we are supposed to be. Been there, learned that, back on the road in Arizona: Cosmic Living 101.

Levi's kabbalistic cosmology added a new imperative—a morality, an urgency—to the mix. Receiving the vibes and being open to the flow, like Starburst and I did, was the first step. He tried to get us to see that we had an active role to play. We had these *mitzvos,* these sockets of connection. It was up to us to grab them and act, seize the moment, and lift up all that was lying dormant, in potential. We little people, our choices and actions did matter, said the good rabbi. Lots. Cosmically. Infinitely.

Egotistical? Exhilarating? Overwhelming? It was hard to imagine living with such a focused awareness and sense of mission. We could see it was a different way of trodding on the earth, for sure.

Once we finally made it to New York and got pizza'd and rested, we sat in on some classes in the *yeshivas* (Torah schools). We women headed over to Beth Rivka, the post–high school women's seminary, entering through the fenced concrete yard into a large, utilitarian building. Climbed up the old, sturdy staircase. The youthful singing and shouting of the elementary kids wafted up from the first floor. We passed the giggling and shrieking high school girls on the second floor. The seminary young women, poised and settled, were way up on the third floor. We were ushered into a classroom with about twenty students, where we sat at small desks and waited for the lecture to begin. Somehow, hearing Torah taught way up there—beat-up lots and garbage-strewn Brooklyn streets below—I had an uncanny feeling that I was perched on top of the world.

The first teacher walked in, an intelligent and articulate young woman. She started to outline one of the Rebbe's discourses. She explained the apparent contradictions in the Torah portion, then offered deeper insights into the text. I sat back, listening and trying to figure this bird out. She seemed strange. Immaculately and fashionably groomed. In my dictionary, that meant shallow JAP: superficial, overly concerned with outer appearances.

But she wasn't a fluff-head; she seemed both knowledgeable and deeply passionate in her faith, with intense eyes and bearing. Cognitive dissonance—this didn't compute. I equated spirituality with rising above the material, not caring about empty veneers. Growing up in an image-frenzied society of paparazzi and beauty queens, my mantra was, don't look at my image; look at my inner essence.

I raised my hand. She looked my way and nodded. I sat up straight and started spouting New Age interpretations and spin-offs to her ideas.

"You said when the Torah was given the people were united like one body with one heart? That means they were in their astral bodies, on the astral plane, where all souls are connected in the oneness... the radiant light...."

The teacher patiently let me ramble. After a few minutes I ended my extrapolation and sat back to listen and watch.

But then something she said triggered another amazing insight that I just had to explain. Of course the girls needed to hear my unique, cosmic inspiration. She really didn't want these young women listening to my traipse through the New Age pantheon, so she politely but firmly steered the class back on track. "Thanks for sharing, ah, what was your name? Oh, Miriam. Um, I have a few more points I need to get through. Maybe you could save the rest of your comments for after class."

Not to worry, the class didn't seem to want to wander into my world. My thoughts were politely tolerated by the young women, along with muted chuckling and eye-rolling. Okay, another wacko, their amused glances seemed to say as I earnestly pontificated. They were used to hungry, wandering souls floating through, some eventually slowing their spinning to settle and get some anchoring.

We were brought to 770, a cavernous warehouse of a synagogue. With its worn-down wooden bleachers, zero frills, it was dramatically different from the elaborate temples of my youth, where style outshone function. Judaism was serious here, a participant rather than spectator sport. 770 was nothing more than a big place where people could get on with the business of learning and praying. There was a certain unique smell and the drone of constant praying, learning, talking.

We girls were directed upstairs to the women's part of the synagogue. Since we were clearly newbie visitors, people made room for us and pushed us to the front where we could see through large, tinted windows. The women and girls crowded into the small place where they prayed and learned with seriousness and strength.

I gazed over the multicolored, taped-up flyers that filled the walls of the narrow passageway. Some were carefully typed and illustrated, others scrawled with a foreign hand and spelling. They silently told the tale of this community's concerns. Apartments for rent, close to 770; babysitter needed; warm, loving playgroup forming; discount tickets to Israel; furniture for quick sale; couple leaving for post in Asia; study and prayer groups meeting; classes and lectures.

Prayer books filled the bookshelves and were piled up on the bleachers. Tomes of Torah were taken in and out of the shelves, learned singly, by pairs huddled together on the wooden benches, and in occasional lectures that seemed to spontaneously take place in one of the three sections of bleachers. Someone stood to teach and a crowd would gather around. A medley of languages could be heard. Hebrew, English, French, Russian, and Yiddish were the primary tongues, but a smattering of others could be heard in this mini-ingathering of Jews from around the globe.

A few young women glared at us newcomers with penetrating stares, looking us up and down. I unconsciously smoothed my clothes and hair. Some gossiped and laughed loudly; many murmured prayers with force and vigor. Not too many wilting wallflowers up here. There was an air of intent and purpose.

These Chassidic women and girls were fascinating, paradoxical. I stared, trying to figure it out. What was the deal with them? Most were quite feminine: made-up, bedecked with jewelry, and looking good. But at the same time, they were strong and confident. I had come to equate femininity with being weak and passive, so I eschewed pink and lace in favor of army pants and hiking boots.

The sex-object thing wasn't the reason for their preening. I had ambled down 11 Mile Road as a young teen, dressed to mirror *Seventeen's* latest dictates. A truck zoomed by and the driver leaned out the window, whistled, and called, "Hey, babe!"

I smiled nervously, feeling flattered, flustered, defensive—feeling like an object, a piece of meat.

Putting it all out there "to catch a foxy guy" wasn't part of this universe. With the schools, camps, and places for praying and celebrating well-separated by gender, these young women were spared so much of that playing-up-to-the-boys tension.

I had tried to play the game, with limited results. Seventh grade, Human Relations class. We were assigned seats alphabetically. That meant I was behind Bob Douglas, the cutest guy in the school. I'd never been within twenty feet of him, but I had admired him from afar. Gawky me knew my chances of getting his attention were slim, but like most of the girls in the school, I was all but helpless, compelled to try.

I figured out a plan. If I raised my hand and answered too often, he'd think I was a teacher's-pet goodie-goodie. So when Mr. Jones asked a question and scanned the class, up and down the rows, I tried my new tactic. Some kids shrugged. Others busied themselves in the book. I dumbed down, and looked away, sitting silent. Then Mr. Jones called on me, so I quickly came up with the wrong answer and giggled, furtively glancing at Bob—but he wasn't impressed by my fluttering-eyelashes ditz act.

However, being a pragmatic guy, he did take action once he realized I was another adoring member of his fan club. He glanced at my paper meaningfully during the next quiz. Of course I moved it to the corner of my desk so he could see my answers. Maybe he'd feel indebted to me and be wowed by my kindness and generosity—just maybe?

But these girls were spared all that. The separation seemed to let them develop more unfettered, straight, and tall in their own women's world. Some were fierce like a lioness. If you did something wrong—said the wrong blessing or stood up or bowed in the wrong part of the prayers—man, they let you know. Even the softer ones who might smile sweetly and show you the page had an underlying determination and clarity. And that aura of mystery, majesty—of something else. A perceptive friend, who knew a little bit about this world, startled me one day with his sensitive observation: "What's with those women that go to the *mikvah* (ritual bath)? They have this special glow."

A unique panorama unfolded in the men's section. We peered through a large plate-glass that looked out over the sea of men and boys one floor below us. They ranged from dewy-eyed toddlers to dignified elders whose intense character could be seen in every gesture. One gentleman caught my eye; he had a peasant's cap and an intense expression, spiritual yet earthy, earnest. I found out that this man, Mendel Futerfas, had been imprisoned in the Soviet Gulag for some twenty years for the crime of spreading Judaism. His lively spark shone, not snuffed out or dimmed by his suffering.

The bulk of the crowd was young men and middle-aged working family men. A sea of black hats, beards, glasses. A hum of laughter and conversation filled the chamber. Waves of song would wash across the room.

The men, left to their own devices without women and girls to impress and one- up for, seemed softer, more affectionate and receptive than the average "guy."

I was amazed to see hugs, affection, kisses even, as friends greeted each other—close body contact without so much male armor. These gentlemen were dedicated husbands, fathers, and grandfathers, responsible for growing tribes. They let themselves be corralled, roped, and committed to their wives and families, with a beautiful soft manliness—a beautiful manly softness.

Suddenly, the enormous room, the thousands of people, became silent. A singular focus and intense anticipation filled the space.

The mob parted, a path opened, and a white-bearded man walked briskly to the front. He wasn't showy or ostentatious; he radiated intensity and focused strength.

I was fascinated and transfixed, peering through the smoked glass. Just like in my Zaidy dream, something like "Jewish collective unconscious", or *neshama* (soul) knowing, rose up and tugged at me. I'd never heard about Moses in any meaningful context, until browsing the prayer book on a few recent Shabbos mornings. I was only minimally aware of this concept of the Jewish people having a leader, following him in the desert, or any of that. Yet, my clear thought was, "This is like Moses."

And not just because of the dedicated throng. I could have rattled off a whole pantheon of assorted spiritual teachers who had followers. Somehow, in those few seconds, from my distance up in the women's section, I could sense a deep and unshakable authenticity, the lack of that blasted ego the others professed to have attained, along with dynamic perceptive intelligence, something rock solid and profound.

The Rebbe sat in front of the crowd, in the middle of a long table covered with a white tablecloth. He spoke in Yiddish, in a sing-song cadence, in a strong and earnest voice that hit me in my heart. Silence reigned in the enormous crowd. Most stood still, some cocked their heads, while others swayed in concentration.

The talks, each segment lasting a half-hour or so, were punctuated by rousing song. Thousands sang together, heartfelt *nigunim* (Chassidic melodies)—some with words, some pure yearning and wordless. Like the Pacific Ocean, waves washed in tireless rhythm. They were waves of intense melody, washing across the room, transporting us from a warehouse filled too-tight with people under glaring florescent lights, transporting us to a timeless soul-place.

We took it all in as best we could for a while; an hour or two sped by in the suspended, primordial time. Afterwards, our group wandered out to meet by a street corner. We were hit by a barrage of cars honking and speeding, jarring commotion on noisy Eastern Parkway.

"Whad'ya think?" Josh asked me.

"It's hard to put into words," I answered. "Whoa."

"Yeah," Sue piped up. "Different. Intense."

17

───⚜───

POWERFUL LITTLE BUGGERS

Back in Ann Arbor, after that strange and fascinating
venture into mega-Chassidic land, something like Judaism
on speed, things slowed back to a Midwestern pace. I
continued hanging around and slowly inching into the observance
thing. As I spent more time in this new/old land, Esther asked if
I'd like to learn to read Hebrew. Me?

Sounded intimidating. Sounded interesting. Dad had tried to
teach me a few times over the years. He had pulled out a *machbe-
ret*, a special notebook for writing Hebrew characters. We learned
the first two letters, *alef and beis*, and how to write them in script.
But we never got further with those mysterious squiggles.

Here were letters again. But now they were more relevant to
my life. Why not, I figured, might as well try. It seemed to be one
of those things people did when they were seriously thinking of
getting serious about their Judaism.

So Esther gathered a group around her table one Tuesday afternoon. Avraham Leaf, Esther's three-year-old son Alter, and I
started learning those mysterious letters. We worked haltingly,
embarrassed in our fumbling efforts, but she encouraged and we
persisted. A new world slowly began to open up, of sounds,

images, and nuanced rich meaning that I never would have experienced the same way in English.

Those letters, those letters...
Powerful little buggers...
Little squiggles, swirls and crowns, ascending up, dipping below.

What about them was so powerful, so evocative; that grabbed hold of me and wouldn't let go? Those letters, dots, and dashes seemed almost atomic, packed full of compressed and unleashed power.

Neshama letters, soul letters, souls in forms, souls on paper or parchment.

Marveling as its treasures shyly revealed themselves, like a sweet young bride would to her beloved, I struggled to court those letters, learn their shapes. At Esther's table, her young son whipped through the letters and vowels, then zoomed off reading with an easy laugh as I sat in the dust trying to put a sound together. That's humbling, university genius. How's your high SAT score gonna help you now?

I struggled through reading *Tehillim* (Psalms), verse after verse. Some days my eyes and lips skipped smoothly through the verses, while on others, they were like lead. I felt learning disabled, disjointed, my parts askew, my tongue and mouth not quite making the right shape, my eyes seeing those jumping dots not quite right.

But I pushed and dragged through, sound by sound. Something compelling and magnetic beckoned that seemed faded and distant when I gave up and went back to English, although I could read and comprehend with agile ease over there, in my *momma loshen*, my native language of *golus* (exile)—wandering American child of plenty and emptiness that I am.

Loshon ha kodesh... the holy tongue.
Those letters... those sounds.

You kind of know what they mean, way before you can explicitly translate them. The black shapes whisper to your eyes, the sounds whisper to your ears; they tickle your soul. There's a gleaning and absorbing, even if you don't know what many of the words mean, and are slowly sounding out gobble-di-gook.

Remember that heron we saw at the lake, standing quietly, then suddenly shooting down into the water and coming up with a fish in its mouth? That deeper realm of meaning and holiness and connection was there, under the water. Nothing seemed to be happening, no understanding. Flash—all of a sudden I got a ping of revelation. Aha! I had a fish, a jewel in my mouth.

These Hebrew jewels slowly became part of my vocabulary. How, when did I absorb them? How did I start spouting these terms? When I had to go back to English—just fell flat. I heard the emptiness, the hard edge and sterility of the English word that came the closest but was still so off the mark.

Brocha... blessing.

Chessed...kindness.

Rachmonus...pity.

The English was a sad approximation. I was hungry to uncover and work into my realm of understanding more and more of these jewels.

What must it be like to pick up a *siddur,* a *Tehillim,* a *sefer* (prayer book, Psalms, holy book), and read them with fluency and ease? I am jealous of my children, natives reading Torah texts at the age when I was reading *Dick and Jane* and *The Bobsey Twins.* I am jealous of Israelis, for whom King David's entreaties read naturally, like a story. Sometimes in our class we ask one of the Israelis to read aloud, just to enjoy the melody of the text read with such intimate familiarity before we jump in to start pulling apart, analyzing, and expounding.

As I sat at Esther's table slowly spitting out vowel-and-letter syllables, going over and over to commit those little shapes to memory, time slowed.

I built up, one halting sentence after another. Read one blessing. Then one fine day, I got to the point where I could try reading the whole first paragraph of *bentching,* the lengthy blessing after eating bread.

Bentching (Yiddish for *blessing*) was one of those beautiful opportunities/burdens, depending on how one looked at it. After most foods I had learned to say a short after-blessing thanking God for the sustenance. But bread was a special food, the staff of life. It required more. A lot more. There was a multi-paged liturgy, full of meaning, but since it was said so frequently it often became a routine mumbled without the thought it deserved.

After a few weeks I'd learned *aleph, beis, gimmel, daled*—all twenty-six letters—the twelve vowels, and then finally worked up to stringing together one, two, even three syllable words. I decided to be bold, and to plow through reading the whole first paragraph of the *bentching.*

I was alone at the Arboretum on a balmy summer day, sitting by a stream, my bike resting on a rock. I took my brand-new prayer book out of my backpack, opened it to page 88, and carefully pronounced (and tried not to butcher) one precious sound, one word, after another. Some ten or fifteen minutes or so later, I finished, savoring the feeling of accomplishment and connection.

Several weeks later I decided to attempt the whole prayer in Hebrew. I was sitting at the Shabbos table after lunch. The Goldstein children had flown through the *bentching,* and ran off to play. The table had been cleared.

Shabbos afternoon after the meal was a golden, relaxed time; sweetness redolent in the air. Folks pushed back from the abundant food and conversation and wandered off for a chat or nap. Some curled up in a comfortable armchair or corner of the couch for casual study with a cup of tea and a favored text or story.

For what felt like an interminable time I sat alone at that table. I stumbled and mumbled and finally finished some thirty minutes later. Bella smiled and commented, "Before you know it, you'll be whizzing through it and be like us, so habituated you'll sometimes have to ask yourself, 'Did I *bentch*? I don't remember.'"

That day came to pass soon enough, when I could casually whip off the words with the best of them.

But that struggle wasn't all pain. The hidden depth of those letters was whispering to me the whole time, singing and encouraging. Like practicing piano, sitting there was a labor, yet the joy of the sounds good company and pleasure along the way. And these sounds were building a path into that hidden world, one letter, one syllable, one word at a time.

18

DANCING ON THE LAWN

The summer rolled on. I was teaching at a day care center, spending many balmy evenings with the Goldsteins. Nacha and Brocha went off to some school in Minnesota for a few weeks. They came back brimming with excitement.

"Miriam, ya gotta go. Minnesota is awesome. There's this teacher, Rabbi Friedman. He's amazing. Come on over, do ya wanna hear one of his tapes?" Nacha urged.

"Can't you take a few weeks off of work, I'm telling you, you gotta go." Brocha implored. And Nacha kept quoting, "Well, you know, Rabbi Friedman says *this*," and "Rabbi Friedman said *that*," with annoying surety.

A women's seminary in Minnesota. Hmm, sounds great.

Not.

When Esther had first mentioned it, I thought: *Well, gee. Sounds as happening as a convent in Iowa City.*

Whoopee.

But Nacha's excitement was pretty intense, and she wasn't a pushover. She wasn't looking to get hoodwinked into something that wasn't for real. She and Brocha kept nudging and insisting it was an experience not to be missed.

I listened to a tape or two and was impressed with Rabbi Friedman's familiarity with current trends and his ability to discuss them from a Torah perspective. He was provocative; he had a unique way of tying disparate ideas together. This guy didn't seem to be in a protected bubble. It might be worthwhile to go there and hear more.

I asked my boss, and yeah, I could take some time off. Packed up my trusty backpack once again, this time with skirts, scrounging to put together enough for a few days.

A few other women and I got picked up at the Minneapolis airport by Rabbi Moshe Feller, the director of the school. A short, middle-aged man, he held one of those cardboard signs with *Bais Chana* scrawled on it, making us feel like VIPs.

I was getting somewhat used to inhabiting a universe of bearded men in dark suits and hats, though I inwardly pulled back and had a heebie-jeebie attack each time I met a new one. Rabbi Feller had a cute, squeaky voice and exuded enthusiasm and energy. He chatted with us on the drive to St. Paul. I alternated between mild excitement and wondering what on earth I had gotten myself into.

We drove to the residential neighborhood of pleasant, older mansion-like homes, and pulled up.

"Go ahead in," Rabbi Feller said and guided us in. I hesitantly followed the other girls in, like a shy kindergartener on the first day of a new school.

We entered a large foyer, framed by a winding staircase on either side. Singing and laughing was heard, a reassuring sound. A young woman greeted us.

"Welcome, how was your trip? Here, let me show you to your room," she said.

We took our bags and went up to the second floor. There were several large bedrooms, each with a number taped to the door. "Here, Miriam, you're in room two," she said.

I slowly walked in. It was a casual dorm room, with several bunk beds and dressers. Someone was sprawled on her bed reading. She looked up with a smile and greeted me. "Hey, I'm Shoshana. How ya doing? These two beds are empty. Take whichever you like." I chose one, put down my bag and got ready for whatever was coming next.

Shoshana sized up my hesitation and said, "Let me take you down and show you around." I gratefully followed her. I knew I was at what had been billed an "awesome place" but what is it actually gonna be like, where do you go, what do you say, and what do you do in a women's seminary in Minnesota?

We went down to the main dining room. The large room, which appeared to have been elegant once, was simply appointed, with large folding tables and chairs filling the room. I looked around. There was a variety of women, mostly about my age; some sporting the hippie look, others more groomed and put-together. In one corner, pairs or threesomes were clustered, huddled over a book, discussing. One woman sat in the back, writing with great concentration. A few scattered groups were sipping tea, laughing, and chatting. The atmosphere was warm and relaxed.

Shoshana gently pushed me into the room and said, "Make yourself at home. It's just about lunch time, and at one o'clock Rabbi Friedman's afternoon class will start."

I rambled over to a table, where the women warmly greeted me, asked my name and where I was from. They proceeded to tell their stories and ask about mine.

Most of the women had a Story—a quest, a journey, a fortuitous meeting or turn of events—that led them to this worn-down mansion, Bais Chana. It wasn't the kind of place you read about in the *Traveler's Guide to St. Paul*. You didn't just causally wander into a Chassidic women's seminary—you had a Story. The women delighted in sharing and comparing theirs.

It was exhilarating to meet kindred spirits—dynamic and diverse women who, like me, sought more and felt the compelling pull of this stuff. Tova had long dark hair and big, doe-like, intense, brown eyes. She sat drawing, radiating a quiet depth. Wow. Her quick sketches put me to shame with their power.

Malka was a medical student, with wild, frizzy hair and over-sized tortoise-shell glasses. She was taking time off of her studies to fill in missing pieces of her identity. She joked around, but had an intelligent and driven look.

Chaya floated around in crinkly Indian skirts, laughing and smiling. She came to Bais Chana from a raw-foods commune in Hawaii, where she'd spent six months communing with nature and spirit. She'd left her oasis briefly to come mainland, gather up a few things, and visit her parents in Pittsburgh. She was planning to settle in her paradise for a long, maybe permanent, stay. Well, as permanent as one gets when she's floating on the breeze.

The way Chaya told it, her mom and dad weren't too thrilled with their daughter's meanderings and her living on carrot juice mixed with bee pollen and every kind of sprout you ever, never imagined. The drone of the juicer and the stars in Chaya's dreamy eyes grated on their nerves. What happened to their sweet girl's ambition and focus? What about her minimum daily requirement of protein and calories? Someone told them about this happening rabbi, who happened to be speaking in Pittsburgh. They shlepped their resistant daughter to hear Rabbi Friedman. She went along just to get them off her back, but was surprised and intrigued at what she heard that evening—enough to postpone her return to Hawaii and come to Minnesota to hear a little more.

But she was worried. The folks in Hawaii had warned her, right before she left, "Watch out for men in black, they are out to get you and derail you." Lo and behold, here they were: black coats, black hats and all. These bearded rabbis seemed a lot sweeter than the lurking evil forces that she had imagined.

"I can't believe it," Chaya said. "It's so weird. I mean, when they told me about the black forces it sounded dangerous. But, it's really bizarre. They're really men in black. And they just popped into my life out of nowhere. I never heard of them before, and now I'm in this school with a bunch of them. How did my guides in Hawaii know about this? And who is right—is this light? It seems beautiful and positive. I'm enjoying what I'm learning. But my friends in Hawaii described something ominous and negative."

Chaya laughed, hesitantly.

She was worried, trying to sort through what Bais Chana was all about. Was she on a path to deep understanding, or being thrown down a dark and menacing hole?

The main event of the school happened twice a day, up in the comfortable library, where afternoon and evening lectures were given by the famous Rabbi Friedman. I followed the crowd of thirty or forty women and trudged up the circular stairway to the second floor. I sat in the middle, far enough back to take it all in from a bit of a distance.

A slim, middle-aged man sat facing us. He had a very long, brown beard, wire glasses, sparkling, intelligent eyes and a slight smile. The *Tanya* sat open on a table in front of him. Rabbi Friedman had a disarmingly simple lecture style. He first read a verse or two from the text, in an ancient sing-song chant. The minor-toned melodic sound was already enchanting, even before any explaining started.

It had the kind of authentic and strangely compelling power I sensed at the similar-sounding Torah reading on Shabbos morning.

"What is this?" I would ask myself, over and over, as they started reading the Torah about midway through the Shabbos morning service. "What is going on here?"

Sometimes I'd try to follow the text by reading the Hebrew, following phonetically, catching a familiar word here or a phrase there. Other weeks I'd try to follow in the English, gathering the gist of the meaning. That meaning sometimes seemed arcane or irrelevant. Or I'd close the bilingual *Chumash* (Five Books of Moses) and just listen. Understanding was good, but even when I couldn't readily relate to the text, more was happening.

Something reached out from that *bima* (lectern), where a handful of men huddled around with their prayer shawls draped over their shoulders or heads. They looked like hovering angels or gulls, poised for flight; with some deep thing happening in those quiet folds. While one man read, others followed and moved into their places in choreographed gracefulness, both protecting and drawing something from the scroll. Something reached over the *mechitza* (divider) and into my heart, making it stand a little straighter, a little cleaner, more connected.

Then came the *Haftorah*, readings from the Prophets. They had this distinctive quality. I'd been wined, and dined on twentieth-century literature and thought, which looked upon the Bible as an outdated country bumpkin. But those prophets—what was it? There was something old, powerful, and, for lack of a better word, Biblical in there.

Years later, as I stood on a rocky hill in Israel watching the goats graze on the stubble under the tenacious olive trees, the word *Biblical* kept floating through my mind. My brother-in- law Marvin stood next to me, taking in the scene. A world traveler, he'd seen many more visually magnificent vistas. But he felt the same pull. "It's something else, isn't it?" he murmured. "It's so Biblical."

Now, as Rabbi Friedman chanted the *Tanya* slowly and methodically, the lines took on that evocative quality. Then he translated, in the same sing-song tune. And explain—with understated dry wit, sometimes almost a monotone, that would slowly work up to selective emphasis. With brilliance. With cutting insight. He took those words from that several-hundred-year- old text written in Lithuania, and showed how they related to the deepest questions and struggles of our own lives, and shone a high-intensity beam of light into our murky beings.

If only I'd been more disciplined in dipping into this unique work in the ensuing thirty years. The landfills would have fewer boxes of wadded tissues. Less tears, more happy mommy days. A better time might have been had by all in my proximity; I probably would have dragged my dear family through fewer meltdowns, stalls, and temper tantrums.

Over the years I've dipped into bouts of depression, of feeling overwhelmed and under-inspired, of feeling like I'm going through the motions in a grinding routine but disconnected inside. Especially around holiday times, when the shopping (nice clothes for all those little people), cooking (trying to live up to the ideal of hosting guests for the two- or occasionally three-days- in-a-row feasts), and planning and organizing demands get pretty intense. My engagement with the *Tanya* has been sporadic, sustained discipline not my strong suit. But when I do get back on the horse and open those pages of Godliness, or nowadays, go to a website, I am once again amazed at the rejuvenating powerhouse that is *Tanya*.

Souls. Worlds. Angels. Missions. Struggles. Light. This book was centered on exploring the very point of oneness I had felt back in that Michigan pine forest. That vision had blown me away on that shimmery August day. But I had struggled to figure out how to integrate it, how to build a life centered around it. These folks had a working game plan, road tested and ready to handle all contingencies. (And I mean all. The Talmudic arguments and debates covered every permutation of possibility, and then some.) They dished up a way to jive mystical reality with a complex world.

Trucking down the road with Starburst, we lived with the premise that all is one—just smile, shine, and groove. "Hi, how are you? I see the divine essence in you. Let's hang out and share the light."

Sounded great, but how long could we have really skimmed and shimmered through the planet like that? In this world, bad stuff goes down too. And there were people and situations aplenty to be wary of. Scammers, rapists, crooks, and shnooks. Platitudes wouldn't always work. There was a need for boundaries, structure, and roots, I was starting to mature enough to realize—as much as boundaries and structure were anathema to my modus operandi of going with the flow.

These weren't the arbitrary human conventions my soul raged against—"We eat at 6:00 P.M., meat and potatoes, place the juice cup on the left and the water glass on the right, then fold your napkin and blot your mouth three times..."—conventions that seem to deaden the creative light. These rules weren't born of fear of the raging river of pulsing life, like Victorian or Puritan artifices. These structures felt like the walls and membranes of a living cell, full of light and integral to making life possible, just as veins and arteries are needed to contain and direct the blood.

This fellow, Rabbi Friedman, had a special knack for taking the issues *du jour*, especially sexuality, relationships, and feminism, and illuminating them with insights from this ancient wisdom. It was liberating. It was a little scary. I sat there smiling, laughing, but scowling too— scratching my head and thinking, "This guy makes it all sound so clear. How can he really be so sure?" He was so darned confident, even when offering provocative answers to some of the women's complex questions and life situations.

His curly-haired toddler would occasionally pop in to school, stroll into the library, and climb into his father's lap for a while, then wander out. Even the hardened cynics among the students would turn into cooing baby-lovers as they called, "Oh, come here, cutie. He's so sweet!"

Rabbi Friedman seemed to relish those moments. He'd use them to poke at our typical notions about how many kids was normal and responsible to have, and how women's work was usually valued outside the home—but not inside it.

He let us know repeatedly that he was the father of fourteen and that his wife was amazing, sharing a favorite tale:

"A group of women came to our house. They wanted to meet my wife and see if she was as oppressed as was commonly believed. They asked what kind of work she does. She told them she ran a home for fourteen unwanted children. These guests were highly impressed at her managerial status and skills. They sat lauding her. Then she interrupted and confessed that the kids were actually her own. They instantly changed their song and considered her a backwater primitive."

At that point, he would tilt his black hat back and wear an expression of mock confusion. "The kids really are unwanted. We put them out on the street, but no one wanted them, so we took them back."

He delivered the punch line with a smile.

"How come raising someone else's kids is impressive, but raising your own makes you a persona non grata?"

Was it brainwashing? Rabbi Friedman was skilled at pointedly exposing us to a definite and different set of ideas than most of us had ever encountered. But we were free to argue, leave, or prove anything wrong. I wouldn't call it coercive, but explicitly influencing. Many of us were perfectly ready and willing to be charmed and convinced, at least to stay a bit longer and dig further.

The classes stretched on for hours, as the women would ask every imaginable question, vehemently arguing, sharing deep struggles, and listening to the rabbi unfold this special wisdom from his pocket and draw us into it. There were other teachers at Bais Chana too, young women teaching Hebrew, Jewish law, and discourses of the Rebbe. They were a relatively minor part of the program compared to the main show—Rabbi Friedman—like a warm-up band.

During the down time between classes, we swam, shopped, hung out... and cooked. The Bais Chana kitchen aptly reflected the many paths trod by this ingathering of searching women. On one counter, Chana was cooking up brown rice and aduki beans in a pressure cooker for her yang macrobiotic repast, talking about the diet's benefits to anyone who'd listen.

Across the kitchen, Chaya was washing and chopping a raw-food mess of sprouts, carrots, beets, and greens, to juice a nutrition-packed, thick, sludge-colored drink.

And, hiding in the corner from the health freaks, Leah was surreptitiously enjoying her chocolate cake and coffee, quickly, before she might be subjected to a sugar-equals-death lecture.

These competing food philosophies shared an overarching commonality. Yin or yang, sprouted or heavily sprinkled with confectioner's sugar, if it was cooked in the Bais Chana kitchen, the cooks learned how to do it kosher.

Like most of the women, I ate whatever the cook set out, general health-oriented fare. I spent many of my spare hours playing the recorder and dancing on the spacious lawn with my new friends, expressing some of the exuberance I was feeling.

Rabbi Friedman held office hours outside, under a tree. He sat on a folding chair, and women would engage him in private consultations. One balmy afternoon, towards the end of my two-week sojourn, I had finished prancing, twirling, and playing my free-spun melodies, and I sauntered up to the shady spot. I asked lots of questions in class, nodding in excitement, smiling, and arguing, but I hadn't spoken much with Rabbi Friedman besides that.

I was trying to decide whether and where to keep learning. Should I head to a *Baal Teshuvah* (special-for-newbies) school and keep up the momentum that Bais Chana had generated? Or should I go back to Ann Arbor and continue my slower, quieter growth with the Goldsteins?

I was pretty sure I wanted to dive in and give this Torah business all-out immersion try. I decided to ask the rabbi his opinion.

"So, this all is pretty cool. I've decided I'm on board enough to want to continue learning more intensively and see where it leads me. Do you think I should go to Tzfat or Crown Heights? I gather those are the two places with study centers for women like me with limited backgrounds."

Tzfat, a mystical, mountaintop town in northern Israel, definitely sounded like my cup of (herbal) tea. An artists' haven, where the ancient mystics would go to the edge of town, clad in white, to greet the Shabbos Queen as she gently descended. With its narrow, winding, cobblestone alleyways, ancient secrets fluttering and floating in the breeze, the birthplace of Kabbalah was considered an especially holy place.

In my mind's eye, I was already there, sitting under the gnarled olive tree in the courtyard of Machon Alte, the women's yeshiva. So many people seemed to think I'd been there or was for sure headed there. "Don't I know you from Tzfat?" I was often asked. The sense of connection to this place I'd never been was uncanny. Maybe I'd been there in an earlier life. Clearly, it was high time for me to return.

Rabbi Friedman smiled, stroked his beard, and peered at me. "I think Crown Heights would be a better choice for you."

I couldn't believe my ears. "You really think so? But I'm so not the New York type. Tzfat is just me. I know it."

We discussed it for a while. I don't remember the gist of his reasoning. Maybe the main reason was to be able to spend time at the Rebbe's *farbrengen* gatherings, a unique and irreplaceable experience. Looking back, I can't help but wonder if he was also thinking, *This girl doesn't need much more spiritualizing and floating, as Tzfat would so beautifully lend itself to. She'd float right off into the mist over there.*

He may have surmised that I could use some solid grounding, even if New York would be a harsh wake-up. Being pushed out of my comfort zone in a fast-paced society that expected its participants to look good and acclimate quickly might balance me out more than dancing and singing as purple-golden sunsets settled over the mountains of the Galilee.

It was a shock, but I thought about his suggestion. After more consideration, talking again with the rabbi and others, I let myself be convinced to give New York a reluctant try. I had friends from Bais Chana heading there as well. It was closer to home, not such an abrupt move. After a few months, I figured I could, and likely would, move on to that little dreamy mountaintop town.

19

SHEDDING THE ONION SKIN

After Bais Chana, the women went back to their homes in various corners of the world. Most took a bit of inspiration to weave into the fabric of their lives. Lisa decided to try making a Friday night Shabbos meal for her family, and ran around collecting recipes before she left for the airport. Sue had argued with Rabbi Friedman about all his emphasis on family and children. Her kids were grown; she was divorced, her life was in a different place. But she gravitated to studying *Chassidus,* finding something deeply enriching there, and formed a class with others from her town.

A handful signed on for more intense immersion, moving to Crown Heights to go to the two programs for us *baalei teshuva* (eager newbies), affectionately known as BTs. Beth Rivka Seminary offered classes in the morning geared to our needs and interests. Many of us had jobs in the afternoon and spent the evenings at Machon Chana.

Chaya and I decided we were too road-seasoned to live in the Machon Chana dorm. We needed a little more of our own space, so we found a walk-up apartment. We enjoyed our classes and the community of *baal teshuva* women. We hung out with them and ate dinners at the dorm, but were glad to have our own, less-intense corner to just be ourselves, go crazy, and process all the changes our own way, at our own pace. Together with our other roommate, an archeologist named Sarah, we stayed up late, singing, laughing, and generally carrying on.

The New York thing continued to grate on us. One day Chaya and I overslept and sat around kvetching.

"I can't take it anymore. The concrete, constant sirens, garbage, all the emphasis on clothes and appearances," I moaned, as we sprawled on the love seat in front of the little bay window. The sun shone into the first few feet of our otherwise windowless apartment and we were relishing the beams, positioning ourselves carefully like cats do, to soak up some morning rays.

"Me neither. I love the learning, but this is just not my scene," Chaya agreed.

"What should we do? I can't handle this, it's too, like, yuck." I yawned and sipped some tea.

"Well, maybe we should rethink Tzfat. I mean we tried New York. There are good teachers, but I just can't feel at home here," she said as she got up off the couch and stretched.

"Yeah, you're right. It sounds so much more, like, mellow, you know... us." I sat up and was starting to get energized and excited. "Let's check out the details. How much is it? When could we start?"

"Okay," my practical friend said, glancing at the clock, "but what about today? It's almost eleven. I don't want to miss that really good class on the Torah portion. If we hurry we can still make it."

"Fine," I agreed, and got up to gather my books.

We checked ourselves in the mirror, a newly acquired New York habit. Chaya locked the grating on the doorway. We went up the three steps to street level and ambled down the long blocks to Bais Rivka. President Street was a pleasant tree-lined avenue with stately homes. Back in its heyday, in the forties and fifties, it had been known as Doctors' Row. We enjoyed the arching trees turning fall colors. Most people were already at school or work, and the late-morning street was quiet.

All of a sudden, as we strolled and chatted, we found ourselves across the street from the Rebbe's house. His driver was standing and waiting in front of his house, the car door opened in anticipation. By now, a few months into our landing in Crown Heights, we'd been to many weekly Shabbos afternoon *farbrengen* gatherings, and had seen the Rebbe speaking and praying quite a few times from afar. But never up close, without a crowd around us. We decided to wait and see what would happen.

After a long few minutes, the Rebbe came out, escorted by another secretary. As he entered the car, he glanced at us, standing quietly across the street. It was a piercing, embracing, encompassing look. Making eye contact with the Rebbe was a unique experience. We somehow knew the Rebbe saw right through us, with deep compassion. It was humbling. He saw and catalyzed our potential. We felt our strength, and our emptiness. It was mere seconds, but it seemed that time stood still.

The Rebbe entered his car. It drove away. Chaya and I stood still for a few moments. "Well," she finally said. "I guess that's why we're here in New York. Dirt, noise, and all."

I nodded, then found my voice. "Yeah, I think I'll hang on and stay a bit longer. There are some, ah, treasures here."

We kept walking.

We had missed the first two classes but arrived in time for the Torah portion class. That was followed by one of my favorites, *Halacha* (Jewish law). Back in the beginning of the term, I'd expected the subject to be dry and stiff. A slight man with a graying beard and horn-rimmed glasses came into the room and introduced himself.

Chana whispered, "Rabbi Osdoba is one of the *rabbonim*, one of the top experts on Jewish law in Crown Heights. People call him from all over the world with questions."

I got ready to be intimidated or bored. Surprise. When he started talking, he cut us up with his wry sense of humor.

There was something completely disarming about him. He looked sedate and conservative, in his dark suit and white shirt. But he also had an impish twinkle in his eyes. He would start explaining the basics of a kosher kitchen, with its separate milk and meat areas and kitchenware, in a straightforward manner. But then he would go off into spinning a fantabulous yarn.

"The mother put the chicken soup up to cook and went out to run an errand on Kingston Avenue. She bought her milk and bread, and came back. 'What?!' she screamed. The soup had exploded, the matzah balls were bouncing around the kitchen, the chickens were flying around the kitchen and getting all over the dairy dishes. She called me in a panic, 'What can I do, rabbi?'"

It was incongruous: this studious man, this learned authority, with deep and complex knowledge under his hat—and his seriously delivered, ridiculous tale that grew crazier by the minute.

At first, we weren't sure if he was joking. Then he'd go on in an absurd monologue, illustrating different situations in the most exaggerated of extreme scenarios. This man just tickled my funny bone. Is it okay to laugh at an authoritative rabbi, a *rav*, I wondered? I didn't want to offend anyone or do the wrong thing. Pretty soon it didn't matter what was right. We just had to laugh.

The rabbi kept spinning his tale. His eyes caught mine, and I saw his smile turn up the corner of his mustache. I burst out laughing so hard I just couldn't stop. Soon a few of us were holding our sides, gasping for breath, and almost falling to the floor. I tried to settle down, but then he'd go off on another riff and I'd lose it again. I guess he was happy that his humor was appreciated, and probably hoped his creative absurdity would engrave the concepts in our minds.

The panorama of different teachers was stimulating and thought-provoking. Rabbi Gordon—quiet, refined, and deep— taught the meaning of some of the *Tehillim* (Psalms). He was the message, even more than his words. His intense humility filled the air. You knew something very real and treasured was here, something that came only through a life of working hard on oneself, reaching ever upward.

My friend Goldie expressed it well: "Rabbi Gordon dripped *chein* (grace)."

Mrs. Nemes and Mrs. Kahn were sturdily built, brilliant, fast-talking. Tough, focused ladies, they delivered the characters and lessons from Jonah and Samuel into us like dentists with a drill. No backseat drivers, them. No danger of them being second-class citizens to anyone. These were Jewish women and mothers with a fierce pride and fiery self-assurance in who they were and exactly why they were doing all this.

Then there was Rabbi Mangel, whose quiet, cultured European accent reminded me of Bubby and Zaidy. His weekly class touched on a plethora of topics. One day he announced our next subject: how we could reconcile faith in a loving God with the horrors of the Holocaust. What kind of mental gymnastics was this going to require, I couldn't help but wonder.

As the rabbi finished his introduction, he took off his jacket, unbuttoned his cuff, and started rolling up his sleeve. I wasn't really paying attention. Maybe he had an itch. After rolling up to his elbow, he lifted his arm and displayed the tattoo, the number seared into his forearm.

Silence. We sat forward and listened with a new intensity, a heightened intimacy in the room. Whatever he was going to say, his credibility had instantly soared. He unfolded a harrowing tale of facing down Mengele twice—miracles and tragic suffering, parables and unique insights— which gave us much food for thought.

Nights found us at Machon Chana, where the classes were more intimate and relaxed, with an undertone of spirited hilarity. This was our own space, just us BTs, not part of the larger seminary. Machon Chana was all of a few classrooms on the second floor of a brownstone.

Rabbi Majeski, the dean of Machon Chana, was a sincere, soft-spoken man. We felt his caring as he patiently listened to our complex tangles of issues and carefully tried to guide us. His fire was more understated than Rabbi Friedman's, but his unshakable dedication warmed and inspired us. He unfolded Chassidic thinking for us with carefully chosen, yet passionate, words, as our gang of scrappy, excited souls gathered round to hear.

Being that we all chose freely to be part of this learning experience, usually after one kind of circuitous route or another, the engagement level was pretty high. The unsaid feeling was, "Let's go. Let's do it. We finally found this way of life, now give us the practical tools and spiritual grease to get out there and do it."

One class explored unique facets of Chassidic life and lore, including the inner meaning of various *niggunim* (Chassidic soul melodies). Back in that first summer visit, we were blown away by the deep expression pouring out of the crowd at the *farbrengen,* that large gathering with the Rebbe in 770. Humming and dreaming, watching and listening to the melodies— some bursting with energy, some slow and yearning—I sat up with a jolt when one got going. What was that song? High voltage zinged through me. I intuitively knew this was an intensive soul experience, a laser beam of higher magnitude than the other *niggunim.*

In Rabbi Majeski's class, the mystery was unlocked. He poured out this heartfelt song and took us on a journey into the making and meaning of a holy *niggun.* Those songs were exponential music—music of the soul. Their function wasn't to be pretty, but rather to express concepts that couldn't come down into words, to lift the listeners and bring them to a deeper, truer place.

That one song *was* different, the holiest of all those moving soul songs. Called the Alter Rebbe's *Niggun,* it was carefully created by the Alter Rebbe, the first Chabad Rebbe. The four movements represent four spiritual worlds, and bring the listener, step by step, to the highest level—way up, close to the essence.

And just when that entranced listener is thinking, "Hey, I like it up here. Who needs cars, bills, grocery lists, bodies?"—when he is practically bursting with sweet holiness—right then, with the more earthy and lively song that traditionally follows, he is gently and joyfully brought back into his body—into time, space, and his place in this world.

"I knew that!" I thought, as I heard the teacher explain. I knew that in my gut as soon as I had heard it, that first time in 770.

That was my overall experience with learning Torah and especially *Chassidus*:

I knew that; I remember that.

There were plenty of new details, some special and others annoying, rubbing against modern sensibilities and twenty-one years of habits and post-modern thinking. The overriding sensation, however, was one of going back to a forgotten childhood, not of exploring an exotic land or immersing in a foreign culture. I'd been there, under the onion skin of the persona I had built up. And the layers peeled off as my soul stretched, flexed its muscles, and woke up.

In high school, my Jewish education introduced me to Camus, Sartre, Bertrand Russell, and Marx, but I'd never heard of Israel Baal Shem Tov, Maimonides, or Chana the prophetess. Finally, we got a chance to meet. I would have missed so much left to roam the planet without them as companions. Pithy sayings from *Ethics of the Fathers* nourished me, ideas I'd been craving—like Rabbi Hillel's famous, "If I'm not for myself, who will be? If I'm only for myself, what am I? And if not now, when?"

I didn't abandon my critical thinking. (*Really*, Mom and Dad. Don't worry.) It coexisted with the feeling of sweet homecoming, of putting down deep roots. I sensed I could trust this whole deal, even though it was so culturally different, even, in some ways, so seemingly backwards. I got that trust from being around and observing the Rebbe.

No, he didn't brainwash me. His minions didn't tie me up and force-feed me chicken soup, drop by drop, until I surrendered, screaming, "Kreplach forever, soup dumplings forever; I see the light!"

It was hard to explain without sounding cultish or scary, but that wasn't it. No coercion. It was more like being around a pure, authentic, and whole pillar of light. I'd have to be a stone to not react. The Rebbe was brilliant and humble, caring and dynamic, but also something way beyond any of those labels. When I read in the Torah about a Moses who could go way up beyond where regular folks could endure, who brought the divine wisdom down for the people, who carried their load and shepherded them, and who ran interference for them with God—it now became somewhat fathomable.

People who weren't conditioned or predisposed to see the Rebbe as a different kind of person felt it, too. My husband, Yankel, once brought his sweet and sincere, but Jewishly unschooled father to a *farbrengen*. His dad came back shaking his head, remarking, "The Rebbe saw right through me. His glance was so powerful. He saw right through me."

World-class scientists and statesmen learned that the Rebbe's advice was more than a well- thought-out stratagem. Something else was there, beyond the greatest conceptualism. I gained a lot of companionship and inspiration from a small memoir called *Return*, written by the leading pioneer in the field of magneto-hydrodynamics, the physicist Professor Herman Branover. He describes his Soviet atheist education, the fledgling stages of his Jewish consciousness, and his growth into a *chassid* who experienced the benefits of the Rebbe's remarkable vision. A brilliant man, Professor Branover wasn't afraid to rely on a vision that went way beyond mortal intelligence.

I tried to walk in his footsteps (often dragging my ego, kicking and screaming) and found that following the Rebbe's advice didn't diminish my free will or thinking, but instead, added blessing and clarity I couldn't otherwise have reached, no matter how high on my tippy toes I stretched.

The humbling aspect of Torah study was refreshing. There were plenty of brilliant minds, in front of the classroom and from centuries ago, whose comments we struggled to decipher. The "I" and ego weren't quite as dominant over here as they were back in the university. It was understood as a matter of course that we had lots of brains. But we used them more collectively, to share, to debate, to glean inspiration and understanding.

And all of our minds, the big rabbis' and the struggling novices', were pretty puny next to the Rebbe's encyclopedic mind and comprehensive understanding, so we didn't get too carried away with our novel and amazing insights anyway.

We were all swimmers in this endless ocean. It went beyond another "ism" of the day, another clever product of the great, but ultimately limited, human mind. Even though no degrees or letters were bestowed after our names for our efforts, our progress, our muscles working to pull us forward, felt good—really good—and that was reward enough.

After I'd been in Crown Heights for several months, Rabbi Friedman came to town to lecture. When I once again heard that sonorous surety in his voice, I relieved the initial sense of wonder I had felt, sitting in that library in Minnesota.

I had come to Bais Chana in a foggy mist, with a hodgepodge of realizations and obstacles: I have a soul, I have intuitions. I have negative thoughts, feelings, desires. I feel intensely spiritual; I feel intensely down, selfish, sluggish.

Through arduous searching and dreaming, sprinkled with copious hints and kisses from above, I grabbed a tenuous foothold on that virgin shore of general spiritual reality, homesteading and laying a foundation to build on—a new and revolutionary premise never heard of in my native land—which set my life on a radically different course: There is a God. Everyone has a soul; a real and sparkling soul.

And if that's so, we've more than a body and nervous system firing neurons... then what? This piece of knowledge seemed to imply a very different journey and destination than the one I'd been groomed for.

Like the early settlers and wanderers on those North American shores, I found this new land an enticing bounty of potential and danger, wilderness resplendent with untapped riches.

PAINTING ZAIDY'S DREAM

Rabbi Friedman and Rabbi Majeski and their buddies, the Baal Teshuva teachers, were like those Native American guides who stretched out a hand to the bewildered settlers. They showed us where to plant and sow; when to water, to lie fallow, to harvest a tender thanksgiving offering.

There is a path, we sighed—its reality deep and strong
The solid ground under our feet felt good.
The solid ground under our feet felt good.
Come tap those riches, they coached. Not in a day, a rush, or ecstatic explosion—
but with one joyful methodical step, and then another.

Right hand here. Left foot there. Count to three.
Now light the candle. Now say this. Now eat. Now don't.

Because our questions were sensitively answered, our guides intelligent
Because of the majestic wholeness of the tribal chief, we felt fairly secure in trusting—taking another step, and still another,

till the tribal dance the blazing fire the niggunim soul songs
the holiday candles burning low
the young 'uns gathered to hear the lore and learn,
with shining eyes, curly peyos sidelocks, pretty Shabbos shoes
bright-eyed does coming of age in innocent strength,
in coy beauty,
till the sweet sip of Kiddush wine, the quiet pause
before the father intones the Hamotzi blessing on the bread
the knife slicing through the challah crust,
dip in salt and bite—soft delight, eggs and flour sprinkled with sesame,
fresh from the oven heavenly fragrant

before the Shabbos multi-coursed too much food it's so delicious meal unfolds
with song and laugher and words from the Torah,
the children answer all the questions and get a treat,
imbibing lore tradition and wisdom with that piece of sweet candy
building another rung on that ladder

before all that becomes part of my blood, my day, my week after week
and year after year

before September is Rosh Hashana more than Labor Day
before January comes to mean Tu B'Shvat and what should I be for Purim
and Friday night means
whose house are you eating at, what Torah portion is it

while Friday night movies and bars and long ambling drives fade away.

20

---❧❦❧---

NEW YORK, NEW YORK

That was *Chassidus*. While the core teachings were pure, transcending time and place, the society was colored by its locale. That buzz I felt when crossing the Verrazano or ascending from the Holland Tunnel extended all the way down Flatbush Avenue into Crown Heights, Brooklyn.

Even though Chassidic practice reigned in Crown Heights, a New York feel permeated as well. Fashion, albeit modest, was of extreme importance. People hurried, with that confident New York stride and cool appraisal of your warts as they passed.

I took up residence in the Big Apple in September 1980. About two months later, I went home to visit during Thanksgiving vacation. Stopping at a grocery, I grabbed a cart and zoomed through the aisles, aggressively cutting in front of other mild-mannered shoppers as they methodically read the labels and made their purchases. Suddenly I realized, *Slow down, honey. You're in Detroit, not New York. No need to push. No one's rushing or grabbing but you.*

Push or be pushed (and never make it to the front of the line) was a rule of life I'd quickly absorbed in the Big Apple, but here in the genteel and pokey Midwest I could let it go.

But even with all of its rushing and glares, Crown Heights was a far cry from the anonymous throngs of Manhattan. There was a mostly upbeat and electric air. A tightly intertwined community meant the streets were full of animated clusters—hugs and greetings, shmoozing and kibbitzing.

Not everyone was in a hurry. Plenty of weary people slowly made their way up the avenue. Some were Old World *Yidden* (Jews) exuding timeless warmth and deep sincerity. The beggars were not your typical panhandlers, but Yiddish-speaking, bag-lady refugees, bundled in babushkas, looking like they'd been flown right from Roman Vishniac's Warsaw. They sat in front of stores and at corners, holding out their paper cups with a plea: "*Tzedaka, tzedaka* (charity, charity)." I often gave pocket change, sometimes a rumpled dollar. People slowed their rushed gait to offer change with a compassionate word.

Some beggars grunted in reply, but others poured on the blessings: "Thank you. God bless you. Good things, much happiness." I learned to not be embarrassed, but look them in the eye and gratefully answer *Amen*. It felt like they had something authentic to offer; their struggles, their air of well-worn Jewish suffering, of having seen too much, gave their words extra resonance.

When I first came to Crown Heights, I reveled in it's almost *shtetl* quality. Kingston Avenue hosted two restaurants. *Ess and Bentch* (Eat and Bless) was a true hole-in-the-wall greasy spoon. Kingston Pizza was the newer alternative, with formica counters and Israelis efficiently serving up pizza, falafel, knishes, and fries. Upscale gourmet hadn't yet arrived.

The little corner grocery, Rivky's, was run by a fast-talking Hungarian woman and her elderly mother. Every inch of the store, from floor to ceiling, was packed with goods; the entire place about the size of my modest dining room. Rivky ruled over her roost with warmth and authority. I frequented her store and was amazed to have her greet me by name: "How are you, Miriam?" And she knew my favorites. "Sorry, we're out of carob rice cakes, but some are coming in tomorrow. There's that whole-grain bread you like." She likewise remembered and kibbitzed with most of her hundreds of customers, and I later learned, after her death, extended credit and charity to many of them.

Most of the neighborhood's establishments were like Rivky's: Homey, no frills, many run by survivors of Hitler or Stalin.

Over the years, Crown Heights slowly expanded and gentrified. Each time I visited, it looked less like a simple village and a bit more like West Bloomfield. New establishments —bistros, sushi cafés, internet cafés, larger groceries with wider aisles and computerized inventories—sprang up. The Chabad.org website and a slew of creative, cutting-edge outreach programming developed as the once-small group of refugee Chassidim morphed into a powerful global network. But I still treasured the scrawled cardboard signs posted on store doors in Yiddish, Hebrew, and English. "Gone for lunch, back in an hour," and other lingering reminders of a plainer, simpler time.

21

---∽✦∾---

ROUND GRAY PEBBLES,
INFINITE BLUE

In addition to 770, I came to treasure another well-known Chabad landmark Known as the *Ohel* (literally "tent"), it was about a half-hour drive from Crown Heights, at the Old Montefiore Cemetery in Queens. The sixth Chabad Rebbe, Rabbi Yosef Yitzchok Schneersohn, was a lion who steadfastly fought Stalin's ferocious efforts to obliterate Judaism. Broken physically by KGB henchmen but still towering in spirit, he subsequently replanted the Chabad movement on these shores. He died in 1950; the Ohel was his burial site. Years later, his son-in- law and successor, the Rebbe, Rabbi Menachem Mendel Schneerson, was buried there in 1994.

Over the years, we would carve out time for a stop at the Ohel every time we visited New York. It was a holy place, an opening for a little closer encounter with our souls and the Infinite. We usually came in the afternoon, timing our visit so we could head off the Belt Parkway on the way back and jaunt over to an empty corner at Rockaway Beach. A favorite part of our trips east were the times we managed to catch some sea expanse— waves, gulls—another universe just a few miles away from the Crown Heights hustle and bustle.

But we'd also show up at the Ohel at wee hours of the morning, or late at night, on our way out of town. Whatever the time, the doors were open, people usually there, and the connection waiting to happen.

Getting there was a trip through many facets of New York. We left the familiar, well-worn, but stable neighborhood of Crown Heights. As we drove down Eastern Parkway, out towards Atlantic Avenue, the neighborhoods got rougher, the gates on the windows rustier and more menacing. The frills that made a neighborhood more than mere subsistence became fewer— amenities like colorful awnings, plants, smiling people. I made sure the car door was locked and rushed furtively in and out if we needed gas or a bathroom stop, hating my fear but feeling it anyway.

We drove down Atlantic Ave-en-uu, as the natives would say. Jostled through the perpetual traffic as we headed east on the Belt Parkway, past the jumbo jets perched around Kennedy airport, left on Springfield Ave. Past alternating pockets of decay and optimistic prosperity, a block of newer condos or row houses, shining in their promise amidst the otherwise tired and weary landscape. Small ethnic businesses called out: Jamaican Treats, Chili, Soul Café.

Turned right at the giant stretch of gated cemetery, past another mile of little boxes of GI houses, lined up neatly, each on their tiny patch of dried lawn, just big enough for a spirited child to do one cartwheel on.

Then we saw it. A small place, surprising in its unassuming simplicity, its functional understatement, its nondescript, out-of-the-way location.

The last house in the stretch, upon close inspection, was a little different than its neighbors, sporting Hebrew writing on the building, a large awning, and an endless stream of people going in and out.

We piled out of the car, straightened our clothes, and came into the small front room with gleaming hardwood floors. This was once someone's tiny living room. I could almost imagine a family sitting on their couch, before their little domain was transformed into a public place that so many passed through.

A video screen stood in the corner, playing footage of the Rebbe speaking to individuals and at the famous *farbrengens* (gatherings) of thousands. Three wooden tables, card-table sized, filled the room. In the center of each table, black Bic pens waited perched in a stand with small sheets of plain white paper.

Round the clock, a diverse group could be found there. Singly or in clusters. Hunched over with age, or young and supple, sometimes with young children in tow. There were chassidim with *streimels* (large fur hats) and curled *peyos* (sidelocks) praying next to leather-jacketed taxi drivers who grabbed a yarmulke from the box at the entrance. Women in tight jeans wrapped scarves over their heads or shoulders. We'd see dreamers and suave hipsters; carefully groomed rabbis speaking quietly to wealthy supporters in well-cut suits. And not only Jews; many others came to the Ohel to find meaning and solace, and to access its unassuming riches. They came from around the world, some alighting from taxis, having come straight from LGA or JFK, suitcases in tow.

A jumble of languages could be heard: English, Hebrew, Russian, French, and a plethora of others, though I would have to listen closely to distinguish them, because the Ohel is mostly a place of quiet introspection and prayer.

We'd stop and gather our thoughts, then fulfill the custom to write a *pan*, a prayer request, which we'd bring into the Ohel to read. *Pan* is an acronym for the Hebrew words *Pidyon Nefesh*, which means, literally, "Redemption of the Soul." A prayer from deep within. We usually wrote them here in the front room, but sometimes in the more spacious back room which was filled with long tables and benches, more pen-and-paper boxes, coffee, tea, water, and cookies, and many people quietly preparing their thoughts or having a coffee when they came back in from their journey to the resting place.

Shelves of Crocs and slippers, scarves and yarmulkes were there for anyone who needed to borrow them. There was a custom to wear non-leather shoes into the resting place, so visitors would slip out of their more-substantial footwear and take from the bin. Empty shoes were scattered on the floor near the shelves of plastic footwear, awaiting their owners' return.

Eventually our kids grew old enough to sit quietly and write their own *pan*, but when they were little critters they would wiggle around and eat cookies, play with the water dispenser and try on the Crocs while we adults quickly scribbled a few lines.

I sat to write. My eyes welled up, there was a lump in my throat. I was writing a request to redeem my soul. That's all.

What was my soul's request, its need? I was about to stand in an awesome place of truth. No façades. No gimmicks.

My loved ones would flash before my eyes; I wrote their Hebrew names. The unlined square of paper slowly filled with loops and wiggles as I listed them one by one, my scrawl ambling across the page. I thought about those names and all they meant, the way these precious ones filled the blank page, the empty slate of my life, my heart, my days. I thought and wrote about my struggles. My hopes and aspirations. The tapestry of my life, viewed from a higher vantage point, a slight distance. I got a glimpse of its totality here.

The first time I went to the Ohel was a crisp autumn afternoon. I had been studying in Crown Heights for about a month. Sara, a classmate, was engaged. It was a few days before her wedding, and she wanted to come to the Ohel to pray. I happily tagged along, with an open mind, no expectations. I vaguely knew that burial places of *tzaddikim* (completely righteous people) were special places to connect and pray. I'd heard that the Rebbe came here regularly to read the thousands of letters and requests he received, to pray and communicate, closer to the upper realms.

The Ohel was empty that day. We walked into the cemetery, past rows of graves, and came to an enclosure. It looked like a little hut, made of slabs of limestone. First we stepped into a narrow hallway that had shelves of prayer books and metal ledges filled with memorial candles. Some had already lit by previous visitors, others sat waiting. We each lit a candle, took a book, and then, with a gentle, respectful knock, stepped out of the hallway into an open square surrounded by limestone walls that were about ten feet high. The enclosure was about the size of a large bedroom. Intensely quiet. A headstone stood at one end, with Hebrew letters carved into the front of the limestone rectangle. Many stones and pebbles were nestled on top.

A Jewish custom is to leave a stone on the headstone when visiting a grave. These gray ovals seemed almost alive, like clustered signs of humanity—rounded, nestled together on top, surrounded by all this flat austereness.

The ground in front of the headstone was enclosed by a wall, about three feet high. All you could see was this interior space of limestone, and the incredibly blue sky above. The square in front of the headstone was filled with torn-up *pan* requests; visitors would customarily read their requests, rip them up, and drop the shreds into the square. Scattered like tears, like flower petals, different colored scraps were piled up, with Hebrew, Roman, Cyrillic, and other scripts, some on lined paper, others blank. The scrawled letters peered up from the heap; thoughts and hopes freed from the paper to fly above. They were fingerprints left behind from the people who had stood here and poured out their hearts, bared their souls. Standing in the place so many others had stood before, I felt I was part of the pulsing sea of humanity, of so many lives filled with hopes, prayers, brokenness, promise.

Sara intently made her way through the whole *Ma'aneh Loshon*, a compilation of psalms and prayers. She paused in the middle of the text to read her own *pan* request. As a young bride about to embark on such a significant chapter of her life, she had plenty to beseech and meditate about. I gave Sara her space, standing a few feet away in amicable quiet. I stumbled through a few *Tehillim* (Psalms), then just looked around and took it all in.

After a long while, Sara sighed, then wiped away a tear. She tore her *pan* and cast the pieces into the center. The ripping sound broke the silence, startling me. The pieces fluttered down into the vast pile.

An infinite calm. The intense white sparkling stone, the azure sky with cumulus clouds, the intimate quiet.

I have visited the Ohel countless times since then. Some hurried, with impatient kids in tow, others meditative and drawn out. Each visit was special, a point of connection, humbleness, and renewal beyond time. But that first encounter was the primal template I always think back to: the blue, the white, the stillness.

Tending the garden

"The purpose of the creation of every person, and of all the upper and lower worlds is to make a dwelling place for God in this world."

—TANYA, CHAPTER 33

"I have come into My garden… into the place in which My essence was originally revealed."

—SONG OF SONGS 5:1, BOSI L'GANI, CHAPTER 1

"Serve God with joy."

—PSALMS 100:2

22

⟞⟨⟩⟞

MY LIFE AND WELCOME TO IT

O ver the next year, my commitment to this Torah thing grew and solidified. I made my way through the rhythmic cycle of a full year of holidays, each rich with foods, prayers, mitzvos, and meaning. I was unnerved, tasting the depth of celebrations I'd casually known as a child.

"This is Chanukah? Where's all this incredible stuff been hiding?" I had thought Chanukah was an arcane military story that was spun into something to keep Jewish kids busy around Christmas time.

Back in elementary school, I was jealous of the carols, tinsel, and excitement. My neighbor Kathy always had a giant tree, full of flashing lights and silvery icicles, with mountains of presents stacked underneath, tantalizing in their colorful wrapping and ribbons. Every Christmas morning I'd saunter across the street to examine the loot. One year her working- class parents went all-out. Ten-year-old Kathy greeted me with a flashing diamond ring, and then spun around to show off her gray rabbit coat, among other treasures.

Our little menorah, educational toys, and new bathrobes paled in comparison. *Well, at least we've got eight days,* I thought defensively, trying to find some redeeming value in our way-too-understated holiday. Sometimes we'd hang stockings on our fireplace. Maybe Santa had a little overstock and could drop some surplus our way.

I was confused in the face of the seasonal bombardment in school, media, and marketplace. I knew Christmas wasn't really my holiday. I felt a gut-level disconnect. I felt the outsider. Kind of. The melting pot was bubbling away, on high heat. It seemed like we were supposed to blend in smoothly, like a cup of "Mm Mm Good" Campbell's Tomato Soup, all morphing into one bland liquid. Should I sit on Santa's lap? Go caroling? Sing "Jingle Bells" in school? What about "Silent Night"—that seemed more hard-core and seriously religious Even though it was just a song, it didn't seem quite right. Where to draw the line? Was there a line? An uneasy time of year.

I never fully realized how disjointed "the season to be jolly" made me feel, until years later when I found myself ensconced in Chaunkah's full beauty. I felt liberated—released from that queasy, free-floating, adrift-in--red-and-green, mistletoe world. Chanukah stood on its own two legs here in Torah land.

I relished the simple beauty of family gathered around, lighting the menorah as the winter night fell, its glow reflected in the children's sparkling eyes. I was blown away by the deep insights into something as simple as spinning the *dreidel* (Chanukah top). How could that child's game be so profound? That old story about the overlooked, neglected treasure buried in one's backyard—yeah, that was my story. That dumb Jewish thing, once dug up, proved to be an extravagantly rich delight.

Towards the end of that immersion year, I was getting itchy, starting to feel ready for the next step. Time to join the generations before me and become, cliché as it sounded, a Jewish Mother. (Woody Allen and Phillip Roth, watch out. You ain't seen nothin' yet.) Of course, in order to become a Jewish Mother and start churning out pots of chicken soup, and little mouths to lovingly spoon it into, I would have to find my soul mate and arrange a fortuitous meeting under the *chuppah* (wedding canopy).

As much as the learning and *farbrengens* were beautiful and meaningful, the core of Jewish life was the home, the couple, the family. Each were symbolized and alluded to on every level, from the mystical to the practical. Male and female symbolism pervaded Kabbalah: the Jewish people were God's bride, loyally following their betrothed into the barren desert. Their union was much more than pragmatic; it was the reuniting of two halves of one whole in unique holiness. And we were not just a raucous bunch of ragtag individuals, but *Beis Yisrael*, the House of Israel; *Beis Yaakov*, the House of Jacob; *B'nai Yisrael*, the Children of Israel.

Most of my working life had been with children—as a camp counselor, tripper, counselor for emotionally disturbed kids and runaways, preschool teacher, and swim teacher. Even when I couldn't relate to much of adult society, I always had a strong affinity for kids. With their innocent wholeness they seemed more real.

And the Jewish world embraced this. Kids were, of course, necessary for the nation's survival and continuity, but it was more than that.

"The world endures because of the breath of children learning Torah," the Talmud states. This society lived out the notion of the depth and unique importance of each individual soul and child. Kids and family were *it*. Hanging around these highly integrated families where little munchkins were infinitely cherished, valued players in this enterprise called Jewish life; well, I wanted part of it. (Of course, all these kids came with a no-runny-nose-or-temper-tantrum guarantee, and each played quietly in idyllic harmony with their siblings.)

And I wasn't just looking for a procreator to make this happen, a breadwinner or compatible companion—but my *besherte*, the other half of my soul, destined for me from the primordial days of yore. What could be more romantic?

Only problem: too many Hollywood movies. On some subconscious level, I was waiting for Prince Charming to sweep me away on his white horse. *Besherte*—destined one. Sounded highly dramatic. His arrival would certainly be heralded with thunder, lightning, swooning, and rapid heartbeat, as "Someday My Prince Will Come" played with full-schmaltz, violins crooning in the background.

But these Chassidim had a unique way of bringing the intendeds together. Instead of Snow White singing for her prince, Tevya's daughters might be heard imploring Yenta the matchmaker to make them a match, to find the choicest find, to catch the cutest catch.

In this world, many couples meet through *shidduchim* (matchmaking suggestions) made by friends, teachers, family, and professional matchmakers. I thought the concept was extremely strange. Where was the spontaneity, the crazed, chance falling in love? But the more I thought honestly about the dating and hook-up world out there—the emotional fender-benders, the pain and confusion—the more intriguing this *shidduch* (matchmaking) approach seemed. I'd seen the wreckage up close, having gone along with two college friends to hold their hands while they had abortions. There was a haunting pain that stayed with them, underneath their nonchalant veneer. Free and easy love wasn't always all it was cracked up to be.

Objective, caring third parties could look farther than that often-misleading initial attraction. A dramatic flash didn't mean the person had the real goods: the important personal qualities and character one wanted. The *shidduch* middlemen (and women) would search out the real scoop, beyond the charm and cute smile. What was he like as an employee, a student, a friend? What were his goals, interests?

If, based on this detached analysis, if *boychik* and *maidele*, the young man and young woman, sounded compatible "on paper,"—*then* the couple would meet. They'd start dating, try to build a relationship, and see if that all-important and elusive chemistry was there—if, indeed, somehow they would sense that ineffable "We are meant for each other."

Like, if the spark, the flame, was there, the structure and groundwork had already been laid to support it. Not the more typical "Wow, a flash!" as two people would meet on the street, and find themselves in deep, halfway in love before they could step back and untangle whether they had enough in common, and whether they even wanted the same thing out of the relationship.

Soon enough, friends told me about an intelligent, fun guy. He was from New Jersey, living and studying in Crown Heights, and had trod a similar path to my own. Parents were the usual detectives in this *shidduch* business, prodding and inquiring. Since mine weren't part of this world I made a few inquiry calls myself, and liked what I heard. A mutual friend reported that the said candidate, Yankel, was "really warm and friendly, knew how to connect with different kinds people and make them comfortable." As he talked, he remembered an awkward situation that Yankel had handled with sensitivity. He told me about it and excitedly added, "Really special. A gem." *Nu* (so), sounded good. Emotional maturity and sensitivity were among the top priorities on my inner "search engine." Sounded like something to talk about. So a *shidduch* (match) was made. We met.

I *liked* Yankel right away. Felt a deep and comfortable connection, like old friends, ancient friends even. I somehow felt very young and innocent when we were together. He'd hippied around too, had been a strict macrobiotic brown-rice connoisseur. Hmm, wonder what I would have thought of him if we'd met out on Highway One? I got a chuckle when this *yeshiva bochur* (rabbinical student) showed me his Brandeis University ID photo, circa 1972—with his shoulder- length hair. We dated a few times.

I found the *shidduch* space a special one. Since so many games didn't have to be played, we could somehow jump right into seeing each other's essence, and seeing what the new essence of an *us* might be like. We both knew we were looking for a marriage partner, we hoped to create roughly the same kind of life—so we didn't have to do the "how committed do you really want to be" game. There was a lovely, golden space where we could perceive, think, and feel more clearly. It was a pure space, an encapsulated, more intense than hours on the clock kind of time.

I liked—really liked—Yankel, deeply, but the violins were humming quietly, not in dramatic crescendos. The fireworks were subtle—too subtle, since if this was *the* one, I assumed that "*besherte*" would surely be flashing in neon lights.

So I broke it off. I got out of the car right after telling Yankel that the *shidduch* was over, closing the door on him sitting in sad and surprised silence. At first I felt a rush of relief. Pressure's off. I went down the steps into the little apartment. Heard the wrought iron gate clang shut behind me. Flopped down on the love seat.

A slowly rising, but overwhelming, sadness hit. Still not Hollywood though: no thunderbolts, no pathos. Not dramatic, soap-opera heartbroken. I didn't soak through even one handkerchief. But I was sad, seriously sad, like I'd lost a special friend. The more I thought about it, the more I realized this Yankel guy seemed to really "get" me. I had a subtle sense that I could lean on him, lean hard, even. Well, it was probably close, but not quite the right one, I figured. Two other guys were suggested, so during the next few weeks I went out with each of them. Once each. I couldn't muster up the patience to give them more time. On each date, I kept comparing them to Yankel, and they fell short. But he wasn't my *besherte*... right?

My landlady saw me moping around, and pried the story out of me. She strongly urged me to meet Shimshon, the quintessential matchmaker. A well-known and beloved character, I had seen him around town. He seemed almost an incarnation of the famous Tevya from *Fiddler on the Roof*, a bit irreverent and cheerily heavy-set. Shimshon could be seen walking right across the tabletops in the men's section of 770, holding a large bucket. He would merrily accost people, shaking them down for donations to the *tzedaka* organization he ran out of his garage with his equally jovial wife, Martha—bringing food and holiday supplies to struggling families.

I hesitantly walked over to Shimshon's house, nervous to suc-cumb to his piercing glance and up-front advice. But he was known for protecting "his girls" and being hard on the guys he dealt with. It might be nice to have a protective poppa bear-type figure watching out for me.

"Come in!" someone yelled as I tentatively knocked on the door. Earthy, robust Shimshon was in the middle of a colorful tirade, mincing no words as he told a pal exactly what he thought about some community shenanigans. As I slowly walked into his comfortable living room, he paused long enough to wave me over to the dining room table. Without batting an eye, he changed gears, turned towards me and took a blank card out of one of his assorted filing boxes, which was unsettling. Was my most person-al, most important quest going to be relegated to a three-by-five card? He fired off questions about my background, my schooling, what I was looking for—my shopping list of important qualities in a husband—and jotted notes as I answered. I tried to describe my imagined Mr. Right.

Then I blurted out, without thinking, "You know this guy, Yankel Karp? Well, I would like to meet someone just like him... just not him."

Shimshon looked at me shrewdly for a few long seconds. He asked me a few questions, read astutely between the lines, and picked up the phone while filing through his stack of cards and pulling one out. This multitasking wheeler-dealer had all kinds of people popping in and out and calling nonstop, so I figured he was working on something else for a minute. I sat back for a breather.

Someone answered his call. He said, "Hello, Mr. Karp? This is Shimshon Stock in Crown Heights. Have your son call me. I have good news for him." I opened my mouth in shock. He had pulled out a card with Yankel's contact numbers and some other bio-graphical stats. I started to get ready to protest. How could this guy have such chutzpah? I had just told him that Yankel was *not* for me. But something told me to let Shimshon take the driver's seat, and go along for the ride. I was annoyed and pleased at the same time.

With Shimshon's help in band-aiding and resuscitating the match, Yankel and I continued dating. Under the ups and downs and ins and outs was a feeling of sweet inevitability. Shimshon's combination of caring chutzpah and sharp intuition helped nudge the tentative young couple over the finish line and seal the deal. I'm not sure where he found the time, but he spend many tedious phone sessions with me, assuring me that Yankel was "a really good guy, special," and that all the ingredients were there for a something much more than a flash fire that could burn out—for an enduring kind of relationship. Shimshon's coaching and just more time together with Yankel, walking, talking, hanging out, and solidifying our growing bond led us to...

Mazel tov! Congratulations! We finally announced our engagement and starting getting ready to build "an everlasting home in [the nation of] Israel." Busy preparations exploded onto the scene —and my supportive and befuddled parents were thrown into the middle of it all.

Until now they'd been guardedly tolerant of my venture into Chassidic life, though apprehensive about its seeming archaic insularity. They were comforted that this trip was a Jewish one, which they could somewhat relate to. Instead of astral plane, color therapy, vibrational healing, washed down with wheat grass juice, it was all about gefilte fish and matzah balls. Ironically, through my involvement with these antiquated Chassidim, I was even learning a bit of their beloved Yiddish, which I never would have dreamed of bothering with.

But now, as parents of the bride, they had to dip their toes in and get more personally involved. They navigated their sudden immersion into my very different world with tolerance (and a little heartburn). They called out the troops, and their enduring gang of family and friends banded together to fete the new and unusual couple.

Yankel found an apartment, while Mom and I hired a band and a caterer. Along with the flowers and fussing, Yankel and I had some learning to do. The Torah guided how we ate, slept, dressed, and conducted business. It was certainly not going to leave something as powerful as sexuality to mere instinct or whatever society's latest take on it was. Nothing was as atomic, as powerful. What else could bind two individuals together in unique oneness, bring a soul into the world, or wreak so much havoc and destruction? So we dove into the Torah's wisdom to keep our "Hey, I remember you from some ancient time" bond deepening and growing—a bond full of potential, but still delicate and wobbly.

I had already learned a little about the practices of *taharas hamishpacha* and *mikvah*—a rhythm of periodic separation and reunification, continual rejuvenation, of holiness and a protected and private intimacy. Now it was time to master the details.

It was more than a bit strange to have this most personal part of my life shaped and guided like this, but over the ensuing months and years, through the hard and delightful parts of this observance, I realized, "This is heavy-duty good stuff. God knows me way better than I know myself."

The marriage blessings they'd read at our ceremony were full of pretty words. The *mitzvah* of mikvah would add a unique framework and inject a drop of golden *Shechina* (divine presence) into our union. Crucial fuel to help the "loving friends as in the Garden of Eden—experience gladness, jubilation, cheer, and delight; love, friendship, harmony and fellowship" and become a living reality that could endure.

The wedding celebration was a night to remember, as the gang was entertained at my strictly Chassidic wedding. Record cold and snowfall defined the robust Detroit winter of '82. Most normal folk huddled at the windows to watch our outdoor *chuppah*, the canopy's four poles held up by shivering family members under the stars. The parking lot of the small Young Israel synagogue had been cleared, the snow piled up at its edges like small mountains surrounding the candlelit ceremony. Only the hardy Chassidim and our immediate family dared venture outside.

Next came frenzied dancing to lively music, men and women cavorting on different sides of the *mechitza* (divider). Young rabbinical students did somersaults and stunts, even lighting vodka- soaked hats on fire. And that wasn't all that was vodka-soaked—I'm sure more than a few of those bearded zealots had downed more than a few. Dad looked disheveled, with a sloppy grin, as though his oldest daughter's initiation to this strange world had been eased with a *l'chaim* (toast) or two.

I can only imagine the old gang's observations and whispered comments as they watched this very different wedding and shared the celebration with a very different part of the Jewish community, whose paths rarely crossed.

Uncle Irving, who outwardly prided himself on being the most cynical, atheist, and left-leaning, must have been beside himself. We kids had always been intimidated by his witty remarks. Irving used to sit at the end of the table at our large family seder, making a show of piling his matzah with the most horseradish, and turning beet-red as he downed it. He'd sing along with such over-enthusiastic gusto that an undertone of sarcasm could be heard. I later learned that his mother was the renegade of a Chassidic family. When her clan fled the Ukraine and headed for Kfar Chabad, a Chassidic farming village in Israel, she headed for America and married a free- thinker.

I can almost hear the jibes Irv must have rolled out, and the smirks, cracks, and sympathy my parents must have received from friends whose mix of support and ambivalence matched their own.

"You must have been brainwashed for someone to convince you to get out of those raggy patched overalls," Mom joked, actually half-joked and half- stated. We had been shopping for modest, knee-covering skirts several weeks before the wedding.

Skirts?

When Grandma Ida had died a few years before, I had to go out the morning of the funeral to find one appropriate garment to wear. I had just come back from the Hazelwood Farm, where I wore knee-high rubber boots and army pants, the better to pitch hay and feed the cows. After that stage, the vintage, flowing dress creations from Salvation Army had come and gone. I moved on to a funky kind of "dressy" for Shabbos in Ann Arbor and as a newbie Chassid. Now I was back to real clothes, from the mall, no less.

Finally, I was willing to go to Hudson's with Mom, to go through the racks, stand patiently in the fitting room, ask her opinion—even sign up for the Bridal Registry.

We wandered up and down the aisles of home goods, check-list, pencil, and clipboard in hand. I had to laugh. This was the last place I ever thought I'd find myself: looking at Cuisinarts, china, and tableware. What was my color scheme?

One hippie met her end in J.L. Hudson's.

Mom tried to show me the nicer china, similar to the classic ivory set she had. Her friends were throwing me a shower and would purchase whatever I chose.

But I couldn't quite make that leap.

"Ma, is it okay? I really like this other kind best. They're just more me."

"Sure, honey, it's your choice. Whatever you like."

I tried to pry open my mind and look at the fancier, upscale lines, but I kept coming back to the thick Platzgraff ceramic dishes, light brown with blue country trim. Hey, they almost looked as though they could have been hand-thrown down on the farm. At least I didn't register for chopsticks and grungy, hand-made mugs. I picked out a real set of matching silverware.

Shopping with Mom—a pleasure she had been long denied. I didn't pout, wave my *Little Red Book*, or head for the mainte-nance-man department. I used to find my overalls and flannel shirts in the J.C. Penney work-gear section. Now, here I was in the fashionable women's department. But at what cost, she must have thought? At the cost of adopting this medieval lifestyle.

I cleverly preempted Mom's resistance when I first told her about Yankel. Knowing her fondness for red hair and freckles, I excitedly said, "Guess what, Mom? Yankel has some red in his hair and blue eyes, just like me." She seemed pleased. "Our kids will probably be freckled *gingies*," I added, using the affectionate Hebrew term for redheads. But Dad was not so easily bought off.

"Remember," he tried to warn me with paternal concern, when I brought Yankel home to meet them, "you're not just marrying a man, you're marrying a way of life."

He must have feared that this was yet another fad or stage, but the stakes were higher this time: I was changing my legal status. I was getting married. And the way we did things, children might be on the horizon soon. No drifting away with no strings attached if this trip eventually grew old or stale.

Throughout my wanderings, Mom and Dad had dutifully shlepped to various Ann Arbor hangouts, each one grungier and more dilapidated than the one before—especially the last, where I showed off our compost pile and handmade tempeh. Wan smiles accompanied their efforts to grasp what I was so excited about.

They visited me at the farm and strolled around, smiling hesitantly and tasting the cheese as they tried to stay connected to my life.

But this time was different, I passionately insisted, when I spoke of my commitment to the Chassidic life. This was serious and for real.

And so, on that frigid February night, the happy? confused? worried? extended family and friends had a *schnapps*, a toast or two, and celebrated together with the rabbis and their wives, bringing joy and gladness to the new bride and groom. They enjoyed the juggling and antics while presumably wondering what cult I'd fallen into.

23

HOLY

"Holy, holy, holy, is the Lord of Hosts, the whole world is full of His glory." (Isaiah 6:3, from the morning prayers)

A new concept—strange and beautiful.

Holy—*kadosh.* It filtered through the prayers.

After those familiar words, "*Baruch Ata...* blessed are You...," the beginning of the blessing said before doing many mitzvos, came the next words... "*Asher kidishanu b'mitzvosav...* who makes us *holy* with His commandments."

Kadish—the famous prayer uttered by a mourner, praising God's *holiness*

Kiddush—Prayer said over wine on Friday night, praising the *holiness* of Shabbos

Kiddushin—Marriage, one special and separate relationship

The starry-eyed hippie blew into Crown Heights on a cloud of oneness. All is one—one is all—the trees the wind the shining moon we're all cosmic light energy.

But where and how to differentiate? To draw lines? What lines? Who says?

These Jews say, holiness means distinction.

Borders separate, but borders set off a special, inner space to fill.

Marriage —a unique, vulnerable intimacy that comes from its singularity.

A ravishing fire, a lustrous flame
Drawing me in.
I feel small, I step back in awe.

Am kodesh—the holy people—"a nation that stands alone,"
solitary and alone.
Even when we try so badly to merge the nations don't let us—:
Jew Jew get out, Jew Jew move back, go back home, go back go

Holy, holy, holy; learn to embrace the difference
embrace the separation
a star has to stand alone to shine up the black abyss
let the empty space the dark night be

A new routine. So now she's *holy.*

What's that all about, the enduring gang wondered. They sat patiently through it all, through the ensuing years, watching me with love, affection, and a touch of condescending confusion when I'd show up to join a family birthday or anniversary celebration—each time with a few more babies, juggling a bit more.

Mom's friend Sherry would smile, a stiff grin plastered on her face, as she greeted me and peered at my burgeoning stomach. "Oh, you're pregnant." She didn't have to add the unsaid but implied, "Again!" I could hear it loud and clear.

"How exciting. How are you feeling," she said solicitously, with barely concealed sarcasm.

Each time I surfaced, I drank up the gang's love and tried to put together a few words, to reach them and help them understand. Who was this girl? What happened to Trudy and Jack's nice kid? Why couldn't she settle down into a nice, middle-class life like we all did?

Over the years, along with the befuddlement, I slowly began to sense a subtle acknowledgment that I might be on to something. These hard-working, first-generation Americans had plotted a life of success for their children. Their kids went to good schools, played in orchestras and teams, and had all the advantages their parents could only dream of when they were young. But the American dream seemed to sour alarmingly often. Strife, unraveling.

My weekly cycle of braiding challah for Shabbos, coming around each year to another season of baking honey cake for Rosh Hashanah and cleaning for Passover, and my old-fashioned kids who seemed less affected by the general malaise, didn't seem quite so outlandish as the years rolled on. Linda, one of Mom's old buddies, told me straight out: she was jealous. Her two grandkids were far off in a distant city. Family struggles had cast a shadow on her golden years.

"All these beautiful kids," she murmured as she stroked my children's ginger hair. "Trudy is really lucky."

But still, there was a gap, a distance. They might have appreciated my values, but the details —the day-to-day rituals and rules we followed to make this happen—seemed formidable. Does it really matter if you eat this or that? Do you really believe all that? Still and all, it seemed a cumbersome mystery. They looked at me with a benign, "Huh?"

Each time I came back from Detroit, from a few days of living with and rubbing up against my family, I would again be torn between the magnitude of our deep bond and our perplexing differences. I saw myself through their eyes and imagined them asking, "What is all this? Why does she have to do it to the nth degree?"

Part of me wanted to fall back and be like them; it was so comfortable and familiar, a well-worn groove. Then I'd be able to really hang and connect with them, without these insidious differences that that separated us.

During one visit to my folks, my sister Viv, my kids and I got together with cousins to watch a Little League game and catch up as we sprawled on the aluminum bleachers. After the game, we passed by Tasty Freeze and saw most of the team lined up outside. Not for us. Not kosher. My accommodating sister said, "Let's stop at Kroger's and get something for you guys. My treat." The kids perked up in anticipation. It was so nice to be spoiled by their aunt.

We pulled into the parking lot and piled into the store, grabbing a shopping cart at the door. Our automatic scanning of labels for kosher symbols suddenly felt awkward, an obstructing hurdle.

"Here," Viv said. "Ben and Jerry's. It's got an O-U."

"Well..." I said, hesitantly.

My teenage daughter Esti explained forthrightly: "It's dairy. We had chicken for dinner a few hours ago. No milk for another three hours. And we only eat special dairy products anyway, and they don't have that kind here."

"Down at the end of the dairy aisle, or over in health food, they usually have Tofutti or Soy Delicious, which are dairy-free," I said, pointing.

Viv generously piled up the cart with all the flavors my kids ever wanted to try, even the coconut- milk kind I usually deemed too expensive. This was pretty exciting. She was so accepting, even though our list of disclaimers and requirements seemed to never end. She smiled brightly as we savored our treats, huddled around the card table in our basement den at Dad's, but it wasn't really the same as sitting in an ice cream parlor. Maybe I was projecting, but I imagined her thinking, "What a pain."

Kedusha (holiness)—what exactly was it already? Why did we have to go the extra mile and make life so difficult? Drink special milk, cover the last inch of our elbows, do all this to the max? Why couldn't we ever chill a bit? We seemed to maintain an annoying separateness from the world—that fine line of loving, empathizing, but not really getting into the fray, not getting down and dirty. "What are ya, super-Jews? Holier than thou? Too good for us? You don't eat our food or drink our wine. You keep yourselves apart and aloof," I imagined humanity challenging us.

I slowly developed a sensor for *kedusha*, just knowing when I was around it. Watching the Rebbe at those large *farbrengens* (gatherings) I felt magnetically drawn in and inspired, yet humbled and reticent.

The more I tuned into this channel, the more it revealed itself to be a unique level of pleasure. People always talked about the saving, shlepping, the contortions they went through to go on this vacation or eat at that incredible restaurant. But vacations, fine food, cars, and all paled in comparison. Yeah, life was more complex with *the holy thing* as the focus, but when you're going for the gold—the ultimate—hassles fall by the wayside.

I guess I wanted pleasure too, but I came to appreciate this more sublime one. And I didn't want to crash, have that morning-after emptiness when the vacation was over or the plate licked clean. A ring of eternity rang out of the *sukkah* booth and from the sound of our family singing and laughing around the Shabbos table. And it lent a protected place of innocence where kids could grow up with a soft glow of wonder, one that didn't dim or turn tough and cynical quite as quickly.

Hey, I wasn't an angel hovering in a nirvana-land. I still understood the attraction of this wine or that delicacy or Paris in springtime or some other alluring delight. (Now, gourmet dark chocolate might make me think momentarily about putting the kosher thing on hold. Not *really*. But I could feel it tug at my long sleeve.)

Seeing old college or high-school friends was usually a mixed bag of emotions. Happy, and tense. We'd hug, chatter, and catch up, but they'd often peek at me hesitantly, like I'd become a bit untouchable. "If we pinch her, is she still there, underneath that get-up?" their looks seemed to say.

"Really, it's me, same old Miriam!" I wanted to shout. "I'm

not dead. My life isn't as narrow as you think." I wanted to stick out my tongue and yell, "Na-na-na-kish-kish! I'm still a nut! Not an apron-clad, kugel-cooking, sedate *rebbetzin* (rabbi's wife)!" I know it might look pretty pathetic, but it's only about restrictions on the surface. It's not jail. It's directed, with a laser-like focus, instead of dispersed, random light leaking all over the place.

It was kind of like the difference between a blaring hard-rock band that played one chord, over and over, beating, beating, beating—and a symphony. I sometimes could touch a higher realm, making other delights seem kind of hollow.

My Shabbos morning routine was telling. Sometimes I'd cuddle on the couch with Bubby's crocheted quilt, a few cups of coffee, a stack of books, and a kid or two. A quiet haven from a hectic week. Other weeks I'd enjoy a leisurely walk to *shul,* our little synagogue. I'd sit towards the back, with my prayer book, praying, thinking, watching the little girls scurry in and out in their velvet dresses and matching hair ribbons, the boys in little vests.

As I swayed and listened to the chanting of the Torah portion, the ancient blessings and scoldings of the prophets, a little voice would occasionally perch on my shoulder and nudge, "Great way to spend your Saturday morning, Miriam. Reading old words, sitting quietly with sedate women and answering *Amen* at the right time. Is this it—the climax of all that intense searching?"

Well, yeah. Isn't it obvious? Praying for hours with a bunch of hoary rabbis as they chant in Hebrew—it's the place to be, like *happening*!

The deep resonance of this staid-looking existence wasn't easy to convey. Sorry, can't eat this, and no, I haven't seen that movie. And I didn't even have a TV—a disclosure that elicited wonder. I couldn't follow the animated conversations comparing notes about this or that show. What a dinosaur.

But I wished my old buddies could jump into my life for a day, be served a large, savory spoonful of the rhythm and sweetness of my universe, somehow understand the beautiful melodies and experiences I was surrounded with when I made even a measly effort to connect. I'd have to push through my laziness and my excuses not to pray or learn. But then I'd find that *kedusha* symphony on my radio dial, in full orchestral splendor. It was there, but invisible and undetectable until I powered on the receiver and tuned in.

24

———⚜———

FLYIN' WITH
THE HOLY ROLLERS

I f my buddies could jump in for a day, I hoped they'd choose a relatively normal one. Not one of the many Holy Roller, hyper-overdrive adventures from my early high-flyin' days.

One recent Friday afternoon, I was transported from my current life back to those days when everything was new and Technicolor. While cooking for Shabbos, I looked for some music to add energy and oomph while I peeled potatoes, got the chicken into the oven, and the salads going. I grabbed a CD and popped it into the player. The bongo rhythm filled my kitchen and I couldn't help but boogie to the spirited riff.

The lyrics—"Goin' Chassidish, I'm startin' to learn Yiddish"— were chanted by a bunch of beat-boxin' young guys, newbies to observance, who seemed to have been around the block enough to appreciate where they were now, hanging out in Torah land.

Listening to the music, I was transported back to a rosy time of fresh beginnings. I looked like a typical observant mom, working against the ticking clock and late-afternoon rays of the soon-to- besetting sun, but my spirit was flying. As I scurried around the kitchen, filling the house with tempting smells—I sang.

As I pushed and pulled my domain, the random debris piled up from a busy week: unsigned homework, Fayga's sweater thrown on the couch, crusty eggs soaking in the frying pan—to transition it to serene Shabbos mode—I boogied.

Listening to the beat-boxers carrying on with raucous laughter and rhythmic chant brought me back to the joy and discovery I felt as a twenty-two-year-old free agent—a young woman with the time to study and explore. Back to the time when I was venturing into the Torah thing, tentatively sticking my toe in, slowly wading, delighting in the refreshing waters, then taking off—swimming, diving, and riding the waves.

Yankel and I, and our other friends who'd made their way to this world, were basically immigrants—like Bubby and Zaidy—charmingly different to the native-born. Naive, idealistic. A little too earnest. And unschooled.

The family loved Bubby's quaint homegrown spelling and heartfelt letters she'd whip off in her campaign to right the world's wrongs. She once wrote a passionate letter to late-night talk host David Susskind, angrily berating him for a segment disrespectfully mocking Jewish mothers. Everyone cheered her on: "Go, Bubby! Take on Hollywood!"

Like Bubby, we "BTs" also tended to take it all *so* seriously, and struggled to get the details exactly right. Over the years, I've accumulated many crazed episodes, sweet in their quaint earnestness, often bordering on the absurd. (Maybe I'm related to those Wise Men of Chelm, innocent foolishness their specialty.)

One day, soon after I got my first *siddur*, Esther went through the first prayer with me. Called *Modeh Ani*, it's a simple one-liner that doesn't even address God by name.

"*Modeh ani l'fanecha, Melech chai v'kayam, shehechezarta bi nishmasi, b'chemla. Rabba emunasecha.* I offer thanks before You, living and eternal King, for returning my soul to me. Great is Your faithfulness."

I slowly mouthed it, syllable after syllable. Esther explained that this prayer should be our first thought when we wake up. In our groggy state, we haven't even washed, gone to the bathroom, or gotten out of bed, so we're not ready to address God formally. But right away, we try to grab our waking awareness and focus. "Hey, guess what? Looks like I'm alive. What a gift. Thanks! God, You rock."

I heard her words, "This should be your first thought." Did she mean that literally? Probably not. Most of us have a few moments as we awaken, of just beginning to come back to ourselves, when it's a little hard to delineate exactly what your first thought is. The basic idea of *Modeh Ani* is: before you go off on a tangent, mentally planning your day, grab your "I am here and awake and breathing" first moment—or second or third will do nicely, too.

As a pure and zealous newbie, however, I had no sense of context or balance or good enough. I carefully got ready for my first *Modeh Ani*. I placed my *siddur* on the night table, page marked, and cuddled under my quilt.

I hardly slept that long weary night. I kept tossing and turning, drifting off, then waking up and startling—so afraid I'd get sidetracked and mess up. I'd drift back asleep and wake up again with a jolt.

"Am I awake? Is *Modeh Ani* my first thought?"

Rolled over. Looked at the clock. 3:14 A.M.

"Oh, it's nighttime, I'm not officially awake." Snore.

Over and over till morning finally did dawn, and a very tired me did corral my energy to push any stray thoughts out of the way—the way my preschool students push other kids out of the way, shouting, "Hey, I'm supposed to be first!" I slowly opened my eyelids and pronounced those precious words.

They were my first words and maybe I really did it; maybe I grabbed and focused and succeeded in making this my very first thought of the day. Yawn.

And then there was *Pesach* (Passover), the springtime holiday celebrating the famous exodus of the Hebrew slaves from Egypt. Let freedom ring.

You want extreme? Bungee jumping? Hang gliding? Cliff jumping? *Feh.* Try Pesach cleaning. It's the Jewish version of extreme sports.

Just mention the "P" word around anyone remotely familiar with traditional observance, especially women, and they might roll their eyes, laugh nervously, or groan.

It's one of those special times we love to hate, but really love.

Growing up, we had a large family seder at Bubby and Zaidy's. We sat around the table, as Zaidy led the show with care, orchestrating and doling out parts to read. Most of the *haggadah* (Pesach liturgy) was from their Yiddish culture circle, the Sholem Aleichem Shule, with poetic readings about freedom flavored with bits and pieces from the traditional text. I thought my cousins Elissa and Stephen were super-religious because they could read the *Ma Nishtana* (Four Questions) in Hebrew. Shelly and Mike read them in Yiddish, while Vivian, David, and I recited in English. We ate matzah at the seder, but bread the rest of the holiday. There were a few zealots in my elementary school that brought matzo sandwiches to school for the whole eight days.

I had heard something about changing dishes and shlepping boxes of special Passover tableware up from the basement, but that sounded completely archaic and over the top.

How was this night, my first Chassidic Passover night different from all of my childhood Passover nights? I came to the seder table with a new focus. I was a burgeoning religious fanatic who knew the deep, mystical meaning of *chometz* (leavened food), matzah (flat, unleavened bread), and freedom from slavery.

Chometz, which we are forbidden to own or eat on Passover, signified rising, ego, puffy arrogance, being full of oneself. Flat, tasteless matzah symbolized humility and being open to Godliness.

And true freedom meant much more than a historical or political event. Going out of our personal enslavement—to our ego, our desires, our limitations—was something else entirely. No "good enough" to achieving that.

"In every generation [and every day] a person should see themselves as if he personally went out of Egypt," the *haggadah* liturgy exhorts. And *Mitzrayim*, the Hebrew word for Egypt, also means boundaries and limitations. So we're told to push beyond our comfort zone, to go forward, push higher. No getting by or complacency here.

Armed with these blazing insights, Chaya, Sarah, and I set out to do our first Chassidic Pesach *right* and began to mount the attack on our tiny basement apartment. Since we couldn't own *chometz*, even a minute amount, everyone in the community spent the month or so before the holiday thoroughly cleaning their domains, especially the kitchen.

But the Torah is for flesh-and-blood people. Is it humanly possible to remove every crumb, especially while raising a gang of cookie-loving children? We do our best, then use the procedure that Jewish law developed to declare tiny crumbs, or any *chometz* we miss, null and void, as if they don't exist. We can close off and sell whole dressers, closets, even rooms, for those eight days—and buy them back after Passover. So regular people can observe Passover with a concerted, somewhat strenuous—but doable—amount of effort.

As a seasoned Passover cleaner, years later, I now have my set routine.

A: I procrastinate as long as possible.

B: I indulge in mentally groaning about what a waste of time this cleaning is, and how I have more momentous and earth-saving things to do. How can I be expected to spend my precious time vacuuming the back corners of a closet, when I would otherwise be saving kids in Darfur? Or discovering the cure for cancer?

I'd possibly, okay, probably be sitting on my duff surfing the web if I wasn't cleaning, but these grandiose images of picketing, protesting, and doing something *big* arise as soon as I pick up the dust rag.

(True confession: A nasty little thought surfaces as I unearth areas neglected during the other eleven months of the year—the piles thrown onto top shelves and out-of-the-way drawers. "Is this cleaning *really* a spiritual task, or a sly trick of those rabbis to get me to finally roll up my sleeves?")

C: As the days march on and the holiday gets a little too close to continue with Steps A and B, I finally get off the arrogant "I'm too good for this" ego train. I push myself to switch gears and finally focus on growth beyond the comfortable—and on getting out my vacuum cleaner and finding the attachments.

Side benefit: This Pesach practice also helps me own my life, and to take stock of and responsibility for those nefarious, multiplying possessions. Spiritual life here on earth means knowing where you're at: your thoughts, your words, even your stuff.

Back then, however, that first full-blown Pesach, we were psyched and primed, game for action. Back in our little bachelorette apartment, we were poised to begin this amazing service. No Cheerio-dropping toddlers or pets could be found. How much cleaning did our humble dwelling really need? A few hours of work, maybe.

But we were eliminating ego, evil, separation! Our zeal went way beyond mere crumbs.

Even though I was usually allergic to all things cleaning, I spent a month of afternoons earnestly and almost microscopically searching for new places to scrub in our tiny pad. I perched on a folding chair in the narrow back hall, way back by the furnace, and reached up to wash each pipe that transported water and heat up into the house.

No food, no crumbs, nothing was to be found on those pipes—except a spongy layer of thick, gray dust. My roommates promised they hadn't squeezed into the furnace room after breakfast, detouring on their three-foot journey from the table to the sink to throw their cereal remnants onto the pipes. But *just in case* some evil or ego might be lurking up there, or hiding in a crevice of my soul, I methodically scrubbed every inch.

Our landlady had finished cleaning her whole two-story house, including the kitchen, and was cooking for the seder. She heard us up late, carrying on at 3:30 a.m.

"What on earth are you doing down there already?" she asked, incredulous. "It's a tiny apartment. You don't even have to clean the stove, the main repository of *chometz*; you're eating the holiday meals with families and aren't even going to use it during the holiday."

"We're cleaning for *Pesach*!" we proudly complained, wiping our brows with the hearty sighs groans and *oy veys* that we felt our intensive efforts deserved.

She rolled her eyes.

By the next *Pesach,* things only got worse.

I was a newlywed, getting the perfect Jewish home going. My Other Half balanced and tempered me in many ways, but he followed my lead in frenzied Pesach fanaticism. After all, before our marriage he'd been living in a rabbinical students' dorm, where others ran the kitchen, but after my pipe-cleaning adventure I assured him I was *experienced.*

As we cleaned the small, but full-service, kitchen in our cozy apartment, I obsessed. All the spatters and splotches from our gourmet Shabbos preparations haunted me. We scrubbed the counters and walls.

"Yankel, cake batter flies off beaters and onto these walls." I paced the floor. "And over there by the garbage can, food sometimes splashes on floor."

Normal procedure was to scrub surfaces that came in regular contact with food. A once-over with cleaning solution was enough to make any remnants inedible— and if it's not edible, then it's not *chometz*. Next step, cover the areas that are directly used for food preparation—with foil, thin sheets of wood, linoleum, or some other lining. Counters—and maybe a few inches of back-splash, too. The actual food prep surfaces. *Not* the walls, floors, ceiling, and cabinet fronts. But that wasn't enough for me! I told Yankel that we couldn't take any chances.

As we chugged through rolls of foil, he considered buying stock in the Reynolds Aluminum Foil Company. He came home one day close to the holiday to find his *aishes chayil* (woman of valor) covering the walls with foil and plastic sheeting. By the time I finished dreaming up possible places where remaining shadows and faint stains from *chometz* might somehow jump off the thoroughly scrubbed surfaces and into our bowls and food, our humble kitchen looked like a psychedelic spaceship. Yankel tried to temper my zeal, but didn't want to upset our newlywed harmony. After all, I was the *akeres habayis*, the foundation of the home. And the tradition did say that even a *"mah'shehu"*—even the tiniest amount of *chometz*—had to go. I just didn't know how far to take it. I listened to the explanations, then came home and did a little more, *just in case.*

This was uncharted territory. We hadn't grown up watching our parents do it—seeing them draw the line and say, "It's clean. It's covered. Enough." We pulled many late-nighters, getting a bit slaphappy, energetically scrubbing, then assiduously covering any remotely possible allusions or suggestions of the said *chometz.*

Yankel tried to support his valiant wife, even if he privately wondered why his friends' kitchens didn't look quite the same. He took his cue from our forefather, Avraham, who was told by God, "All that Sarah says, listen to her voice," and he kindly, respectful-ly, shrugged and smiled.

Our guest for the second seder was Yankel's brother Ken. Ever the amazingly polite good sport, he listened quietly as we took him on a guided tour of Pesach on Spaceship Mars. Ken didn't comment, but I imagine he must have been thinking, "Great religion you got here guys!?" All we needed was that little Martian from the Glad plastic-wrap commercial to jump out and chant, "Man from Glad, Man from Glad."

At least I didn't come up with a way to deep-clean the air, which might have had remnants of flour dust floating in it. Hmmm... there's always next year!

Perhaps we tended to take it all a *tad* too seriously, as many gently smiling rabbis tried to intimate when answering our earnest and convoluted questions.

"Its okay, that's good enough," they'd say.

"How could that be?" we'd argue back, and try to prove all the reasons that their suggestions weren't good enough and they weren't being strict enough, pure enough, in their answers. We didn't want any shortcuts, loopholes, or dumbing down. We wanted the complete, pure essence.

It took quite a few years till we could accept their wisdom and "*Chai bahem*"—learn to *live* with the *mitzvos*, instead of making ourselves and everyone around us a little crazy with our overdrive.

After escaping pogroms, smuggling through borders, waiting anxiously in Bucharest for the right papers to arrive, weeks of travel by ship, getting clearance on Ellis Island—young Bubby finally set foot in New York. Her suave, Americanized sister's beau greeted her, and handed her a banana, the first she'd ever seen. What do you do with such a fruit? The new immigrant started eating it, peel and all. The young man grabbed it and peeled it for her, with a cutting and disparaging, "Here, greenhorn, you ignorant one, this is how you eat a banana."

We, too, made it to these shores by the skin of our teeth. We grappled to acquire the skills to at least read the basic texts, but the nuances, the absorption by osmosis, the between-the-lines, this- is-just-how-everyone-does-it naturalness—we lacked.

The daily routine of *davening* (praying) never got firmly implanted in me. And I can't swim through the texts with ease. I'm mystified at the natural firmness these women employ to run their homes and discipline their children. I am still a greenhorn in many ways.

When the kids were little and the chaos would pile up extra high, I'd sometimes crack. I'd crawl up to my room, lock my door, sprawl on my bed, and start bawling, with a brew of self-pity and self-directed scorn because I couldn't get it together like everyone else seemed to. Yankel earnestly helped manage our flock and our domestic duties, but along with steering our rollicking ship he had his hands full with the demands of full-time teaching.

"Look, God, I'm doing the best I can, and it's not working. I wasn't raised this way. I never saw my mom churn out the equivalent of a Thanksgiving meal every Friday night and Saturday lunch, no nights off at a restaurant or bringing home take-out, never enough money or energy to deal optimally with all these kids—laundry, food, homework, and appointments. I grew up with quiet, order, my own space, and cleaning help trailing after me several times a week. I chose this. I want this, I believe in it, and usually love it, but... dealing with the nuts and bolts and one hundred toenails and fingernails and thousands of socks and shoes and Lego and other sundry pieces under my guardianship is quite, freakin', daunting!"

(Had I accepted the Rebbe's practical and insistent urging that women hire lots of help, things would have run much less ragged. But I always told myself that the kids would undo the newfound order in five seconds, we couldn't afford it, I'd rather spend the funds on more permanent home improvements, and so on. Smarter than the Rebbe I wasn't.)

Hmmm, come to think of it, I wiggled out of other guidance from the Rebbe that would have lent more calm and order as well. He urged all the Chassidim to find a *mashpia*—a personal mentor—and check in with that person regularly, asking for feedback and advice. I did call Bella and others occasionally, but ego, shyness, and embarrassment kept me from fully mining this treasure-trove of support. Excuses galore: I can't find just the right person. This one doesn't know about life outside of New York. That one's too religious. That other one's not religious enough. She's way too busy. And who could really understand me? Etc.

I gotta say, my grown kids who fully engage in this opportunity and have an active *mashpia* relationship—which really amounts to their own personal coach—are much more even-keeled. I careened through a challenging life unhealthily stuck in a stubborn, habitual, "I can do it myself, I'll just put down my head and bulldoze through" independence.

Life on the fringe: a perspective that never totally left us. Growing up, underneath the pleasant, capable exterior of a good girl from a nice family, I was nagged with a subtle feeling that I didn't quite fit in. I couldn't party and mingle with ease. I was compelled to try to figure out life on this planet from an early age, not able to just take it naturally, live it and enjoy. I'd rummage through the biography section of the Huntington Woods Library, carting thick books home, poring through other people's lives, trying to figure out how others figured it out.

As a hippie, growing increasingly estranged from an overly materialistic society, I felt an affinity with the souls hanging on the edge in Ann Arbor, and struck up friendships with mimes, street clowns, and Shakey Jake, an old-time jazz musician character. The day I gave him a ride to Detroit was incongruous, seeing this wizened charmer sitting seat-belted in Dad's orderly Chevrolet sedan.

And in the observant world, Yankel and I still tended to gravitate to those on the margins. When we lived in Crown Heights, we sometimes invited the scruffy, bag-lady *tzedaka* collectors over and brought them food.

But the edge was cushioned in this more integrated and connected society. While the Chabad world had its fast-paced side, with polished business people and dynamic educators, it retained a personal, homey touch. There were extremely empathetic givers, filling the gaps, holding up the wobbly, discreetly providing food and money to struggling families and support to new mothers, impoverished brides and grooms, and others in need.

Like all infatuated honeymooners, we eventually came down to reality with a thud. There were plenty of amazing things about this Chassidic society, and plenty of raw edges, imbalances, and major problems, too. To starry-eyed dreamers like us it was incredibly disheartening to encounter some of those same egos, excuses, and power-hungry grabbers that had populated the "old country" of our pre-Chassidic lives.

One summer I was feeling down and discouraged. Feuds and petty politics were rife; rot seemed to be eating at our community. Hamas terrorists had captured three soldiers and were bombing northern Israel, that precious strip of land I felt increasingly and viscerally connected to—a connection surprising in its stark intensity, at least to my logical mind. Iran saber-rattled and the world yawned.

My usual concern for the travails of that little land was ratcheted up. This time it was intensely personal. Two of our kids were there.

Chaim had just finished a trying two years serving in the army as a foreign volunteer soldier. His Israel experience started abruptly, when he was called to respond to a blown-up café during a summer jaunt volunteering for Magen Dovid Adom, the Israeli version of the Red Cross. My kid had been through a lot. But the beauty and grit, the pull of our land, won out over fear; he was making *aliyah*—becoming a citizen in the midst of this new war.

Devora Leah was there, too. She had just finished a year of study in Jerusalem, and was invited back to work as a dorm counselor. They were out of the range of the missiles, so far.

Emotional exhaustion and a creeping cynicism pulled at me. I was tempted to—at least internally —throw in the cards and go back to default mode, the rational and realistic mode of thinking I grew up with. I was angry and discouraged.

Belief? For fools.

Negative thoughts festered. One afternoon, I was out alone in the car, on a ninety-minute ride to a pickup at the Indianapolis airport. As I drove down the quiet highway, I tossed a CD into the player. I liked the country-blues-rock-n'-roll-funk combo of Yood, a band of three dynamic, young BT guys I had recently interviewed. Maybe some music would lift my spirits. At least pass the time and dull the ache in my heart, the churning in my stomach.

The familiar twang of the lead singer's guitar started, as song #4, usually my favorite, got going. Ha. Ironic. The refrain and the title were two words: "I believe."

Should I fast forward? I wasn't sure I wanted to stop sulking and listen to that drivel. Why do they say believing is an opiate? It's hard work. I wanted to give up and be safely and comfortably cynical.

As I sped past the budding corn fields, I envisioned the community leaders I was so disappointed in. I had expected more from them, a higher level of integrity as they worked out their differences. Their failings tore a hole in my heart; disillusionment festered in my soul. And I envisioned that tiny, exquisite, battered and beleaguered land, friends and family running frantically into sweltering bomb shelters.

I thought of Sherwin—Rabbi Wine—who had just died in a car crash in Morocco. He was no dummy. Didn't believe, so he wasn't deflated with what a cold universe dealt him, even a violent end, far from home. "What did you expect from your irrational attempt to put together a puzzle that has no solution?" I imagined him chastising me with a knowing smile. "Welcome back from your cloud, naive child. Welcome to the real world."

But I wasn't ready to turn my back on those sweet treasures, even though they seemed awfully fragile. I wasn't ready to throw in the towel and swing all the way back to Sherwin, at least not yet. I ached for him: his sudden death, his spiritual paucity.

The song kept playing. In spite of myself, I listened. I hummed. It had a message for me. More than that, it massaged my being. The slowly building country song, its straightforward refrain "And I believe..." sung with simple sincerity, poked a tiny hole through my cloud.

I rolled down the window and started belting along at the top of my lungs as I cruised down the highway. "And I believe in the power of a song... And I believe, there's hope within humility..." I sang through the tears and the pain, working to excavate the tiny crystal of hope still there.

Okay, girl. Hang in there. Songs, words, and ideas *are* powerful. Humility too, even if it's not out there in abundance.

It's not naive. It's good and whole and human and right to stand up, feet on the ground—stand up straight and affirm, "And I believe."

Eventually, Yankel and I came to accept that we were all quite human, all works in progress, individually and collectively. As the famed lover and defender of the Jewish people, Reb Levi Yitzchak of Berditchev, would argue: "God, You've put Your great wisdom in the books and all the temptations and character flaws on the street and in the people. What kind of a chance do You think those struggling folks have? How about putting Your wisdom and holiness out there in the open and tucking the temptations away in the bookshelves?"

We eventually slowed down, sobered up and became more realistic and tempered, in for the long haul. And a long haul it was gonna be, to take all those lofty ideas and grasp onto them tightly; not let them slip away as too airy-fairy, but slowly pull them down to permeate, transform, and reveal that inherent potential in our magnificent globe.

We couldn't just flood ourselves, our kids, or our society— much less that big world out there— with the light. Couldn't turn the hose on high, pour it on, and swim happily and harmoniously away. More like a slow and persistent IV drip, we'd have to keep on trying to saturate and integrate, keeping the drops of light, goodness, and inspiration trickling, building step by step. Once in a while there were joyful skips and leaps, moments of blazing inspiration, but it was usually two steps forward and one back, or teeny-tiny baby steps. But forward we trucked, forward we trudged.

25

—⚜—

NESHAMALA, NESHAMALA— SWEET, PRECIOUS SOULS

I n the early days of heady excitement, burgeoning spiritual awareness was stretching and transforming the contours of my known world, poking holes in its staid surface. I relished the revolutionary notion that people were more than separate entities, more than their distinct and sometimes difficult personalities. I longed for physical connectedness: more interdependence than each family making their money, buying their domain, and sequestering themselves off behind their closed garage door in their private oasis.

Learning to look at others with "*neshama* glasses," trying to focus on their shining soul—made it easier to forge connections, even with folks who superficially were "just not my type." While I might not always *like* them that much, seeing their soul first made it easier to look beyond differences. They might be too square or domineering for my floaty persona. If I could scratch beneath the surface—like that scratch-off-the-black-crayon-and-find-the-colors- underneath art project that kids love—their *neshama* (soul) was there, in full panoramic color, pretty darn beautiful.

Take Uncle Irv. As a child, I giggled at his biting humor and know-it-all grin but nervously stayed out of the direct line of his sharp jabs. Later I matured enough to realize that under the cavalier bravado hid a caring and sensitive man. Under his tough veneer, a glimpse of a soft, vulnerable *neshama* beckoned. Superficially, we were worlds apart, but from time to time we connected in a quiet and personal way.

In 1992, about ten years after my wedding, Uncle Irv began his battle with cancer. Dad kept me posted as the disease progressed. Finally, the news came. Irv was rapidly weakening, and in the ICU. Even though our relationship was pretty undeveloped, I wanted to be with him. Irv was in a Center City Detroit hospital, while I was in Boston, ensconced in the daily drama of five little ones, with no extra cash flow to boot. But Yankel and I were nothing if not impulsive, ready to jump into an illogical but heartfelt urge.

So, with Yankel's encouragement, I quickly charged the last-minute ticket, packed up baby Yeshaya, made hasty arrangements for the kids, and flew to Detroit.

Top secrecy was employed, as my pragmatic dad would have probably disagreed with the importance and economic sense of this trip and tried to dissuade us from coming.

Rented a compact red car, and tried to guess/maneuver/ remember my way to the hospital. Weaving through vacant lots and burnt-out neighborhoods with tough-looking guys aimlessly wandering was a bit scary for a sweet little mom with kid strapped in the car seat of the buffed, shiny rental car. We finally made it to the hospital complex. I parked, popped Yish in the stroller, and found our way in.

We appeared on the hall, like an apparition. Found the family holed up in a small waiting room littered with crumbled cups and empty potato-chip bags. Bleary-eyed and restless, they were worrying and kibbitzing to break up the monotonous tension.

"Miriam!" Aunt Ruth cried. "I can't believe you're here! It's a sign, a good luck sign!" At that point, any omen was grabbed on to as a good one.

I couldn't wave a magic wand or utter a kabbalistic formula to turn back the cancer's destructive course, but my redheaded toddler and I were glad to bring any bit of fresh air and diversion.

I sat with Irv, sharing what I could from my world, and sang the *Shema* prayer. My robust, ever-wisecracking uncle was weak and thin and could barely talk. No sarcastic jabs. Love and connection filled those few timeless seconds.

Irv had shown subtle signs of respect for my trip over the last few years. A respect that meant a lot to me, because he wasn't being polite. He was all about bravado and a cutting edge; he didn't care about being politically correct or nicey just to be nice.

He had reached out to me several years before, when Zaidy died. The whole family had gathered at Mom and Dad's house for several evenings of *shiva*—mourning and condolences. Family members were sharing readings and thoughts. I had pulled some ruminations together, eager for the chance to try to poke a few holes through that invisible barrier—the wariness that my new religiosity seemed to trigger. But Irv had already hightailed to a side room when he saw a rabbi arrive to lead the memorial service.

My new way of life was especially hard for my precious Bubby. I could no longer eat her food packages—chock full of love, but not kosher—a sad new reality I don't think she ever made peace with. She'd still offer her cookies, and shrug and try to smile when I apologetically declined.

Though my family sensed a chasm, I felt much closer to them than I had in years. I had come to see Bubby and Zaidy's passion for Jewish life in a new light, no longer writing it off as insular nonsense. I thought about Zaidy, the tireless communal shaker and doer—the speeches, the endless committees, the hustle and jostling for *kavod* (honor), positions, and funds. If he'd put all that effort into building up his business, the Ambassador Hand Laundry, he could have become a magnate. But he poured his *kishkas* (guts and passion) into the Jewish community, for nary a dime, but plenty of frustration.

I was starting to wise up to the joys and troubles of taking on communal woes. I'd moved beyond my starry-eyed days as an idealistic innocent. Back in college, when I first met the Goldsteins, I had dreamily romanticized them and the Chabad Chassidic community. *When I get to New York it will be a whole united group of people, delving deeper into Torah, transcending their egos, serving God together...*

Ha. Ha. Ha. Two Jews, three opinions—the saying goes.

One of my first rude awakenings came after I'd been studying in New York for a year. I was asked to help run a girls' summer camp. One of my principals, Mrs. Green, smiled knowingly. "It will be a good experience for you to see more of what really goes on." What could she mean?

Camp revealed some less-rosy parts of this world. I was confused. Why were some girls so cliquish and mean, and some counselors so blasé about all the rituals I was breaking my head to master? They seemed to think I was an over-earnest goody two-shoes. Later, working in Jewish education and in the community, it wasn't long before politics and turf battles arose.

I sadly fell back down to earth, and realized that these Chassidim were three-dimensional human beings too—fallible, real people with egos and warts along with their beautiful hearts and souls. The Jewish communal life I was becoming a part of was not all that different than Zaidy's world.

My stalwart Zaidy was right in there, part of a long tradition of community service, stretching back to our forefather Avraham, the first Jew, who busied himself with communal needs.

I tried to weave these ideas together in a word of Torah to share with the family at Zaidy's *shiva*. But Irv wasn't there; he was holed up, watching a football game till the rabbis were gone. When he finally shut off the TV and rejoined the group, he realized he'd missed me speaking. He turned to me with real sincerity and disappointment and said, "I would have come out if I knew you were talking, not just them."

And it wasn't just because I was his cute little niece doing a tap dance or reciting a poem. He seemed to want to understand more of the puzzle of who on earth I had become and what I was thinking. He seemed to want to hear something authentic, not prefab words for a *shiva* by rabbis who did it because it was their job.

And so, our few interactions here and there struck deep, creating a bond I wanted to honor now, in the ICU, even though he could barely respond.

It was more than me being one of his three nieces, more than him being one of my two uncles. I wanted to be there because of who Irv was and because of our unique relationship, our scant but meaningful connection over what might appear to be a cavernous gap of world views—the Marxist and the *chassid*—such a wide gap that it made, paradoxically, an extra closeness.

26

ARE ALL THOSE KIDS YOURS?

My tribe. My baseball team. My family?

Back in Huntington Woods where I grew up, among the proper families of two or three children, there was one Catholic family halfway down the block who had five or six children— kids poppin' all over the place. It seemed a little primitive, unruly. They all squeezed onto a bench around the kitchen table at dinnertime since enough chairs wouldn't have fit, waited obediently for their father, and bowed their heads to say grace before digging into their meal. The discipline, the order, and the kid farm they had struck me as quaint.

Yet, here I am, some forty or so years later, a veritable matriarch in Israel, my husband and I blessed with a caboodle of progeny. Thank God. *How God?* How and when exactly did this forest of vigorous saplings happen, we ask in wonder, when we're fortunate enough to have them all gathered around the table – or tables– our old battered dining room table plus a folding table or two.

"How many children do you have?" the nice lady asks, making pleasant small talk in the waiting room. As grateful as I am to have them, as humbly proud of these fun and good, really good, young people, I still hesitate when asked that common question. Sometimes you want to let an anonymous conversation wash over you, contribute your two or three words, and move on quietly; you don't feel like making waves.

"Do you really want to know?" I respond.

She looks confused; she was just being polite. She wasn't asking anything that risqué, like my age or my weight, for goodness' sake. What could the big issue be?

"Ahh, sure..." she says, raising her eyebrows.

Here goes. "I have ten children, thank God."

Her jaw drops. "What? Are they all yours? With one father? From one marriage?" She calls her friend over to examine the exotic creature. "Sue, come here. You wanna hear something? This lady has ten children!"

They flock around. Sue looks like she'd like to feel my forehead, to make sure I'm not feverish or hallucinating. They eyeball me. "But you look great, you don't look that old." (Or broken down or decrepit, their expressions imply.)

Medical professionals do not usually react favorably to this interesting disclosure; many barely conceal their scorn. A doctor once asked in a kindly voice if I knew the facts of life. And that was relatively early on in this venture, when I was expecting Yeshaya, child number five. I was tempted to reassure him: "Of course, Doctor. The stork comes every two years or so with a special delivery. I know what I'm having by the color of the blanket that the baby is wrapped in—pink or blue."

So, if we *do* know the facts of life, we don't have a Swiss bank account or an oil well in our yard, and we have the same amount of energy and hours in the day as everyone else—why do we assiduously, religiously, and thoroughly do our part to "Be fruitful and multiply"?

Why is one question. *How* is the more mysterious one. I'll answer that one first. I honestly have no idea. When I think over the hard data—the months pregnant or nursing, the sheer number of diapers, meals, spills, and shoes, the nights of interrupted sleep—it doesn't quite compute.

Raising a large family had a marathon quality to it. My experiences hiking up mountains, portaging canoes, and swimming miles came in handy—good training for all this. Back in the day, as a sixteen-year-old camper, I was deep in the wilderness of at Isle Royale National Park. Trudging haphazardly over a rocky path through thick woods, I precariously balanced a heavy aluminum canoe on my shoulders. *This is not fun,* I thought. Sweat poured down my face and back. The only way out was to hang on, keep going, stay focused on the goal. Finally, stumbling to the end that seemed like it would never come, we threw down our backpacks, lay on the beach, and basked in a rush of exhilaration and accomplishment.

Growing my tribe—like building anything enduring—was honestly not that hunky-dory-comfortable at many moments. Snapshot: two kids fighting, one crying, and another needing my attention *right now!* But hold on, next frame: Yankel shepherding his flock on another one of his fresh-air-and-exercise campaigns, rosy-cheeked kids rollicking, throwing leaves, and playing football in the yard, laughing so hard they could barely play.

Chassidic homesteading was a dichotomy, a paradox. Filled with extreme work, *mil'matah l'maalah* – from below to above, as the expression goes. From down here, feet on the ground, we toiled, prepared, tried to build secure fences; yet they had to be transparent – to allow for that opening from above. There was a divine blessing that kissed our efforts and took them on wings, further than we could ever reach on our own.

In some ways it wasn't such a stretch. After all, I was an American: a hardy builder and conqueror of new frontiers. Challenges? Bring 'em on! But I was also an American: indoctrinated by glossy ads to want easy and smooth pleasure, now. As a disorganized mom of a multitude, my house never looked like the ones in *Better Homes and Gardens,* no matter how many hints from Heloise I read.

"Okay, I've got a plan. If I just place a cute wicker basket with a color-coordinated ribbon in the entry of each room, to collect all the clutter, then organized harmony will follow."

Uh huh. Dream on. I knew it was ridiculous to compare my bustling laboratory of life to Madison Avenue images of gleaming floors and designer decor, representing values I'd rejected long ago. But those images haunted me, adding to the subliminal chatter that tried to subvert me, murmuring, sometimes scolding, and then yelling, "This is a disgrace! What would _____ [fill in the blank, whoever's judgment would bother me most: Mom, my neighbor, my second- grade teacher, or some organized, calmly smiling diva] think if they saw this mess?" I'd try to catch myself and smother the smoldering fire: "Don't browbeat yourself or explode. C'mon, breathe. Focus. Look at the big picture."

The big picture was packed: abundant yumminess, the kind that keeps parents going and generations happening. Oodles of first words, first steps, and shmushy kisses. Feathery-soft, baby-fat-padded cheeks, rapidly growing bodies to squeeze and hold, soft waves and ringlets to stroke, exquisite faces to adore.

I gravitated to Yiddish and Yiddish-sounding spin-offs to express the deliciousness of these little folk: "Come here bubbala, shpoodle-doodle, zieskeit, yingle-bingle, Rochkele, Chaimke, Layli-bayli." My kids didn't like it too much when I'd disregard their embarrassment and use these shmaltz-laden endearments in public. "My mom just calls us these weird names," they'd explain, shrugging, to their friends' questioning glances.

All right, cuteness and all, I admit it—ten kids does sound overwhelming. To me, too. Whenever I'd hear about families a little larger than mine, at any given stage, it seemed completely daunting. No matter the number we were up to, I'd be madly in love with the children I had, worried about being able to attend to their needs without losing my tenuous sense of self in the process.

With each pregnancy, I'd panic and think, *But I have a good balance now. I'm finding my stride, getting it together. How will I possibly manage another?* I'd fret and worry, fearful of letting go, of letting a bigger plan sweep through me. It was hard to relinquish my feeble attempts to be in control. I'd be jealous for the current youngest, hesitant to disrupt our bond—that singular, gaze-in-my-eyes, I'm-your-baby bond. *How can Esti not be my baby anymore? I know it will never be quite the same.*

I was often ambivalent—anticipating the intense joy, but also the struggle, of the first few postpartum months, which were like groggily swimming underwater. So tired. So hazy. I wrestled to find that place of acceptance, of openness to a blessing so vast it came with a proportionate challenge to my sense of security and equilibrium. Underneath all that, I heard the quiet inner voice of excitement and trust—it would be okay, it would be good. Blessings were on the way.

Yankel learned to hear me out and give gently positive support, without crossing the line into nauseating, Pollyanna positive that I would instantly reject with tears or sarcasm.

"I can't get anything done," I whined as I lay on the couch vegging.

"Don't worry, you're doing the most important thing ever by just lying there," he patiently repeated.

I eventually learned to not take my panic too seriously, getting to know my mental and emotional shtick. Today's matinee: *Fear #234, Panic Attack #75*, now playing.

Once labor accelerated, and that new one born, we felt we'd been waiting for him or her forever. How did we ever feel complete without this squirt? They were *our* kids, not a number, on a kiddie assembly line. Not random faces. Chaya and Chaim, Devora and Mushky, Yeshaya and Mendy, Esti and Motti, and Fayga and Chana—each a totally indispensable part of our lives.

What does it *feel* like to bear ten kids? I'm in the flow of life— a deep womb, primeval space of woman-power. I'm walking my faith, I'm living my faith, my body is my faith and my temple. I'm living and breathing and eating to build a kicking and expanding and breathing and pulsing nation, *mamleches kohanim v'goy kadosh*—a nation of priests and a holy people—transmitting and building as I lie on the couch and doze, hands on my pregnant, kicking, living, expanding, stretch-marks-of-love belly.

I am connected.

I am vulnerable.

I am strong and eternal. Down here on earth, raising these kids, movers of the heavens.

I often wrapped my mind around the Chassidic concept of "expanding the vessel." I didn't wake up one fine day with ten kids. Like most moms, I struggled mightily to manage the overwhelming adjustment of that incredible first—the searing beauty of a deeper bond than I ever imagined, as Chaya's blue eyes gazed into mine in the recovery room.

It was so hard to get used to being on constant call—to surrender so completely to this squiggly, beautiful, demanding being. "She's crying again," I moaned, bursting into tears. And I wanted to mother perfectly, in harmonious, organic, bonding bliss, not letting precious Chaya stress or fret. Especially after our traumatic first few days.

She was born in a busy Brooklyn hospital, run like a no-nonsense army platoon. "It's 12:00. Feeding time. Nursing mothers, prepare yourselves," a drill-sergeant nurse boomed over the loudspeaker. They rolled in the babies, and then whisked them back to the nursery a crisp half-hour later. What about bonding, nursing on demand, cuddling and cooing? My perfect child would be scarred for life, I fretted, sure I'd be kicked out of the Earth Momma Society. I wobbled and teetered down the hall after the heartless nurse who was wheeling away my darling—tears, milk, and hormones flowing, pleading and demanding, to no avail.

After the first few weeks, we settled into enjoying Princess Chaya. Months later, the urge to have another melded with the *mitzvah* mission to "bring another soul down" and we excitedly welcomed number two, delightful redheaded Chaim, born some eighteen months later.

Three? Beautiful Devora Leah was a delicate sweetheart. Our ability to keep several plates spinning got more sophisticated— Yankel and I couldn't each hold one child and have everyone accounted for. I couldn't hold three on my lap at once. Slowly, one by one (except for our twins), our capacity—our vessel— expanded, with our ability to juggle, to manage, to nurture.

Our garage and attic were like a battered Toys R Us: baby swings, high chairs, walkers, car seats, different- sized bikes and skates were in the gear aisle, while plastic bins of clothes were stacked in another aisle, organized by size and gender. I climbed the wobbly attic pull-down stairs every few months to bring up the outgrown clothes and forage for the new size.

We also acquired the hard-earned experience to (usually) weather each developmental stage with greater equanimity and perspective as time went on. The Terrible Twos didn't seem so formidable when older sibs were becoming Terrible Teens. Com- pared to adolescent intensity and high drama, a few temper tantrums over the wrong size pretzel or a lost pacifier were a cute respite.

As the kids grew, the normal, wearying, sometimes intense sibling rivalry morphed into a wondrous bonding. Now they call and coach each other, share jokes. Yet I'd worry. They didn't choose to be one of a *minyan* (quorum of ten). I'd think of the well- rounded palette of lessons I had as a child: dance, piano, violin, skiing, tennis, art. I had my own room. Were we shortchanging our kids? Would they get *enough?* Individual attention? Chances to develop their unique talents? Space?

A true middle child, Mendy (now nineteen)—positioned smack in the eye of the storm as child number six—was bewil- dered by this question. Mendy looked over my shoulder as I wrote this chapter and interjected, "What do you mean, Mom? Being in a large family is awesome."

And he meant it. These rugrats are there for each other with a fierce, unbreakable bond. They're gonna go out in the world with a team behind them. I sometimes talk about the vacuous emptiness I felt as a teen, like a free-floating atom adrift in empty space. The kids listen, nod, but don't really get it. They hopefully feel connected to a loving God and vibrant tradition and people, but on a most personal level, they're part of a tribe that's blood and soul and DNA and shared craziness.

Biblical babies, *B'nai Yisrael*—those wandering, troublesome, loyal, and challenging Children of Israel rise up off the pages

"Maaaa, where's my sock?" one of the tribe whines.

"She grabbed my doll!" another cries.

My biggest challenge was mental, that space between my ears. Those messages I mumbled to myself could leave me joyful and connected—or short-tempered and resentful. At times I was cruising, getting support from friends, teachers, books, and magazines, fortifying myself with positive imagery.

For ideals, for justification, one only had to look back a half century. Hitler's unspeakable decimation left the world bereft of a few million Jewish kids. We were busy creating living "Holocaust memorials," who we tried our darnedest to raise to be passionate, knowledgeable Jews and light-makers—people who'd add more to the world than they'd take.

While many might sympathize with our people's need to rebuild, they are concerned about the dent a large family makes on rapidly depleting natural resources. Chaya and her growing young family live in ecologically-minded Seattle, where anything above 1.2 children is almost an abomination, considered an intolerable drain on the ecosystem. When given questioning or dirty looks, Chaya and her husband have an apt reply ready: "Some people invest in bonds. We invest in lives."

I was in Seattle for whimsical Levi's *bris* (circumcision ceremony). I'd already hit Target for the gauze pads and antibiotic ointment. Shortly before the ceremony, we realized I'd forgotten an item, cloth diapers. So I ran to a nearby baby boutique, which had brown organic cotton diapers for an exorbitant price, for the cooperative baby who doesn't excrete too often, I guess. The cashier gushed, "Thank you for being so conscious." I bit my tongue and *didn't* say, "Sorry, I'm not a greenie today. These diapers are for child #4's 'primitive bloodletting ritual,' thank you very much, and he's going to be wearing disposables. His parents are also a natural resource, gotta keep them from depleting."

I knew about population explosion and cared deeply about our environment. But I looked first and foremost to the Torah and the Rebbe for guidance. The Rebbe, a Sorbonne-trained scientist, conveyed the Torah's wisdom with a full understanding of today's reality. The Rebbe also knew this past century's Jewish challenges most intimately. Reb Levi Yitzchok, the Rebbe's father, died in the Soviet Gulag, his life destroyed by Stalin, while the Rebbe's brother was killed in the Holocaust.

This illustrious luminary was emphatic—what these souls accomplished by coming down into bodies was crucial to our world's development; crucial for them individually, crucial for humanity. I leaned on the Rebbe's vision, (which reached a whole lot farther than mine—to the end of my nose on a clear day).

The numbers didn't really add up for me, either. But a higher plan was unfolding. I tried to suspend logic and trust forces that were greater than I could measure.

Listen, I'd tell the green critics in my head: my family drives used cars, has mostly "distressed" furniture, well-loved toys, and our share of vintage, a la previously enjoyed clothing, so our carbon footprint is relatively small. And I'm the recycling queen of our street. (Well, I was until Wendy Sue moved in a few doors down. She's dedicated enough to bring bags of empty soda bottles home from the synagogue, so I've had to relinquish my title to her.)

Other mental menaces would worm their way into my mind and chip at my commitment to enterprise Karp Kidz Inc. These noxious thoughts bothered me even more than the diapers we contributed to the landfills. Living outside of major communities of like-minded folks, the negative attitudes towards large families wore at me. I had to struggle not to see myself through society's negative stereotyping.

Barefoot, pregnant and in the kitchen—that's you, an inner voice would nag during the late months of pregnancy as I'd follow my burgeoning stomach around the house. *You're so much more than your womb and your milk, but that's what you've let yourself get reduced to. When are you gonna use those talents of yours? God gave you those, too, honey.*

"Oh, shut up," I said to my inner Miss Critical, who turned her nose up at my quaint, domestic (very domestic actually) homemaker (ugh) status. "I'm not Betty Crocker. I'm a Woman of Valor who girds my loins with strength and flexes my arms. Strength and dignity are my garb. What's more, I open my mouth with wisdom and the teaching of kindness is on my tongue." Thanks King Solomon, for penning such a great song about us women, hear us roar—fiery creators of Jewish destiny.

Chana stayed home from prophesying to nurse her son Eli. She was a traveling prophetess—like a Biblical rock star—yet she wanted to be with her kid. And that was before washing machines, Pampers, or frozen dinners to streamline her days. I, too, was trying to build a *mikdash m'at*—a small sanctuary of warmth and holiness (there's that word again), a solid platform of security. You try raising ten kids, Ms. Professor Alter Ego. Whoever I'd be, were I not a Chassidic Woman Central Pillar of the Home, few jobs would call on the strength and smarts I summoned up daily. Well, most days.

Hey, I was legit—a card-carrying working woman, teaching part-time during most of those busy baby-booming years, juggling with the best of the multi-taskers. I'd scribble lesson plans on shopping lists (and shopping lists on lesson plans), throw on some clean clothes and lipstick, greet the babysitter, and run out the door to enjoy a few hours of appearing to be a competent and poised professional. Other people's kids, i.e., my students, were usually more compliant and impressed with me than my own.

But this niggling chorus wore at me. It knew just when to rear its nasty head and dampen my enthusiasm, in particularly vulnerable moments, even sow despair.

Late afternoon was often a testy time. My blood sugar was low, my energy lagging, just like my tired and hungry kids. The debris of a busy day piling up. On better days, I pulled a Chabad women's magazine off the bookshelf, spent five minutes laughing at Harriet the Harried Housewife—a witty spoof that encapsulated the absurdities of a mom's life. Buoyed by the camaraderie, I sat down on the floor and listened with more attention to the details of the kids' days. We read a story about sharing. Mendy and Yishy went off to build a Lego menorah.

I decided no one would die from eating the "I don't feel like making dinner" special—once again—of noodles and cheese. The kids helped set the table and we sang as we sat down. Yankel came home and shared some Torah stories and jokes. He managed cleanup and bedtime while I went out to a class for some relaxation, socializing, and a bit of learning.

Other days were not so golden. When the 4:30 low hit, I stormed to my room, pushed the unfolded laundry onto the floor, closed the door with a not-so-gentle slam, collapsed on the bed and churned black thoughts about undone paintings, unwritten books, and the genteel and oh-so-hip-and-cultured life that I was most decidedly not living.

After sulking for a while, I came out and yelled at Yishy and Mendy—"Get those Legos off the floor! I'm tired of stepping on them!" Then snapped, "No, I don't know where your green sweater is. Take care of your own things!" I snarled when someone asked what's for dinner. Threw some bread and cheese in the dairy oven. Realized it wasn't going to be filling enough. Put up a pot of noodles. Same old, mac and cheese. Too bad.

Set it out and sat scowling. Yankel came home, tried to share some Torah stories and jokes with the kids, but it was hard to penetrate the black cloud I'd cast over the table. He managed cleanup and bedtime while I locked myself in the bathroom, read a vapid magazine, and fell into bed in a huff.

241

"Sorry, dearest sweeties," I murmured when I came out later, pushing back their curls, kissing their foreheads, and tucking the blankets tighter around my precious ones sleeping in innocent loveliness. I unearthed the green sweater, fold it carefully, and lay it at the foot of Esti's bed. *Tomorrow will be better. Thank you God for these gifts. Help me do better by them.*

Same basic story line. But my inner dialogue, my choice of frame and attitude, could lead to radically divergent outcomes. Sometimes, if I couldn't muster up the positive inspiration, I'd not-so-nobly take it from the bad. A negative times a negative equals a positive, right? That principle proved true in the math book of my mental games.

Someone else's *tzorus* (suffering), may God cure and help them, would push me to appreciate my challenging but manifold blessings.

When I was forty-two, we were gifted—out of nowhere, no family history—with twins. At five months, the midwife recommended a sonogram for this so-far routine pregnancy, since I was a bit "mature." I lay on the table, cold gunk on my abdomen, as the technician scanned. Suddenly, she announced, "Why, I think there are two in here." I drove home trembling, in a daze, and stumbled into the house.

"Yankel, sit down. I have to tell you something. It's... it's ... twins..."

He gazed blankly for a second. Then he broke out in a dizzy smile and laugh.

"*Kiflayim l'toshia* —double for salvation!" he exclaimed.

"But how will I manage?" I whined.

I made my way to the phone and called an old friend, Chana Gittel, who had twin daughters. I remembered her pregnancy, when she waddled around in tent-like garments, from the extra-extra-extra-large department.

"Chana Gittel, help! I'm expecting twins..." I cried.

"You're so lucky!" she said with intense excitement. "It was so special. I wish I would have twins again."

242

Really? I thought, dumbfounded. *She not only survived, she'd like to do it again?* I slowly started to calm down, wrap my mind around this, and realize, maybe we *could* do this.

When Chana and Fayga were infants, the miracle of "Wow, there are two!"—double chubby, delicious, copper-haired mush—usually kept me going, even when Yankel and I were beyond the beyond with exhaustion. Weary with fatigue, I'd crash, lying in bed, night after day after night—nursing one bubbala, and trying to summon the resolve to roll all the way over to nurse the other.

Then I remembered. Jews getting blown up in Israel, in cafés, on buses, as the Second Intifada roared. A close friend lived in Tekoa, where two sweet boys, barely past their Bar Mitzvahs, had been brutally butchered as they explored a cave in a wadi near their home. She shared the agonizing details. I sat at the computer reading her firsthand account of the frantic search, the funeral, and the *shiva* of the shattered families and community, in shocked tears.

Heartbreaking agony—but also a slap in my face. I was worn to the max from good stuff: healthy children. When they headed off to school in the morning, I didn't have to dig deep into my faith, wondering if they'd make it back in one piece, please God. I prayed for those Israelis under fire. And I humbly, gratefully accepted my piece of Jewish life, my "challenge."

Launching these lives went way beyond art-school creative, a transmission of something more essential and deeper, purer and better than I could put into words or brushstrokes. Each kid expressed different physical, emotional, and spiritual aspects of me, of Yankel, and of their own unique souls and signature selves—each with a smattering of freckles, blue eyes, and a wide-open smile.

Torah was about making a *dira b'tachtonim*—a dwelling place for God down here in this lowest, most physical world. A world where toothbrushes, lollipops, homework, Cheerios, and assorted paraphernalia were the building blocks of the modern-day sanctuary. (True, the acacia wood and hewn gold of the Torah's tabernacle sound much more romantic than size 10 purple Converses, three boxes of macaroni on sale this week for ninety-nine cents, and two bottles of shampoo.)

And the education these Chassidic kids got was *crazy*. I was driving thirteen-year old Motti to school one spring morning. We were engaged in a discussion about different aspects of physical vs. spiritual vs. emotional vs. intellectual realities. When I pulled up to the building, he smiled and waved, "Have a good day, Ma."

He ambled off, with a shy, confident, sweet, grown-up, young teenage smile. I remembered how proud I was at sixteen to be learning Philosophy with Sherwin. This kid was dancing jigs around the few straight-forward concepts we copied verbatim from Sherwin's dictation. He was already holding a map that's so rich and broad.

I'd been so excited by my major discovery: Spirituality is real. Three cheers for you, Ma. Duh. This little *pisher*, affectionate Yiddish term for wet-behind-the-ears young 'un, was doing figure eights and loop-di-loops around me He had a full array of precision tools, insights, concepts; a diamond cutter's fine saw, while I was still pounding a nail into the wall with my all-purpose Home Depot hammer.

I flashed to Bubby and Zaidy, ironing pants in the Just Rite Hand Laundry, laying the groundwork so their kids could go to Harvard. I struggled to stay afloat, believing and doing, keeping those Shabbos meals coming, so my kid could fly like an astrophysicist, in this pulsating quantum galaxy. And sometimes I managed to shuffle and dance a bit too, trying to listen to intense Torah CDs as I ran errands, with layers of jokes and references in Hebrew, Yiddish, and English, rich ideas pouring out of the player. I was growing at my suburban mom pace, maybe not quite at a rocket scientist's level, but at least a glider pilot's.

I'm creating with You, I'm diving deep into the void, a void deeper than that terrifying blank white canvas or empty computer screen. I'm diving deep into the primordial purple sparkly empty void, pregnant with possibility—pun intended. Let's sing, let's dance, let's create.

Dear God, Your kids are amazing, spawned from a people of thinkers, doers, fighters for light and justice. They're worth the pain and the worries. It's an honor to be able to do our part to let them sing their song down here.

(But next time You create a world, check with me first. I've got a few ideas to make it a bit easier for us Earthlings: like, lighten up on the pregnancy and labor thing, childrearing could go a bit smoother, too, and could You please send a little more cash along with each kid? And one more thing, my pet peeve: how about shoes that grow with the child, don't get worn out, and can't get lost, especially in the morning when the carpool is honking?)

We found ourselves on a different path to tranquil serenity than the one I had once sought in ashrams. In many cultures, the tragic hero stands alone. The ascetic sits on his mountaintop in perfect solitude.

We Jews teach and feed and nurture and shlep our *kinderlach*, our children. It's family. It's family. Around the Shabbos table the weekday dinner table they sit—the food, the kids, the books. We read, we debate, we question, we sing--our table is our altar, our home, our school, our bedrock—our survival that vanquishes empires and armies come and gone. Our haven from a hostile world.

Doe-eyed souls, old souls in new bodies, mommy's milk filled with ancient truths—they're older than their days. I look in their eyes and see the blown-up, gassed, orphaned, burned at the auto-da-fé, forcibly converted *kinderlach* of the sweet and gentle, strong and terrible, pure *ner tamid*, eternal burning light.

"It is a tree of life for those who take hold of it." We're grasping, we're hanging on tightly for dear life, dear God. We've floundered and wandered, been chased and buried alive in Babi Yar pits—but we're holding on tight to Your word, a sweet and good elixir.

PAINTING ZAIDY'S DREAM

My kids are carrying You. Already branded, by the *bris*—Your
covenant. They're scrappy survivors, caring doers—living,
breathing Jewish kids.

Alef beis gimmel dalet kids
Vov zayin ches tes kids
Boychicks running merrily, *yarmulkes* perched perilously
on their round heads,
tzitzis fringes hanging out from T-shirts, flying in the breeze
as they fiercely bike
Earnest voices singing *brochos*—those blessings
on their cookies and milk
Chubby dimpled hands giving *tzedaka*, coins clinking in the can
And kissing the *mezuzah* scroll, reaching up on tiptoes

Spin little dreidel, dance on into eternity,
spin that heavenly light down into my living room
spin off living room, spin to Poland, Morocco, to Jerusalem
spin spin spin where children sit
hunched over nuts over chocolate coins, spinning that top
as the candles burn down low

Kinder, mein zissen kinder murmurs the graying bread lady
at Mertz Bakery, stooping
to give a cookie—
My dear children, she sighs wistfully, at the sight of
innocent *Yiddishe kinder*
Jewish children that remind her of
a sweet one; she sighs for that little one who never
saw another butterfly
But *alef, beis, gimmel, dalet*—these little ones
still sing those letters, even now

Keep singing

27

—⤝⊶⊷⤛—

THE ROAD TO ANYWHERE

The wander lust of the hippie days wasn't totally drowned in chicken soup. We liked to venture out, even with our abundant brood. Family trips were a slice-of-life snapshot of the logistics and chaotic fun that defined our mega-family hippie-Chassidic mélange.

Every time we boldly, foolishly, attempted to embark on a family trip, a song from my idyllic summers at Camp Tamarack echoed through my mind. I'd relive the rousing voices, the banging on the lunchroom table, the exuberant youthful spirit.

We're on the road to anywhere, with never a heartache, with never a care.
We've got no home, hey, we've got no friends,
We're thankful for anything the good Lord sends [or: our mommy sends].
We're on the road to anywhere, each milestone seems to say, Ouch my toe!
The road to anywhere, the road to anywhere will lead to Tamarack someday.

Something about being on the road made life seem simple and carefree. No laundry piled up. Work details and deadlines were left behind. Which way, California or New York?

It was simple and carefree, that is, once we'd actually taken off. That moment of excited departure was the culmination of hours of ferocious packing, washing dishes, getting the house ready to lie fallow, and untying ourselves from the web of daily commitments. Who would take out our elderly neighbor's garbage? That bill will come due while we're gone; better get it paid. The myriad details and pieces involved in packing and transporting our family were daunting— enough to make me pine for the simple spontaneity of an earlier lifetime, when I'd sling on my backpack and head for the West Coast. Hitch a ride, blend into the vibes of the driver. Wherever they let you off, it's meant to be, man. Take it from there.

Packing. Oy. Feel the heart palpations at the mention of it. No more jeans and T-shirt thrown in a backpack. Now it was weekday clothes, sweaters, diapers, bottles, rain gear, kosher food for the trip—what if we get stranded in *Yehupitzville* (in other words, the middle of nowhere)? If our trip extended over the weekend, an extra level of packing was necessary: bringing Shabbos clothes.

Toys, books. Yankel didn't feel packed without toting along one or two milk crates of *seforim* (holy books).

So much paraphernalia, holy and secular. As the kids grew and started flying the coop, we scaled back down from a fifteen-passenger monster to a more modest minivan. We outgrew car seats and diapers. The kids could largely pack for themselves. Thank goodness, sighed this weary fifty- something.

But at our peak, we were a veritable traveling three-ring circus.

About ten years ago, the kids were home for Sukkos. Mid-holiday, I had an insatiable itch to take my family to Lake Michigan. Like, they-have-not-had-a-proper-childhood-unless-they've-been- there kind of itch. Like, it's only five or six hours away and we *must* go.

So, I trolled the internet late one night until I found a little off-season cabin in the southwest corner of the Michigan. Bright and early the next morning we started loading (actually overloading) the family van. We strapped in the car seats. During Sukkos, Yankel followed the custom to do all his eating and drinking in a sukkah, even simple snacks. So into the van went our portable sukkah, built of three plywood boards hinged together, and some evergreen branches. They would serve as the *schach*, the branches that make up the sukkah roof.

The kids were running in and out toting supplies. Chaim was the master space organizer, arranging everything just so. Grill. Charcoal. Frozen hot dogs, hamburgers, and chickens. There were few, actually zero, kosher butchers in St. Joseph, Michigan, and quick fixes at McDonalds wouldn't cut it. Sweaters. Bathing suits. At least we could do this whole trip in casual attire.

When we pulled in to a rest stop, we looked like one of those clowns-smashed-into-a-telephone- booth routines. Kids just kept piling out. And lots of pieces got rearranged as stray shoes and wrappers spilled out of the overflow.

What if Yankel was hungry or thirsty? No problem. Mendy and Yeshaya pulled out the sukkah, branches, and a folding chair at the rest stop and set it up on the grass. While we were there, bathroom- ing, stretching, and getting in some Frisbee-throwing, Yankel had to finish up his morning prayers. Clad in *tallis* (prayer shawl), *shuck- ling* (swaying in prayer)—he did his thing, as truck drivers and their peroxide-bleached wives threw a glance or two our way.

VW hippie vans and Ken Kesey's happening bus paled next to our generously dented, 1995 white Ford Econoline, fifteen- passenger, Jewish-life-on-wheels wonder with the rumbling truck motor so loud we had to shout to hear each other.

We finally got to the cabin, dumped down our bags with a cursory look around, and headed down to the beach. Those vacation days were filled with complex sandcastle villages com- plete with turrets and flags, long beach walks, campfires, wave jumping, burying siblings in sand, and dreamy sunsets. That Lake Michigan adventure proved every bit as magical as I'd hoped for— family bonding time with simple, natural fun, away from schedules and distractions.

In retrospect, it turned out to be a precious last time we were all together before family life got more complex. Soon after the trip, Chaim moved to Israel, and the big guys started getting married, which made getting everyone together much more difficult.

Amazingly enough, our crazy road shows did more than raise eyebrows; they often aroused dormant Jewish sparks. In some remote parking lot in Western Pennsylvania one October afternoon, Yankel and the kids heard a knock on their portable sukkah door. A debonair, antique- collector Holocaust survivor with a handlebar mustache was passing through from Minnesota. The last time he'd sat in a sukkah was during his childhood in Prague, in a different universe decades before. He surprised himself, he said, feeling freed by the openness of the road, and stepped out of his lay-low Jewish modus operandi and into our little holiday hut to make a *l'chaim.*

But the family outings to parks, museums, and little vacations here and there were kid stuff. The hardball, epic Karp family trips were the Cincinnati-to–New York "pilgrimages." We tried to go with the kids at least once a year, but it was a Shlep with a capital S. A twelve-hour-plus marathon of potato chips, Twizzlers, and dog-eared maps—which later evolved to Google Maps printouts, and, finally, that annoying lady barking directions out of our GPS. I dreaded that trip. Little free spirit there—more like a grueling ordeal on that wearying Pennsylvania Turnpike that never ended. "Are we *still* in Pennsylvania?" the kids would periodically whine.

We started each trip with strategically placed garbage bags and promised to keep order, but the van was inevitably a squished cracker-barrel of wrappers, crumbs, and rotting bananas by the time we piled out in front of 770, looking like bedraggled country bumpkins in the smooth, slick Big Apple.

One exclusive travel perk: we had our own Motel 6, where the lights were always on, the door open. Yankel's big sister, El, and

THE ROAD TO ANYWHERE

her jovial husband, Marv, were our New Jersey pit stop. They inherited the job from my dear in-laws, whose bemused, bewildered, toasty-warm embrace of our tribe included accommodating our crash landings in their retirement village. We piled in, took up most of the floor space, and spilled out into the normally quiet paths with our kiddie entourage.

Bubba and Zayda from New Jersey plied us with the best green beans, freshest corn, and juiciest melons they lovingly harvested from the Garden State's bountiful roadside stands. They sat with us at the round, Formica kitchen table, asking gentle questions about our lifestyle and where this ship was heading. What future did we have in mind for these beautiful and different grandchildren of theirs?

It was when Bubba and Zayda started to get infirm and then passed away in the '90s that we moved the show to El and Marv's. No trip east was complete without our flash mob descending on their hospitable home, usually in the middle of the night. They greeted the intrepid travelers with warm-hearted humor, carefully chosen kosher food, and a spread of sleeping bags and spare mattresses. (And after our whirlwind stay, they waved goodbye and returned to a quiet abode, ferreting out the stray socks and pieces we left behind, probably with a sigh of relief.)

28

SURPRISE IN HEBRON

Israel. A war-torn place of aggressive, hardened guys like that counselor Zev. Deserts and camels. *Kibbutzim* where kids were raised in the communal children's house. That's the image I'd acquired. Not for me. So, as a savvy seeker, I looked for enlightenment in other places: I climbed Mt. Shasta, traveled the West, and thought about maybe checking out India.

But now, my mind was bathed in continual references to that far-off land, suffused with evocative images like "land flowing with milk and honey." We faced east to pray, towards Jerusalem, prayers replete with requests to "rebuild Jerusalem, Your city, with mercy." King David exhorted, "Jerusalem, if I forget you let my right hand forget its skill."

Was it the power of suggestion, repetition, or indoctrination that changed things, making that land grab a prominent place in my thoughts and reverie—not just as Israel, but as *Eretz Hakodesh*, the Holy Land?

My teenage friend Julie used to daydream about living *la dolce vita* in some tropical paradise. She'd often walk around singing about "Hawaii" or "Guadalajara" with a rhythmic lilt in her voice, whenever suburban Detroit seemed too gray and flat. But somehow this place came to replace Hawaii, even Tahiti, taking dominance in my consciousness as the number one travel spot on my wish list.

I entered countless raffles that offered a ticket to Israel as the grand prize. I'd envision my trip as I filled out the entry form. How did the non-Zionist apathy of my youth morph into this passionate feeling of intense yearning and connection?

Seemed like a natural condition of a healthy Jewish soul—to dream about Zion. That *neshama* seemed to have a DNA, a certain structure, that resonated like the taut strings of a tuned violin—to *mitzvos, niggunim,* and words of psalms, and to that little dusty piece of land, wedged over there in a challenging neighborhood. Beyond politics, Beyond posturing. Just a soul thing.

Like a bottle of champagne that lay in the cellar collecting dust, cork tightly wedged in place, my tie to my homeland lay dormant, hidden, for many years. Once the cork was pried open by Jewish lore and living—pop!—the contents of the bottle fizzled up and couldn't be pushed back inside. A natural, deep bond. I pined to go there. I knew I'd been there, in some form, in some *gilgul* (incarnation). I'd wandered those winding streets, tread on those sun-baked stones. When trouble hit that beleaguered country, my heart was there, vulnerable, beating with anxiety.

"My heart is in the East, but I am in the uttermost West," penned the twelfth-century poet Judah Halevi, from his home in Spain. Yeah, I can relate. I'm American. I love this sweet land of liberty, its precious "We hold these truths to be self-evident, that all men are created equal" values. I know its history and geography. Can still rattle off the big fifty: capital of Maine is Augusta, capital of Idaho is Boise. I feel its pride and pain and sometimes tear up listening to "The Star Spangled Banner." When provoked, I've been known to belt out my own gutsy, off-tune rendition. But this Zion pull—it coexisted with the red-white-and-blue, but it was of a different magnitude.

I wanted to go there. I longed to go there. But lots of little kiddies and big expenses kept my dream of touching down on that soil in the realm of someday. Finally, the time just came, cash in hand or not.

In 2003, nineteen-year-old Chaim went for a summer jaunt as a volunteer paramedic, which grew into thinking seriously about joining the Israeli Defense Force as a foreign soldier. Our son was struggling to grow into his own person, stepping out of the *yeshiva* world, asking hard questions, trying to forge his own way (much like some graying lady and man he was related to did way back when they were his age). But he wanted our guidance and support. Yankel and I figured it was time to get out the credit card, and one of us would just go. He had work obligations, so I started to pack and plan.

Arriving at JFK on a flight from Ohio, I excitedly made my way toward the El Al terminal. Where was it? Passing multiple airlines with all kinds of exotic accents and peoples lined up, I turned a corner, and boom—El Al. Lots of buzzing people on their way to the homeland, man. Yacking and shmoozing and jostling and warmth. Yarmulka-clad travelers pushing toddlers in strollers—hordes of excited Jews milling around.

Going through the intense security, the agent asked me a spitfire array of seemingly innocuous questions, carefully noting my body language and expression as I answered. "Why are you going to Israel? Who are you visiting? Where do you work? What's the principal's name?" His penetrating gaze must have categorized me as a flustered, spaced-out, but honest, Jewish lady.

The snaking line of post-interrogation passengers boarded. Friendly chaos ensued, very different than the impersonal, polite quiet normally encountered on a plane. An older gentleman caught my bemused stare at the chattering people and happy pandemonium.

"First time, eh? A *balagan* (lively madhouse), isn't it?"

I laughed. He went on: "I travel for business. Last week I flew to Japan. The jumbo jet was full, yet everyone was quiet and reserved throughout the extremely long flight. This is different. It's one big family." And it was—real families, like his extended gang of a dozen or so offspring traveling for his grandson's Bar Mitzvah, or figurative family, bouncing around the plane sharing stories, contacts, and nosh, men forming *minyanim* (prayer quorums) wherever there was an open galley or corner.

We finally arrived, flying over sand, palm trees, and bustling Tel Aviv, coming in for a landing accompanied by cheers. Ben Gurion Airport seemed small, a bit worn. (It's since been extensively remodeled.) In fact, much of Israel sported a surprisingly small, tired, 1950s or '60s appearance, not the top level of glitz and gloss we Americans come to expect. But a quiet, deep charm and beauty unfurled that slowly seeped into my bones--- not Miss America glamorous, Grand Teton magnificent, bang bang wow wow knock your socks off beauty. Subtle.

Chaim met me at the airport and guided us to a *sherut*, a communal taxi-van, heading to Jerusalem. *Jerusalem!* Of gold. Of dreams. Its very name meant city of wholeness, of peace. As we drove on the highway—winding upward, climbing hills—my eyes stayed glued to the window. Pinch me. I'm here—with almost a déjà vu sensation. We found our way to a friend's sparse apartment and got our few bags unpacked, then headed out by foot for a half-hour evening stroll to the *Kotel,* the Western Wall—that landmark, that fulcrum, that central point I'd seen in so many photos and paintings.

The *Kotel* was... undersized. Plain. Not that mighty or magnificent. *That's it?* I said to myself. I pretended to be excited, not wanting to be disrespectful, knowing intellectually all that the *Kotel* stood for. We prayed, then sat on a wall on the side of the plaza and looked around, enjoying the pleasant evening breeze, watching the people strolling, praying, crying, meeting up with each other. A buzz of energy seemed to pour out of those stones and the night air.

Over subsequent visits to the *Kotel,* this modest yet becoming maiden slowly revealed her beauty, gradually enchanting me with her charm and might. My relationship with her may have started formally, with me just going through the motions, but eventually we bonded. She shared her secret power, and I grew to trust her and let her whisper to me and open my heart and soul. I did what everyone does in the pictures: I put my hands up on her, laid my head against her—to just feel her energy, to try to soak it in. I prayed. I meditated. Tears welled up. Walls usually separate, but this was a wall of connection masquerading as cool and silent stones.

Those eight days were way too short to even begin to experience it all. But enough for the land to start to percolate into me. We spent a few days seeing different parts of Jerusalem, and traveled to the port city of Ashkelon so I could see the apartment Chaim shared with three other paramedics and visit his ambulance base. Elegant and magnificent Ethiopian immigrants shared his building, the children waving shyly at Chaim and his friends.

Tzfat beckoned--that mystical haven, where I almost headed back in 1980. During my visit, this sleepy mountaintop town hosted its annual Klezmer Festival: three nights of live, free music, with bandstands scattered throughout the town.

Chaim and I boarded the bus for the several-hour trip, heading out of Jerusalem, past Tiberias and the Sea of Galilee, into the mountains, up crazily narrow highways winding up the side of the mountain. Hope this bus driver knows what he's doing. Hold on tight, don't look, pray. The town was buzzing with visitors: tents pitched all over, excitement hovering in the air. As twilight loomed and a golden haze settled, we followed the sun's last rays and headed down into a valley, an ancient cemetery where the Arizal and other great mystics, the early masters of *kabbalah*, were buried.

We walked down the million steps, deep into the valley, and came to the Arizal's *kever* (burial site). It was startlingly informal. A rough-hewn boulder painted luminescent turquoise blue marked the site, the Arizal's name painted roughly by hand, in white cursive scrawl. I said a few psalms and stepped up on a ledge, right next to the blue stone, not for any particular reason—

just because I was there. It seemed right to go up close and touch it for a second or so. Electricity shot through me. I could feel a physical sensation of pulsing voltage that left my legs shaking. After a few surprised seconds, I stepped down to terra firma—relatively speaking, as no piece of earth was one hundred percent solid in that enchanted town of dreamers and visionaries, of mysterious blessings and wandering sages.

Chaim and I were both swept up in that twilight magic as the colors deepened. We started climbing the multitude of steep stairs. About halfway up we saw men over on our right, hurrying in and out of another famous site, the Arizal's *mikvah* (immersion pool). Set within ancient stone arches, fed by a mountain river, this mikvah was legendary. Physically freezing. Spiritually rejuvenating. It is said that if one immerses in it, he will have thoughts of *teshuva*—wholehearted return to God. We walked past the entrance, and, on the spur of the moment, Chaim decided to dunk. He came out some ten minutes later, shivering and glowing. We continued climbing.

We finally reached the top, huffing and puffing. We turned back to enjoy the ethereal beauty of the fiery gold-red orb gently setting behind the valley. I calculated the time and called home, across the sea, to my family, those sweeties who seemed so far and so close.

Back in Ohio, it was mid-afternoon. Chaya was heading out on her first date with a young man who sounded just... just... just like he might be the Right One. It was *Tu B'Av*, a special day on the Jewish calendar. In Biblical times, maidens of Jerusalem would don white dresses and dance in the vineyards, and many young men found their intended brides among them. While I spoke with Chaya on the phone, I could hear the MCs at the Klezmer Festival wishing the crowd a wonderful *Chag Ha'ahava*—holiday of love.

Chaya and Elie hadn't based their date on the Hebrew calendar; August 12th had just worked with their busy schedules, but it seemed a fitting premonition of good things. I beamed them *Tu B'Av* wishes from up on the mountain, down to Dayton, where—

as we joked in the subject line of our emails as we made arrangements—Chaya would pick up Elie from the airport and they'd have their first "Date in Dayton."

The sky turned inky and the stars bedecked the sky, as the sounds of instruments tuning and microphones testing floated through the air. Crowds strolled freely from bandstand to alley to amphitheater, taking in a lively array: klezmer riffs, Chassidic tunes, Sephardic crooning, large rockin' ensembles, intimate acoustic groups. Close to midnight, a crowd gathered in a central courtyard. Young, old, punks, dreamers, observant were all milling, singing, and dancing in the full moon's glowing light. The ancient courtyard was surrounded by terraces, balconies, nooks, perches—jammed full with an appreciative audience swaying and singing. The moon smiled down; we felt closer to the heavens, up in the mountains, in that soulful town.

It was hard to believe the intifada was raging. In the day-to-day world, buses were being blown up with impunity. A visit to a café could be deadly. Most everyone standing in that courtyard had served or currently was serving in the IDF, or had loved ones in active duty, trying to protect their families and communities from the newest version of terror: suicide bombers. But up there in Tzfat, where it seemed we could almost touch the stars, these thousands of Jews of every persuasion stood shoulder to shoulder and sang passionately. Not for blood or revenge. Voices rose to sing for peace, for unity, with a wholesome sweetness that took my breath away.

We headed back to Jerusalem the next day. The bus wound down the mountain. Across the aisle, a withdrawn, morose-looking man made me nervous. Was it my overactive imagination running wild or true intuition screaming: *Something's wrong here.* I certainly didn't want to raise alarm or make a total fool of myself. But this was how a *pigua* (terror attack) would happen... people sitting on buses... No one else—no experienced, street-smart Israeli— seemed to take notice of the man, so I kept glancing over anxiously but bit my tongue.

About halfway through the trip, Chaim and I returned to our periodic discussion: should he join the army? We had already made a list of the pros and cons. He now opened up a bit more; he said was leaning heavily towards doing it, which didn't surprise me. He sat pensively for a few minutes, finding a song as I gazed out the window. He handed me his earphones. A country-western ballad was belting out about "the heart of a soldier." The singer crooned her praise of her man's bravery, fortitude, his loyal service to his country. The refrain, "the heart of a soldier," kept repeating over and over. I listened for a few minutes. Chaim glanced at me out of the corner of his eye to see if I got his message—his decision. I knew she was singing about his heart too.

What should I say?

I was a mom. Of course I was worried. Scenes of carnage and disaster instantly arose from my morbid imagination and flashed before my eyes. I looked over and saw him nervously waiting for my response, like a little boy who did want to please. I saw a brave, determined, and idealistic young man. I didn't feel he was really asking our permission—more our blessing. Yankel and I had discussed it at length and were prepared to back him. We didn't want Chaim's determination to be soured by defiance. His heart was set on doing it—better to be behind him.

But now it was moving out of the theoretical and into the real. Tears ran down my cheeks as I tried to gather my thoughts. I glanced at his copper hair and milky skin. After only a few months in Israel his delicate complexion was already ablaze with *nekudei chein*-- "drops of grace," as the Israelis so aptly and poetically call freckles. I focused my Jewish-mother worriedness on what those desert ultraviolet rays could do, and left the larger, overwhelming worries unspoken. I smiled through my tears, like a drama queen in a B-movie.

"Promise me one thing," I gulped. "Promise me that you'll wear sunscreen."

The week passed so quickly. Loaded up with inspiration, hopes, gifts, and memories, I headed back to the States. Chaim did indeed serve for two years—of growth and pain. He eventually made *aliyah* (became a citizen) in 2005. After working his way into the language and culture, he earned a degree in social work.

A special milestone arrived soon after. In spring of 2010, Chaim became engaged to Ayelet, a vivacious musician and biologist. True Israeli kids, they met at an archaeological dig, carting away buckets of dirt as they helped excavate King David's palace.

We were so excited. So proud of Chaim for enduring and building a new life. And we faced a dilemma. Should we, could we, all go to the wedding? Now we were talking major credit-card debt. But Chaim insisted and threatened that he couldn't get married without all of us there. We knew he was right. How could anyone be left out?

So with deals and Sky Miles and this and that, we pieced it together as best we could. Generous friends lent us their spacious home, a half-hour from Jerusalem. This time we would have two wonderful weeks.

We roughly sketched out an itinerary. Where did we want to go? Hebron came up several times. Everyone was excited. Everyone but me.

My heart fluttered. We'll see how things go, I hedged. The pang of conscience: I *should* go. We should bring our family. It's one of the holiest places. And visiting gives strength and support to those who live there. I tried to brush off my fears.

I should go.

I didn't want to go.

In all honesty, I was embarrassed to admit it: I was afraid to go.

This was an antiquated, angrily disputed place—quite small, really, though you'd never guess it by the media attention it drew. I had pushed it to the back of my mind, but it lingered there, unresolved.

Hebron didn't really speak to me. I had seen photos of its ancient sites in books and in my daughters' neatly arranged photo albums, but for me it lay flat, mute. It didn't jump off the page, beckoning, imploring me to wander through its nooks and crannies, kiss its stones and soak up its energy, like Tzfat or Jerusalem had. Setting foot in those unique places felt more like a reunion than a first date. I had the uncanny sense that I'd been in those two cities way before I ever arrived in our homeland; their charm, mystery, smells, and sounds had been almost tangible in my imagination.

Hebron's main historical and religious site, the *Me'arat HaMachpelah* (Machpelah Cave) was different. It looked too large, square, solid, and imposing. True, it was the burial place of our forefathers and foremothers—Adam and Eve, Abraham and Sarah, Isaac and Rebecca, and Jacob and Leah—but even that didn't make my soul tingle. I knew intellectually that Hebron was one of the four holiest cities, but I felt little magnetism, no pull or attraction.

Well, I did actually feel one visceral connection; something resonated when I heard the word *Machpelah*. Grandma Ida was buried in a cemetery in Detroit that bore this Biblical name — near the Michigan State Fairgrounds, in a rundown neighborhood, surrounded by bars and pawn shops.

Devora Leah and Mushky spent quite a bit of time in Hebron during their seminary years; Mushky decided it was her favorite place in Israel. Hardened Israelis looked at her in bemusement. What? That place of discord and violence? She even dreamed of spending a year learning and living in that embattled compound.

Okay, my daughters and I were cut from a different cloth. If Hebron was a holy place, they'd go there and do what they could to actively support it. While I pined after peace and tranquility, I imagined they loved the challenge of Hebron, the gritty courage of the Jews who lived there, and the feisty spunk of their kids— long sideburns flying in the wind, scruffy sandals scooting up the narrow alleyways.

The girls spent a lot of time with Chaim when they studied in Jerusalem. But they didn't tell him about their forays into the

Hebron Hills, going down from Jerusalem on the heavy, green, armor- plated Egged bus. At least not until they were safely tucked back in the dorm.

Chaim knew the other side of life in Hebron's twisting alleys. A large chunk of his two-year service was spent there on tedious guard duty: hours of grueling monotony while he hovered, poised to catch a sign of trouble. One afternoon, a comrade on guard duty was picked off by a sharpshooter just a few feet away from him. Another night, Chaim had to arrest a terrorist, while trying to minimize the fears of the wide-eyed kids whose house he searched. Big brother wasn't happy with his little sisters' passion for Hebron. Too many bad memories and close calls.

They usually told me when they were planning to spend a Shabbos or holiday there. What should I say? The same idealistic passion that drove Chaim to defend his people and overcome the many difficulties in moving to Israel led Devora Leah and Mushky to boldly explore. I lay in bed praying, worrying too. How could I dampen their flames, the youthful sparkle in their eyes? Real life has a way of tempering dreams soon enough. We had tried to raise them to be full of faith and love for their people. They took the ball and were running—flying. How could I clip their wings?

Back on that first trip in 2003, I had ventured partway into Judea: to Tekoa, a settlement south of Jerusalem. My good friend Chana Rivka had moved there with her family. We met up with her husband Dave, in front of his Jerusalem office, and drove to their new home. It was weird to be driving down the same Highway 60 that occupied too many news shows with reports of grisly attacks. Was I brave? Scared? A bit of both... mostly floating in surreal calm.

Dave seemed the same as ever—tan, funny, matter-of-fact— though he now packed a gun for self-defense. After all, they did live in the "Wild West... Bank," as Chana Rivka dubbed her new home.

Me, in the infamous West Bank? Many Americans couldn't understand how I could visit that "war zone". Hey, I figured, attacks were happening everywhere, and we weren't about to give up the whole country. Was going into Judea that much more dangerous or different?

I saw daily life go on. My friend's children, transplanted from Boston, were taking root, hearty and healthy. When I stood facing Chana Rivka's stucco home with its red, sun-baked tiles, I felt I could have been in Southfield. The sights and sounds of young families—bikes strewn in yards, kids running in and out, screen doors slamming—a typical suburban scene. When I looked across the street, however, I saw the barbed-wire fence surrounding the settlement, and the arid land around it, which seemed increasingly menacing as night fell. I slept lightly, startling at the sound of occasional shots and rustling.

Chana Rivka took me to a natural spring in nearby Bat Ayin. We drove around, viewing the olive groves and vineyards. Caravans clung tenaciously to the sides of the stony hills. The achingly and elegantly simple synagogue in Bat Ayin moved me; its natural, hand-crafted wood sanctuary sang with an understated, earthy holiness. There was an outpouring of creative Judaic art in the Gush Etzion gallery.

Chana Rivka's neighbor, a transplanted Frenchman, nurtured a boutique winery. He refused any mechanization, proudly producing pungent bottles of fine vintage, handcrafted the old French way that he'd learned at his father's side—complete with stamping the grapes barefoot. He hovered protectively over the grapevines, which grew along Tekoa's perimeter. These "West Bank settlers," too often depicted by the media as rabid, intransigent radicals, seemed a creative, individualistic, and dedicated bunch, who deeply loved the land. Many felt their resolve in "holding down the fort" helped make Israel safer for those within the Green Line.

During that first visit, going farther down the highway, all the way to Hebron, was too much of a stretch for me, however; more than a tad outside my comfort zone. I sent a donation to Jewish educational efforts there from time to time. I admired (from afar) the valiant pioneers who maintained a Jewish presence.

264

Abraham had purchased the Machpelah Cave to bury his beloved wife, Sarah. Modern-day Hebron residents live adjacent to
the first parcel of land in Israel that was legally purchased by a Jew,
documented bill of sale and all. It seemed almost as if Abraham
foresaw the day when they'd need every legal and historical claim,
when that hot spot would be continually embroiled in conten-
tious dispute.

I understood the need to maintain the connection, knowing
intellectually that Hebron was an important part of our heritage.
But it was an abstract conviction; I didn't relate personally. From
what I had read in the news, the place seemed shrouded in anger.
It was hard to imagine that a unique light might be shining and
nurturing those inhabitants, that their resolve was based on more
than militant pride or Jewish stubbornness. It was for tougher,
cowboy types—not softie scaredy-cats like me, I mused.

But by the time we visited Israel again, seven years later, three of
our kids had spent considerable time in Hebron, and everyone
else was clamoring to go.

Thursday was another scorcher. The kids were up early,
scrambling around with Yankel. Hats. Water. Sunglasses. Snacks.

"Hey, Ma! We're taking the bus into Jerusalem and catching
the afternoon bus to Hebron. Are you coming?"

"I guess," I mumbled, letting myself follow rather than think. I
quoted the book of Ruth: "Where you go, I will go . . ."

We met up with Chaim at the Central Bus Station. His mixed
feelings seemed to match mine. He came along, to somehow
protect us if we were dumb enough to go, and to see what would
unfold. Chaim and Yankel had visited Hebron together some six
months before, which seemed to begin a healing and more benign
feeling about the place for him. We found the right bus port and
boarded, the kids duly subdued and impressed by the bulletproof,
smoked-glass windows.

It was an uneventful trip snaking through the striking, ter-
raced Judean Hills. I murmured psalms and took in the Biblical

landscape. Could almost see David the shepherd tending his flock, there, under that tree. We arrived. Drove through a checkpoint, around a curve. Concrete blocks, barbed wire, and lively music greeted us as we disembarked.

I braced myself for a feeling of fear, anger, determination. I was going to make a stand for Jewish pride and resolve, and march resolutely into the Machpelah Cave.

But I didn't expect... this.

The air, the energy was festive. People strolled on the grounds, but there wasn't a swarming crowd to explain that uplifting feeling. Something intangible but very real hung in the air. A delicate joy. I startled, almost bristled, when I first heard the music as the bus doors opened. At first it seemed incongruous, but as I picked up the vibes of the place, it seemed somehow appropriate.

The Cave looked different in real life. Not forbidding. Perched on the grassy hill, it didn't beckon shyly, but instead exclaimed joyfully. It was Momma, waiting to reunite with her *kinderlach*, her returning children, with open arms and hand-baked goodies warm from the oven. I couldn't wait to ascend the steps and enter her welcoming embrace. The air sparkled, sang. I felt light and young. We all walked up together, admiring different views, and entered through security, bantering with the soldiers and guards.

Inside, we wandered from one resting place to another, looking, reading, thinking, praying, and soaking in the special atmosphere. Quiet. Intimate. Relaxed—yet intense in a very natural way. Sweet, comfortable. Homey.

We ended up in the central area, used as a synagogue. A group gathered for the afternoon prayers, pulling over stackable resin lawn chairs. Prayer was usually an effort for me, but now it flowed, welling up naturally. I wanted to bring a cot and sleep in there— just soak up the comforting, inspiring energy that rooted me deep and reached to the heavens, like a pillar.

I saw Chaim, sitting on some steps in a corner, pouring out his heart in a moment of deep introspection, gathering strength and heavenly help for his upcoming marriage and new life. He seemed to be tuning into the riches this place so generously offered.

Coming out later, back into sunlight, back into time, I thought of the words Jacob uttered after his dream of the ladder ascending: "How awesome is this place."

By the time we headed back, night had fallen. We sat quietly on the bus, dozing, thinking, dreaming. I was touched deep in my bones, by the glimpse of a pulsing holiness that had moved and surprised me. Hebron's complex issues hadn't melted away. But I kept visualizing that simple and magical afternoon prayer, thinking about that tangible sweetness, connectedness. Now I understood, on a gut level, that this extraordinary place was a vital part of us.

Several days later, I shared my surprise with our cousin Sheryl, a former American living in Jerusalem. "You won't believe it, it was just so special. Even more inspiring than the Western Wall, in a way."

I expected this moderate and levelheaded woman to be dismayed—both at our foray to Hebron, and at this unusual impression. She paused, and surprised me by nodding.

"Well, you know, Alan was there and he said the same thing. I guess I'll have to go there, too."

The next day a few of us took the bus to Rehovot, to help Chaim clean and prepare his and Ayelet's new home. They had found an impossibly cute little nest, a cottage in the back of the yard of a Yemenite grandma and grandpa. It seemed like a relic from a simpler, sweeter era. Verdant gardens surrounded the yard. Prodigious, blossoming growth: vines and plants and numerous grandkids of the extended clan filled the garden, the family homestead.

Yankel's cousin's son, Alan, his wife, Sheryl, and their three lovely children had become Chaim's Israeli family. Veteran *olim* (immigrants), they opened their hearts and home to Chaim, helping him maneuver his way. They were his crash pad and refuge during his army service, and loyally came to his swearing-in ceremony and other milestones. They had lived in Jerusalem's German Colony, a few blocks away from the popular Café Rimon. Chaim's ambulance was called to the café one evening when a suicide bombing ripped through it. After the carnage was cleared, Chaim knocked on Alan and Sheryl's door and fell into their arms. They spent the night huddling and crying together, and continued to support each other through other events, tragic and beautiful, as Israel's journey continued to unfold.

Now they joyfully rolled up their sleeves to help with the myriad wedding details. Alan and his kids joined us to spend the day, washing windows and floors, spackling and painting, putting together IKEA bookshelves and unpacking boxes, in the thick August humidity. I took a break after painting the living room, perched on a lawn chair, and let my mind wander. I imagined the newlyweds living here only a few days hence.

Dwelling Together
Pomegranates hanging, luscious and ripe over your roof
figs and mangos budding succulent
Gan Eden mi'kedem
Like the first couple
in the pristine beginning

Unravel the ages, *chatan v'kallah*
your flaking paint, cracking plaster paradise
Coo, turtle doves
Pad your nest with CD towers, internet-wired,
my children of the future

Ayelet: graceful doe gazelle
You labor by day
in sterile labs of genome frontiers
microscopic splitting-hair precision

Chaim: take bus thirteen to the pained and downtrodden
Bringing life,
a compassionate ear
The same meticulous care with which
you smooth the spackle, fold the clothes

At night—*ba'laylah*

let the moon shine into your window
let your dreams spill into the inky darkness
let the ancient crooning melodies
the wrinkled Temani *savta*
the curly-haired children
the figs and the olives bedeck your garden

Gan Eden mi'kedem	the Garden of Eden in the beginning
Chatan v'kallah	groom and bride
Ayelet	gazelle
Chaim	life
Ba'laylah	At night
Temani	Yeminite
Savta	grandmother

The wedding night was pure magic. We arrived at the small artisan winery, on a barren hill north of Jerusalem. As the day drew to a close and excitement mounted, friends and family gathered. The clear sky was kissed with streaks of pink and purple. Yankel and I walked Chaim to Ayelet, where he covered his bride's face with the traditional veil. We each blessed them, as did Ayelet's parents. As Yankel and I placed our hands above Chaim's head, it was a charged, timeless moment of hope, love, and forgiveness, when all hurts and misunderstandings seemed to fall away.

Ayelet's aunt had come all the way from Hawaii with a beautiful silk *chuppah* (wedding canopy) that she'd painted. It flapped in the brisk breeze as Ayelet's mother and I escorted the bride to the *chuppah*. The sky showered us with a rich palette of colors, from lavender gray to deepening turquoise to inky indigo. By the time the ceremony was over, night had fallen, abundant stars clapping as we danced.

Days later—after a heady, cozy Shabbos of celebration with Ayelet's family, our kids, and El and Marv in their village of Kedumim—the time came. We cleaned, packed, and quietly headed to Ben Gurion Airport, leaving a piece of our hearts behind.

Arriving the next morning in New York, I was shocked to see puddles. Unappreciated, lying in the gutter as taxis drove through, and rushing travelers splashed carelessly past. After two weeks of living in sweltering heat and mostly arid land, it seemed an extravagant indulgence: all that water, sitting unnoticed and unappreciated on the pavement?

TLV to JFK
Approaching New York in foggy spatters of morning rain
puddles glisten on the pavement
wallowing in careless watery delight

No summer rain
in Israel

Parched stoic land
stones piled in crumbling terraces,
enduring
waiting
Through conquering armies advancing,
zealous crusades ravaging

Sheep frolic under the shepherd's watchful gaze

SURPRISE IN HEBRON

searching for
a well of fresh water
gnarled tree offers up shade
respite from the blistering sun

Trees shed their leaves in summer
in Israel

Unceremoniously curling up brown
Vermont blaze of glorious fall splendor
an unaffordable luxury

So little water the tree must choose—
support leaf or fruit?
Fruit wins
clinging tenaciously to the branch till harvest

Those hardy, scrappy, enduring Jews
too must choose
struggle, send down roots
grasp nourishment
Find the well
in an arid world

Difficult land
spawning innovation
squeezed out of struggle
like golden oil flowing
from the crushed, bitter olive

The easy, resplendent green of America
floods with too many choices
vacuous pleasure
abundant emptiness
lush foliage of plenty

Not the climate to grow a Maccabee
a pungent olive
a Rabbi Akiva
whose Torah quenches an expiring soul

Tzoma L'cha Nafshi
my soul thirsts for You
like a parched traveler in an arid desert
without water.

29

———⌾⌾⌾———

SHE IS PURE

The years went on; the kids started to grow up. We gave away our last few disposable diapers, at long last. What a different phase, in so many ways. "Little kids, little problems—big kids, big problems," the saying goes. It's true that as the children grew into more complex beings, their issues weren't solved with a lollipop and a kiss. I did miss the dizzy, delicious baby-on-the-hip days, much as it was a blur. But we savored and enjoyed the richness of our emerging people.

Finally, all the kids in school, all day. I had time to branch out in new directions. A good friend regularly performed the *mitzvah* of *tahara* (purification)—preparing a Jewish body for burial. I'd wanted to try this important task, but kept putting it off for... later. This *mitzvah* was usually handled by more mature women, because of their freer schedules, and probably also because of the said maturity. As I rounded the corner on fifty, mortality wasn't a far-off, abstract notion that really had little to do with me. My mom was struggling with dementia and decline. I had lost some close friends. So when Tamar asked if I might be willing to try it, I gulped and hesitantly said yes.

"Good," she said briskly. "Malka told me you were thinking about it. The first time you mostly just watch, and the women will help guide you. How about tomorrow morning? We need a fourth. Na'ama will pick up you up at nine o'clock. Okay?"

"Sure," I answered, sounding more confident than I was.

Early the next morning, Na'ama honked right on time. She took side roads for our half-hour trip, avoiding rush-hour traffic. We pulled into the funeral-home parking lot, going around to the back. Na'ama punched the code to the rear door and we entered the quiet building. Several empty caskets were in the hallway.

I followed the women into a utilitarian room with a cupboard, sinks, concrete floor. We washed our hands and put on plastic aprons and latex gloves. They read over the Hebrew name of the deceased. I recognized it—I had visited her several times during her month of decline. I knew her somewhat; what would that be like?

No time to think. Ruth opened the heavy door of the walk-in refrigerated room that adjoined our work room. We entered.

There she lay.

Everyone else faded into the background.

I took a deep breath and followed the three women.

Two *meisim* (newly deceased) lay in the chilly room, covered with sheets. I recognized Rachel's bulky shape.

As the women wheeled Rachel into the preparation room, I followed, a bit nervously.

Back in the early days of my Chassidic immersion, I had been touched and intrigued when I first heard about this ritual. Soon enough, Yankel and I were pouring all our energies into building a Jewish homestead. I was focused on pregnancies and nursing, busy with the kids and their constant needs, nurturing life—not yet physically or emotionally ready to deal with its end.

But now I felt more or less ready, and somewhat obligated to try. Obligated because purifying a *meis* was a sacred ritual performed with care by Jews all over the world. Some unknown *tahara* team had done it for my grandparents and in-laws, *aleihem hashalom* (may peace be upon them). In our small community, we all shared the joys and responsibilities of Torah life, and every set of willing hands counted.

Aleihem hashalom. According to Jewish law and tradition, the living helped the soul get ready to rest in peace, by preparing its earthly home—the body—with well-defined rituals of cleansing and dressing in simple shrouds. These rituals were done with the utmost dignity, privacy, and respect. Rather than making an attractive façade for the funeral, they focused on purity and simplicity, each step suffused with deep kabbalistic meaning.

I knew all this. In my head. But I still wasn't sure: could I really do it?

Helping the dead was called *chesed shel emes,* true kindness— you gave with no possibility of being paid back. To be honest, I wasn't there just for altruistic reasons, beautiful and compelling as those were. Beyond noble acts and community responsibility, I wanted to expand my spiritual horizons.

Maybe I'd hone in on the real essence, become a truer wife and mother, waste less energy on trivialities; swallow and internalize a greater appreciation for the gift of life. Less kvetching even. Perhaps this encounter with mortality would make me a more sensitive artist and writer.

I was now a reputedly respectable figure, a rabbi's wife and Jewish educator busily mining the treasures of Jewish mysticism and living. But every now and then I still longed for those "wow man, far out" intense experiences—albeit in a Jewish way. Surely helping a soul and its body in this transition would fit that bill. The burial committee was traditionally called the *Chevra Kadisha*—the holy society. With a name like that, I reckoned, they must be privy to some deep, mysterious truths.

The *tahara* turned out to be like most of Jewish life, where searching for rarefied or transcendent "spirituality" wasn't exactly the point.

Was it profound, quiet, hushed—*spiritual*? Yes, and no.

The *tahara* felt surprisingly prosaic. Earthy. Even ordinary.

Naama, the group leader, a brisk and efficient woman, helped dispel my initial discomfort by referring to Rachel as *her*. "Move her over here," she instructed. "Hold up her head."

There was nothing macabre about the scene, though my subconscious offered up images from horror movies accompanied by a Gothic organ's pitched tone. It wasn't a staged "religious service," with a choir marching quietly in perfect formation. We were about to help a real woman, a *she*, a person. We had a job to do.

Watching my experienced partners' faces for a cue in this new universe, I felt both humbled and relieved: humbled by their ability to just step up, assess the situation, and figure out the best way to proceed, with an earnest and everyday kind of caring. Relieved to see them show signs of compassion, even distress, at some of the bodily signs of the suffering Rachel must have endured these last few months. It was hard for them, too. But they each took a breath and continued.

The first glance at her was hard. The first touch was hard.

The other women started washing Rachel with washcloths, keeping as much of her face and body covered as possible at any one moment, respecting her privacy, even now. Initially I stood back, watching with hands folded. But I knew it would be best to jump right in, so as they turned Rachel to wash her back, I reached out tentatively and held her hand to keep it from flopping over.

The words *dead weight* and *rigor mortis* echoed through my mind. Rachel's hand was cold, heavy, and stiff. I imagined holding a living hand that had the pulse of life flowing through it. This was different.

I helped more and more as we proceeded, following my friends' spoken and intuited guidance. As we gently washed her body, a body that had lived and loved and borne children, it seemed almost like bathing an infant, with its total dependence on our care and protection.

Trying to talk only when necessary, we gave each other instructions in subdued, focused voices. The quiet was punctuated by coughs, sighs, the sound of water filling the buckets, the snap of latex gloves.

We took off whatever bandages we could, along with other substances that would block the purifying water, so it could cover her as completely as possible. Removing her frosted-pink nail polish was like stripping away her earthly life. I imagined a kind nurse or grandchild sitting patiently with Rachel and applying this reassuring, slick coat of certainty and vanity on her worn, fading hand.

That was all behind her now.

In an unbroken sequence, Na'ama, Ruth, and Malka poured cascading buckets of water from the *mikveh* from her head to her toes.

"*Tehora hee, tehora hee, tehora hee*—she is pure," they intoned rhythmically. Over and over in almost a chant—asserting, defining—the sound of the water splashing against the metal table, accenting their words.

Pausing at several points, Na'ama murmured several prayers and parts of Psalms, the familiar sounds of the ancient Hebrew washing over Rachel and clothing her in a cocoon of comfort. We listened, understanding the intent, even if we couldn't translate each word. Our wishes for this woman cushioned and cloaked her as well.

We gently patted her dry. Ruth brushed her still-wet, gray-white hair and I watched it spring into soft, fine curls. This tender act was touching, like giving a small child that final mother's touch.

Working together, we dressed Rachel in *tachrichim,* simple white linen garments—tunic, pants, gown, bonnet—each put on and tied in a special way.

We carefully lowered her into the unadorned wooden casket. Fulfilling the Biblical declaration, "From dust you came, to dust you shall return," holes had been drilled into the bottom of the casket, allowing the body to have contact with the dust of the earth.

Na'ama placed a shard of pottery on each of Rachel's eyes and on her mouth, symbolizing human frailty. Golden sand from the land of Israel was lightly sprinkled over her. We covered Rachel's face with a piece of linen, then asked her to forgive us for any unintentionally rough or disrespectful handling, and wished her a speedy journey to *Olam HaBah*—the world to come.

Lifting the heavy casket cover and positioning it onto its fastening pegs felt like an act of finality. Ruth opened the door to the refrigerated room. The whoosh and blast of cold air was startling, breaking the meditative mood. We wheeled Rachel inside, where she would wait for the next step of her voyage.

Stepping out of the quiet, windowless room into daylight, we collected our purses and cell phones, and stepped back into our day—a sunny summer one.

The casual chatter on the drive home seemed strange after such intensity. But I soon relaxed, realizing the conversation offered a soothing transition. What we had shared did not really need to be put into words.

Easing back to reality, I drew a blank when Malka asked me, "So, how was it for you?" I had to stop and think. How was what? Oh, yeah. I just did a *tahara*. "It was okay," I said quietly, downplaying my feeling of accomplishment and my inner relief that I'd made it through.

I felt buoyed throughout the day. Catching up on the phone with Devora Leah, now a new mother, I told her, "I did my first *tahara*."

She gasped. "Really?"

But, the *tahara* wasn't a gasp type thing, not of horror, and not of an *Oh wow* mystical high. It was an ordinary, extraordinary thing to do.

Rachel's image flitted though my mind once or twice. Not in a morbid way. Just an image of a friend I was glad to have helped.

Early Thursday, I awoke and remembered her. I said *Modeh Ani*, expressing thanks for the new day. No rote recital this time; I really felt it. Rachel was in her place in God's universe, stripped down to her essence, purified of her worldly concerns. And I was thankful to be in my own place —unfinished business, chaos, imperfection, and all.

30

━━◈◈◈━━

Praying with Gittel Rivka

ittel Rivka—Mom's Hebrew name. During Mom's last months, last days and hours, it was Gittel Rivka whose hand I held, and who I sat with. Trudy Driker, the articulate, competent persona, was all but gone. Her physical life was pretty much a shell. She was emaciated, hadn't stood or walked in months, and had labored breathing and could barely speak. But she was there. Her *neshama*, her soul, was there. That's what I focused on.

Mom's death was not unexpected. First there was a sudden onslaught of dementia, her confusion apparent as soon as she came out of anesthesia after surgery for a heart valve replacement. That had been about six years before these final days.

She'd been home, cared for by our stoic and stalwart dad, during the ensuing years of her gradual decline. Vivian and I tried to offer suggestions and interventions from our homes in Phoenix and Cincinnati, but our sporadic, well-meaning attempts didn't make much difference.

During the last six months of her life, our always-skinny mom grew ever more fragile; she could barely stand on wobbly legs and grew easily confused. But almost to the end, her sharp perceptions would surface unexpectedly.

We sat in the kitchen one January day. Mom's aide, Barbara, and Viv and I were having a lively discussion about politics. Mom sat quietly at the end of the table in her wheelchair, her fluffy white robe drawn around her, seemingly lost in her foggy reverie. Suddenly she interrupted with a determined voice: "Talk more slowly! Why are you all shouting? I can't follow what you're saying!" She still wanted to be part of it, and she would add comments to the conversation— details a bit off, but insightful.

We three kids visited more, talked on the phone more, wrung our hands, and mourned our slow loss of her. This bad time had drawn us into more frequent contact and a web of connection. We were in and out of Detroit as the bitter Michigan winter slowly turned to spring, hovering and helping a bit with her two hospitalizations, her downward journey in a rehab center, and finally to hospice care in a nursing home.

The respectful, loving, but detached distance between me and my folks—which I had maybe erroneously felt they'd wanted— had evaporated. For years I would call them weekly. Our brief conversations followed a set pattern.

"What's new? How are the children?" Mom usually sounded chirpy and glad to hear from me. I would give a brief update about the latest comings and goings.

"How's the weather?" Our most reliable topic. We could complain about too much snow, or not enough rain, or praise the few short days of perfect Indian summer. Mom would ask me if the weather was similar in Cincinnati, and I would assure her it was.

Dad and I would have a few words along the same lines, and he'd sign off, saying, "Thanks for calling." I longed for more intimate sharing, but they seemed content to be in comfortable contact without being burdened with too many details of my chaotic and unusual life.

But now I no longer worried about Dad's dignity and privacy; I called him daily for updates, to commiserate. As a guilt-laden, out-of-town daughter, I tried to at least cheerlead and support him from four hours away, a straight jaunt down I-75. And we sibs, as the adult children, strove to find the new balance between following the ever-certain lead he had always provided, and stepping in. It seemed like yesterday that we were kids at the zoo, munching on cotton candy or an oversized, rainbow-streaked lollipop, running after him as he marched with confidence to the next exhibit.

The table was turning at too fast a speed. We were tiptoeing with unsure steps into guiding our parents and taking up a bit of the slack. Dad was still in charge, but with increasing exhaustion and his own grief, he seemed to welcome leaning on our shoulders a bit. I sat on the couch in Mom's room in Henry Ford Hospital, expecting to quietly listen and support Dad with my presence. I was surprised when he introduced me to Mom's doctors and sat back. He seemed relieved to let us kids query them.

We tried to get them to tweak this or that, but her health continued to decline. Even though she seemed barely there, I wanted to sit and just *be* with her. In a way, I shared more of my real self with Mom during those winter and spring months than I ever had been able to before. I shared my real world, which her persona and more conscious self would have dismissed as gibberish.

It was so hard to walk into the hospital room and see her. Increasingly thin, agitated, unsure of her surroundings, withdrawn. But a core was there.

She was childlike. She was Dolly—her mother's pet name for her—a sweet little girl you could tease and joke with as you got her to take one more bite, with a combination of coaxing and gentle sarcasm.

"C'mon, Mom. C'mon, Dolly. Take another bite. Mmm, this soup looks good. The milkshake is a little thick. What kind of a joint is this? How can they give *my mommy* service like this?"

Or:

"You've got a real scam going here, Trudy. Vanilla ice cream for lunch? Man, oh man, how'd you pull that one off?" She'd giggle and open her mouth conspiratorially, forgetting she had bitten the spoon in resistance one minute earlier.

As she faded more and more, I often couldn'r make contact with Dolly, the wide-eyed girl with bouncy black bottle-curls who rode the Oakland streetcar downtown to Hudson's, her small, white- gloved hands clasped in her mommy's.

Now I could talk to Gittel Rivka, the *Yiddishe neshama*, the sweet Jewish soul I had included in my prayers for years, but had never been able to directly address—because Trudy didn't believe in souls or any other non-rational, non-quantifiable beings.

We switched roles. It was my turn to tuck her in, with sweet whispers on the evening breeze. As she drifted to sleep, I sat by the hospital bed (and later the nursing home bed) and sang. *Yiddishe* lullabies—Jewish words and melodies. I sang *Shema*, the basic prayer we say at the end of each day—and at the end of life—affirming our connection to and belief in one God. I guess I was trying to arouse her soul; to feed it, water it, give it vitamins and nourishment, much as we kept trying to get another sip of Ensure or another spoonful of yogurt into her body.

"Just trying to get some nourishment into her," Dad would wearily report each day when I'd call. He went to the nursing home three times daily, to sit and coax another spoon or two of pudding or applesauce, a sip of water.

Ess, mein kind—eat, my child—the timeless urging of the Jewish mother. As her body was clearly diminishing, coming round the curve to the finish line, I wanted to give nourishment to her soul. It would be there anyway, when she got to the next stage, but I wanted to make it feel safe, acknowledged. It was like teaching someone a bit of the language before they take a trip abroad. Her soul knew the language, of course—it's inherently there—but it had lain dormant for so long that I wanted to befriend it and guide it along. I hoped to help Mom feel a little less scared and ease her transition.

I still wanted to make up for my big mistake when Mom's mom, Grandma Ida, died over thirty years earlier. I was already ensconced in general spiritual thinking by then. I'd been reading Kübler-Ross' *On Death and Dying*, in which she described near-death experiences, universally reported as being a vivid experience of going through a long tunnel into a great light.

We were at the hospital the night Grandma Ida was dying.

"I'm afraid, I'm afraid," she called in a quivering voice, over and over. No one knew what to do. Flustered and upset, they called the nurse for more medication.

But I knew the turf a little. At least I'd read the tour book and I knew where she was going. I held her hand and sat next to her.

"Don't be afraid. You're going to a good place. God loves you," I said quietly.

Grandma Ida came from a traditional family. She had clung to a few Jewish practices throughout her life, such as fasting on Yom Kippur, even though her husband was an avowed socialist and our family considered such things outmoded superstitions.

"You'll see Grandpa. You'll be with your mommy and daddy. It will be good," I murmured to Grandma.

I think she called out for her mother.

I ignored my family's questioning looks and kept repeating. "God loves you, He will take care of you. You're going to a good place."

I was nervous, venturing into unknown territory, especially since everyone else seemed to think I was nuts, but it just seemed like the right thing to say. Grandma calmed down a bit. I pulled up my chair next to her bed, ready to camp out for the night.

Mom, comforted when everything was in its place, wanted me to come home with the rest of the family. I didn't want to make waves at this stressful time, so I complied reluctantly. Grandma died alone that night, in her hospital bed. Her fear and aloneness still haunted me.

Now, facing the end of Mom's life, I didn't want the same thing to happen again. I wanted Mom to be with a loved one, and I wanted to be the doula—coaching and encouraging her as she transitioned to a different realm.

Besides being with Mom as any child would, and in addition to giving Dad a break, I felt I had a mission. True, I had never died, thank God. But I knew what Jewish tradition offered up about it, and was now well-versed in *neshama* language. I was determined to at least try to ease the transition—to be there. To talk to her soul, as I never could before, when we could only discuss the kids, the weather, books, politics, and other common ground. But now, I could let that superficial veneer go. We could meet on a soul level; this would be our common ground.

Who was running for president or which book was a *New York Times* best seller was irrelevant here, in this bed in this modest room under the alcove, with this wizened woman laboring for another breath.

Her blue-and-gold-striped quilt, a touch of home, had been crocheted by Bubby Faygie. A few other personal belongings were scattered here and there. But the little corner room had few amenities: a bed, an armchair, the oxygen tank, and a dresser. More or fewer things didn't matter. The plant her friends had brought sat forlornly on the windowsill, ignored, unable to give her the desired perk at this late point.

This once-sophisticated woman was now just her bare essence, soon to leave this world from the sparse nursing-home bed. Her carefully chosen art, her lovely furniture back home, were of little use or comfort now. I tried to shower her with the kind of love I could offer: praying, ushering, escorting this rational nonbeliever over the threshold to join her momma and daddy, to let her *neshama* free.

I held her hand and talked to her as she dozed. I forgave her for whatever hurts I'd held on to, and asked her to forgive me. My eyes welled up as the words stumbled out.

"Mom, I probably hurt and disappointed you with my different choices. I chose a life that's hard for you to understand. I'm not the daughter you thought I'd be. And I know I was too busy with the kids and my world, and I didn't visit or connect with you enough. But I did it out of love for you, wanting to honor you the best way I know how, and I hope you will have real *nachas*, real satisfaction and gladness from it."

My confession tumbled out and surprised me. Someone had advised me to ask her forgiveness, so I started it somewhat routinely, because it was a good thing to do at this juncture—and stumbled into a well of feeling.

I didn't usually think about her perspective that much, but there must have been a hurt, an empty hole, for many years. I lived far away. My promise as a future professor or therapist was never fulfilled; I spent my days mumbling old-fashioned blessings and having one baby after another. I wasn't able to compare notes on travel and shopping. We both shopped, of course, but Mom frequented Saks, so I didn't think she'd want to hear about my finds at Walmart. My shopping was pretty much utilitarian—due to my tighter budget, higher volume, and less-materialistic focus.

I couldn't even go out to eat anywhere but at the greasy kosher pizza store, and share Mom's simple pleasure in enjoying a gourmet meal and fine wine at a great new place, for goodness' sake.

As my older kids started leaving the nest, I came to know the emptiness that lingered in their space—and that was with my kids and I on pretty much the same page. How much emptier it must have been for her.

It seemed like Mom squeezed my hand a drop. Perhaps on some level she was acknowledging and accepting my words. I sang Jewish songs, prayers, and psalms, mumbling and chanting, hoping that the Hebrew syllables were a balm, a gentle massage to her being. In my extreme mindset, as I sat by her side, every psalm seemed to be full of heightened meaning, alluding to souls coming and going.

"Even if I walk in the valley of the shadow of death, I will fear no evil, for You are with me... Only goodness and kindness shall follow me..."

If this wasn't the valley of the shadow of death, I didn't know what was. *Fear no evil*, I emphasized, saying it a bit louder, a bit slower, as though my words were a command to her. Dear Gittel Rivka, sit up and take notice! God is with you, my dear Mommy. *Only goodness and kindness*, only sweetness, for you—an end to the darkness and confusion of this perplexing world—as though my words were a command to God. Please, I begged, shower and comfort and protect this sweet soul in golden, soft goodness.

"The Lord bless you and guard you. The Lord make His countenance shine upon you and be gracious to you. The Lord turn His countenance toward you and grant you peace."

Please. Pour Your blessings on Mommy, and let her feel Your closeness, Your shining countenance, Your innerness. For some reason, You've let me taste a bit of Your presence, of Your grace—oh, I wish there were a better English word. It's time to let her taste and know and get strength and comfort, too.

"Our Father, let us lie down in peace. Spread over us the shelter of Your peace. Shelter us in the shadow of Your wings; and guard our going out and our coming in for a good life and peace from now and for all time."

The image of men quietly praying under a *tallis* has captured me since I first saw it. I've painted the soft folds and mysterious shadows, the *shechina* (divine presence) that seems to be hovering under there. That's something like what I imagine the shelter of Your wings might be like. Just protect and love this innocent, little-girl soul, let her sit close to You, like a child in the shadow of her mother's skirt.

I wanted to be awake and with her when Mom would pass on. She was agitated and clearly approaching that moment, her breath rattling and irregular. I reached through the bed railing and held her hand—not too tight, but there. Kept dozing off and pulling my eyes back open. But around 11:00 P.M. I collapsed into an exhausted sleep in the recliner that I had pulled close to her side.

With a sudden jolt, I sensed the nurse coming to check her at 1:00 A.M. One glance and I knew, before the nurse could utter the words.

"She's passed."

Mom was gone. That tiny remaining bit of enlivening life force had left.

I was shocked and frozen. She looked like an empty shell, like the newly deceased women I had helped prepare for a traditional burial. I sat there for a moment, then picked up the phone to call Yankel and Dad, hands trembling.

31

———⚜———

THE CAR SERVICE

During the next few days we transitioned during the blur
of *shiva*. Family and friends filled the house to pay
condolence calls on Friday and Sunday afternoons, with
laughter, tears, reminiscences, and just being there. We'd spent
countless birthdays, Chanukah parties, and celebrations with
these same faces and voices. Their buzz of conversation spun a
cozy cocoon of familiarity. The large Farberware urn was filled
and plugged in, a ritual that signaled company coming: a significant gathering. The kitchen was filled with the sound of bubbling
water, the soothing smell of perking coffee. The time-honored
trays of bagels, lox, and bakery goodies were assembled. Platters
coming and going, Saran Wrap stretched on and off, like any other
party.

The house was comfortingly the same, yet dramatically altered
in the subterranean sea change. Without Mom, without Trudy, it
was unfathomably and vastly different. Dad's portrait of her hung
over the fireplace. Her lovingly chosen objets d'art were carefully
placed everywhere, her touch felt in each nook. There was an
underlying empty space. What would the new normal be like?

The moderate-sized condo was bursting with kids, grandkids,

and great-grands over Shabbos—a welcome reprieve that Dad seemed to savor.

Day by day, the house emptied out. One group of my kids left with Yankel on Sunday, another on Monday. Our two married daughters, Mushky and Devora Leah, decided to stay an extra day to cushion the ever-quieter emptiness. Their husbands drove east together on Sunday, and they planned to fly back Tuesday to their homes in Baltimore and New York.

"Dad, what taxi should we call?" I asked as we got their plans together. "Where's the *Jewish News*? They have a bunch of car services listed in the classifieds," he said.

In Detroit's woebegone economy, lots of people were putting out a shingle and looking for a way to bring in a few extra bucks, it seemed. Dad scanned the numerous ads. "Only one ad lists a set price to the airport. Why don't you call them? You won't have any surprises," he suggested.

We made the call. At the appointed time the next morning, a man showed up. He wasn't Russian or Israeli, like most drivers who post in the *Jewish News*, but middle-aged American. He stood in the vestibule waiting, surveying the scene as Mushky and Devora Leah got their last-minute bits and pieces together. Food. Baby seat. That bag, oh yeah. Dad and Vivian were in the kitchen.

The driver peered at me. "Do I know you?" he asked.

I laughed defensively. "I don't think so, I don't live here."

"I think we're related. What's your maiden name?" he persisted.

I shook my head. "I really doubt it. You're probably thinking of someone else. I come from a small family. But, anyway, my name is Miriam..."—he said the last word along with me—"... Driker."

I was startled.

He said, "Remember me? I'm Eddie Rappaport."

It took a second for my brain to open to this familiar-sounding name. As it clicked, I was shocked. I tremulously called, "Dad, Dad! It's Eddie Rappaport!"

Dad looked up from the paper, startled by my urgent tone of voice.

Eddie followed me into the kitchen, looked down at my dad and said, "Hi Jack. It's Eddie. Eddie Rappaport. Elsie and George's son."

Everyone gaped.

Mom was an only child. She grew up in her grandparents' house, in the bosom of her large extended family, playing with her many cousins, most older than her. As kids, we saw several of her cousins and their children sporadically, every few years at the most. In later years, those loose bonds weakened even more. The cousins were inevitably preoccupied with their immediate families, and, later, their own challenges of aging. Between the gap in the family chain—they were cousins, not siblings—and the consuming occupation with Mom's care and decline, our contact with her relatives had been all but lost.

Dad didn't even know if any of her cousins were still living. A bit numb during that short period between Mom's death and the funeral, we weren't up for a research project; we only called people we could readily reach, who we were in active contact with. So no one from her side of the family was in the loop or at the funeral.

Gregarious Elsie Rappaport, Eddie's mom, had been one of Mom's first cousins, one we actually knew a bit better.

Viv regained her composure first. "Do you know why we're here? I don't believe this. My mom died last week. We're in the middle of *shiva*."

We had this other-worldly feeling. Viv, the rationalist, piped up again—laughing, but a tad serious too. "I guess Mom and Elsie got together *up there*, and wanted to have their side of the family involved. So they brought you to us."

We shmoozed and commiserated for while, and then remembered the girls had a flight to catch. In a daze, we saw them off. Eddie promised to return for dinner, with his Bar Mitzvah albums in hand.

And he did. He happened to have an avocation as *the* Lipchinsky family historian. He came back that evening with yellowed albums, sixties chic in full glory, along with family trees, cemetery records, and tons of lore and minutiae. We pored over pictures of people long gone, caught in a moment of celebration almost a half-century ago. Eddie knew obscure details we'd never heard of, about relationships, characters, marriages, business deals come and gone. We were drawn back into a world we'd been far removed from, drawn closer in than we'd ever been.

On a normal day, we might not have even been that interested, but now, some scant days after Mom's passing, we savored every detail, every piece of her. We felt a completion of the circle. Mom's family had indeed been brought to us, on a silver platter— literally to our doorstep— represented by the one person on the planet who probably knew the most about it, in remarkable detail.

A link in the chain. No circle left incomplete. Dad kept shaking his head and mumbling, "Remarkable. Unbelievable."

32

HOLDING GITTEL RIVKA

After Mom's death the summer rolled on, first ever so slowly as we eased out of the driveway, out of our cocoon of mourning. Then, gradually picking up speed to a gentle thirty-five miles per hour or so down the road of return back into life.

Dad started exercising. He pried open his dried-up paints, re-stocked with some new colors, and lifted a brush to the canvas. He was picking up the musty and neglected threads of his life, shelved during the caretaking crunch. By the end of the summer he ventured up north for a few days at Lake Michigan, his first time away from home for years. My brave dad adapted and started healing.

I started writing down these recollections, and painting—as the summer months crept by, sunny June days morphing into late August, tinged with impending hints of orange and burgundy, right under our noses.

Our kids were busy with the ins and outs of their lives. Yeshaya and Mendy were overnight camp counselors, using what they'd learned from growing up in the middle of our pack to tame a bunch of rowdy kids. Esti was a spirited day camp counselor in New Hampshire. Chana and Fayga went off excitedly to overnight

293

camp for the first time, giving us a taste of an empty nest as we pitter-pattered through the quiet house. Chaim, in Israel, finished up his social work degree and started looking for work. Motti took a trip to Seattle to spend time with his sister Chaya and his nephews and nieces—and I tagged along for the chance to get some squeezes in. Devora and Levi, both dedicated educators, were moving to Cincinnati to work with us. We couldn't wait to have some of our grandchildren living right down the block.

And Mushky's tummy grew.

Mushky, our fourth child, had over the years developed a special closeness with my parents. She called them every Friday afternoon—from Chicago, where she and her young husband studied and worked, or from New York, Jerusalem, Seattle, wherever she was—to touch base and wish them a Good Shabbos. In her matter-of-fact way, she pushed through any distance or formality and forged a unique bond. They came to expect her regular greeting. I usually remembered to call my folks in the last minutes of the Friday rush. As Dad picked up he'd say, "Oh, I just got off the phone with Mushky."

As the kids marry and start their own adult lives, it's pretty cool stuff.

Our perspective shifts. The big picture is more visible. When they were little and crying and fighting, when I'd run out of diapers and someone was merrily dumping Cheerios on the floor, some annoying matron would inevitably pipe up: "The days are long and the years fly by." Then she'd smile calmly and wish me that elusive Jewish blessing—to have *nachas*. Sure, lady, can you grab a broom? Here, take two kids and read them a story or something.

I was thinking about only one thing: survival. How much longer till bedtime?

Nachas?

Pleasure. Satisfaction. Pride. It's something like that, but more.

It was pretty darn hard to get much of a sense of the tapestry that was being woven while pulling the thread for dear life and hoping it didn't slip through the webbing. That troublesome knot is in my face. Will this kid ever grow up or that character trait ever mellow or change, we'd desperately wonder?

As they married—we could see it. *Nachas.* They've emerged from the fray a veritable *mensch,* a person of integrity—and even more, found a lovely *mensch* to be their life companion. They took the values we didn't realize we were giving over, enriching and personalizing with their own particular stamp. And they were stepping up to the plate and trying their hand at that glorious task of starting their own families. (Would you like to see pictures of my brilliant, beautiful, and talented grandchildren?)

Mushky married Binyomin, a good-humored, mild-mannered, wild-dancing young man. She called me in a panic Thursday night.

"I think my water broke. What should I do?" I could hear that certain unmistakable tone of voice —flat, pained, zoned in, zoned out—hear the intensity of the labor she wasn't even aware she was already in.

My little girl. I wanted to say, "I wiped your nose and changed your diapers. Get off that delivery table, I'll do this for you, too! It's too ouchy and too much for you!"

That didn't happen, but two hours later a dazed Mushky called back to say "It's a girl!" Seven pounds and six ounces of pink. We all rejoiced in the healthy birth.

For Mushky and Binyomin, a new world of parenting opened up with that first shrill cry. Their lives were forever and wonderfully changed. So many major and minor details to navigate for that little one. One of the first was deciding on miss sweetheart's name.

Our tradition was to name daughters at the first Torah reading after their birth, which in this little bundle's case would be on Shabbos morning.

It was also a tradition to name after those who had passed on. Their legacy and being would continue in a sense, and we're taught it's a comfort to the soul.

We didn't know for sure what name Mushky and Binyomin would choose. The Hebrew letters that form the name are the particular conduit for that soul's life force to come down; it's the name of the soul, a spiritual force. We believed that whatever practical factors seem like they were going into the process, such as "we like that name," or "we want to name the child after this or that person," at the end of the day, the parents would have a *n'vua k'tana*—a small degree of prophecy—it would all come out as it was meant to be.

So it was heavy stuff. And grandparents and other interested parties backed off—at least Yankel and I did. I didn't feel a compelling drive to push my mother's name. They'd choose what seemed right to them. And the little girl would get the name she was supposed to have.

It didn't come as a surprise when they called us after sundown Saturday night, but it was touching and gratifying, sad and fulfilling nonetheless. They called to tell us the baby's name, given to her as her Daddy stood at the open Torah scroll.

Gittel Rivka *bas* (daughter of) Mushka.

A circle is closed. The chain goes on.

I'm sitting on the Megabus, Chicago-bound, the next day, Sunday afternoon. A young mother across the aisle is shushing her wiggly toddler. Most passengers are electronically engaged in their own world via earphones or laptop. A pedestrian enough day. But the calendar says otherwise.

9/11/2011.

Ten years after devastating darkness and havoc made it to this side of the pond with a horrific roar, on another regular day—a sunny Tuesday morning, after which life would never be the same.

I had scrambled to plan lessons for the sub, and get carpool and other myriad details in enough order to pull out from my routine and head out for a week of baby-holding, new-mommy nurturing and coaching—and bubbying.

Anxious to get there and meet this little one, this Gittel Rivka.

On 9/11. A time to pause.

Life is precious.

We're trying hard to squeeze a bit of light out of our busy chaos, to add a few more drops of healing to our aching world. We're following in the way of our forefathers and foremothers, an ancient way that reaches forward to wholeness and rings true to us and our children—who are finding their own way on our people's well-trodden path.

An incredible, dreamlike feeling.

Mom, I feel your presence.

Zaidy, the chain is continuing. The chain of Jewish life you hinted at in that dream—that blue, purple, hazy dream.

And look where that dream has brought me.

Sowing with more than a few tears—but building generations, each one of these kids their own special self.

Yes, I can say, reaping in joy.

EPILOGUE

Searching
  Wondering
    What people do—
Fragments looking for wholeness
Halves looking for each other
Humanity looking for revelation, for healing, for fullness

Hints. Drops of dew. Kisses. Clues.
The gingerbread trail of tantalizing crumbs teases the hungry heart.

I was placed in one home, one mindset,
a product of societal forces, history,
a soul product of my people's collective yearning,
moving forward through the generations, driven to fill in the gaps

To earnest first generation emancipated Americans:
rationality beckoned.
Economic promise.
And then, my gang, the boomers, boomed and clamored onto the stage.
For whatever inner reason,
some of us resonated to
a different tuning fork.

I was born a product of my times. I was born a hungry soul.
I was born a product of an ancient people of prophets, wanderers,
with a mission and a vision of fixing and connecting.

Now that I've laid out a few of the quirky particulars of my journey,
in which I was
pulled and pushed and propelled to
scratch beneath the surface, to connect the dots...

I'm a little scared.
"Why are you writing all this?" a friend asked.
"What would you do if your kids tried this radical crazy shtick,
and wandered and hitched and left you wondering
where on earth they were?"
Am I inviting them to emulate stories better left untold?

No, my dear *kinderlach*, my children. Learn something different
from me spilling my guts and leaking my dribbles and drabbles.
Please.
As I share these meandering adventures, I hope you'll take the spirit
of searching for truth, the perseverance, the hanging on for dear life
for what seems right and true to you.
But hoping you can piggyback on what your Tatty and I managed
to figure out,
on the new/old land we found and foraged for you,
and that you'll be spared and have enough sense to skip the
crazy crazies.

Yes, my dear *kinderlach*. Learn to listen to and honor your soul,
and let it lead you to good and whole places.
I've been lucky to be led to a place where I can stand on my
tippy toes and reach
to the thinnest, highest, most radiant atmosphere of light,
and shown how to bring it into this world—where being in a body,
stirring the soup, mommying in a house on a Friday afternoon,
is the sweetest thing, the sweetest spirituality—down here
with sesame seeds and lettuce and tomatoes and hair ribbons
and candles
and fresh cake smells
and flowers on the table.

Acknowledgments

I t takes a village to raise a child, and I've learned that it takes one to get a book nurtured, written, finished and out there. There are many people whose support has made a tremendous difference.

The idea of sharing my story—its inspirations, stumbles, warts, divine providence and light— has been percolating for years. The structure of the Individualized Masters of Arts Program at Antioch University enabled me to focus, persevere, and finally bring it to life. I would like to thank my mentor and instructor Rebecca Kuder for her patience, keen insights, warm encouragement, and belief in my voice. My memoir instructor Matthew Goodman's insightful questions and challenges helped me develop the sketchy ideas into fullness. Matthew has given my writer's toolbox many valuable tools, and is a *gantze mensch*.

Rabbi Shmuel Klatzkin, Ph.D., graciously served as the external mentor and an instructor for this program. He has shared illuminating insights into the creative process, the role of the Chassidic artist, and *Tiferes*—the spiritual force of beauty—and has offered much vital support and direction. I'm humbled and honored to have his sensitive foreword grace this book.

Diane Young, my pumpkin and soul sister, has catalyzed my middle-aged return to the paintbrush and has been an enthusiastic cheerleader for my muse. She introduced me to many special creative souls, among them Rita Wasserman. Rita is a wonderful painting teacher and mentor, always encouraging and suggesting the next step.

Rabbi Manis Friedman, Tzivia Emmer, Chana Finman, Yosefa Gross, Shterna Kalmanson, and Adrienne Varady have generously given of their time to read the proof. Their thoughtful questions and constructive suggestions have helped refine and enhance the book. Many thanks to Rabbi Friedman for taking time from his busy schedule to offer guidance and clarification.

Yael Resnick has been a most talented and careful editor, bringing deep and sensitive insight, smoothing the rough edges, and polishing a rough manuscript. Her cover design has aptly captured the book's spirit.

To Diane, Esther, Hagit, Marcia, Miriam, Shterna, Tehila, and all the other women who have sat together in our Shabbos afternoon class throughout the years—eating chocolate, learning, sharing, laughing, crying, and keeping our souls nurtured with Torah and deep friendship—thank you.

To all the many Torah teachers, dedicated men and women of great spirit, heart, and intellect, especially the Rebbe's dedicated *shluchim* (emissaries) and lamplighters, who've shared so much with me over these years, *chazak!*—may you continue to be strong and shine. I hope this little messy work adds a bit to the great light you've put out there.

To El and Marv, you da best, truly! Your loving support for us and our kids, (and following them around the world), has kept us going in so many ways. To Viv, my sis, you got my back—thanks for being there through it all, and for your insightful comments. David, you are an inspiration.

Acharon, acharon chaviv, the last is the most precious—to my dear husband Yankel, and our precious jewels—our wonderful children, children-in-law, and delicious grandchildren—for all your patience, laughs, love, and great ideas during this rather crazed book-writing preoccupation, and in everything. May we all give *nachas* to the Rebbe and to the *Aibishter,* the One Above. I hope in some small way these scribbles find their way to help our collective task, bringing our beautiful aching world to that long-awaited time when all hidden light will be revealed, the meaning of our journeys made clear, each of us savoring peace in abundant fullness, under our fig tree.

Made in the USA
Charleston, SC
22 January 2014